D1614251

STRATEGIC
INFORMATION
SYSTEMS

STRATEGIC INFORMATION SYSTEMS

Competition Through Information Technologies

Seev Neumann

Information Systems Department, The Claremont Graduate School
Claremont, California
and
Faculty of Management, Tel Aviv University
Tel Aviv, Israel

Macmillan College Publishing Company
New York

Maxwell Macmillan Canada
Toronto

Maxwell Macmillan International
New York   Oxford   Singapore   Sydney

Editor: Charles E. Stewart
Production Supervisor: Margaret Comaskey
Production Manager: Su Levine
Text and Cover Designer: Lourdes Gerace

This book was set in Garamond and Helvetica by Carlisle Communications, Ltd.
and was printed and bound by Book Press.
The cover was printed by Book Press.

Macmillan College Publishing Company
866 Third Avenue, New York, New York 10022

Macmillan College Publishing Company is part
of the Maxwell Communication Group of Companies.

Maxwell Macmillan Canada, Inc.
1200 Eglinton Avenue East
Suite 200
Don Mills, Ontario M3C 3N1

LIBRARY OF CONGRESS CATALOGING-IN-PUBLICATION DATA

Neumann, Seev.
    Strategic information systems : competition through information
technologies / Seev Neumann.
        p.   cm.
    Includes index.
    ISBN 0-02-386690-X
    1. Management information systems.   2. Information technology.
I. Title.
HD30.213.N48   1994
658.4' 038' 011—dc20

                                                                93–17343
                                                                CIP

Printing: 1 2 3 4 5 6 7 8   Year: 4 5 6 7 8 9 0 1 2 3

To Rona, Eilat, Tom, and Lee
and to Fruma, Ephraim, and Chaim Neumann.
Sleep well, dear ones.

Preface

This book provides a comprehensive treatment of all aspects of strategic information systems (SIS), those information-technology–based systems that support organizations in their quest to survive or succeed in their competitive arenas, to gain a competitive edge, to sustain one, or to lose a competitive disadvantage. The organizations may be business firms in a fiercely competitive market, regulated monopolies, not-for-profit institutions, fledgling entrepreneurships, or mom-and-pop stores. What is common to them all is the potential for using information technologies to improve their relationships with their stakeholders—customers, creditors, employees, competitors, communities, stockholders, regulators, and suppliers.

To paraphrase Yogi Berra, the future of information technology ain't what it used to be. The tremendous advances of information technologies have outpaced our recognition of the opportunities (and threats) embodied in them. Many managers are recognizing that information technology is central to driving the organization, requiring resources that are viewed as investments rather than as expenses; many read or hear about SISs and want to get one but don't know how. For some, the only thing they know that is going on is that no one knows what is going on. This book is for the confused, the unaware, layperson, the astute, the skeptic, the practicing manager, the aspiring manager (current students), and the sage (researchers and instructors). It provides conceptual frameworks and a practical guide for everyone interested in understanding how information technologies can provide a competitive edge, how to identify SIS opportunities and risks, how to manage organizational SIS applications, and how to sustain such a competitive edge in a global environment.

You can prove and disprove almost anything about information technology—its impact on the individual, on organizational structure, or on scouting for NFL teams. That is why this book is not an attempt to formulate empirical results or to be a prescriptive manifesto. Samuel Johnson observed that it was insufficiently considered that men more often required to be reminded than informed. This book intends to come one up on this observation—to remind and to inform persons (and not just men . . .) about SIS opportunities and ideas (bearing in mind that there are no copyright laws pertaining to competitive advantage and no way to patent a good idea).

The book therefore includes case studies, war stories, and anecdotes. It is comprehensive yet flexible enough to be used in different settings, from a full semester MBA or information systems course to a short executive seminar, a corporate management retreat, a filler for TV commercials, or a session on your life cycle.

Not many schools of business offer a complete course on strategic information systems, but many have made it a popular elective in recent years. Peter Drucker once said that when a subject becomes totally obsolete, we make it a required course. In that sense, strategic information systems is definitely still an emerging subject.

The contents of this book are intended to benefit a variety of readers. If you are a practicing manager, my advice is to think about your own organization and function as you read each chapter. Think about whether and how each chapter can help you see opportunities or threats for your organization. I have provided a list of references at the end of each chapter to point you toward more information about the ideas that interest you. If you are an academic who is teaching or studying and doing research, you may meet new explanatory frameworks, observations that have not appeared in the existing literature, and ideas for empirical research.

I wish to thank the following doctoral students in the Information Science Program of the Claremont Graduate School, whose assistance was instrumental in writing this book: Victoria Goodrich, Ruth Guthrie, Detlef Matthies, Ben Mortagy, Subramanyan Murthy, Justus Schlichting, and Roy Sprague, who was first among equals.

I also want to acknowledge the financial support of the Claremont Graduate School and the Mexico Chair for Management Information Systems at Tel-Aviv University, and, finally, the careful typing by Ruth Neumann.

Finally, I wish to thank the following reviewers: Arthur Rasher, University of Tulsa; Jae Song, Saint Cloud State University; Jacqueline Wyatt, Middle Tennessee State University; Ephraim McLean, Georgia State University; James Senn, Georgia State University; Michael Ginzberg, Case Western University; Ed Stohr, New York University; and Paul Gray, Claremont Graduate School.

I now invite you to a tour of Strategic Information Systems.

Seev Neumann

Tel-Aviv, Israel

Brief Contents

Contents

CHAPTER 4
The Impact of Strategic Information Systems on Industries, Firms, and Strategies

CHAPTER 5
The Impact of Strategic Information Systems on the Internal Structure and Processes of Organization

CHAPTER 6
The Impact of Information Technology on Strategic Alliances

1

Introduction and Overview

*Find ways to change the rules of the
game . . . so that we can use
our IS resources to win.*

Corporate CEO

This executive call to action,[1] elicited during a research interview, best summarizes the goal of a *strategic information system* (SIS) and also the key challenge of developing such systems. This book is about effective implementation of strategic information systems in organizations.

What are strategic information systems? The definition of SIS used in this book focuses on the *use* of the system—the primary function of an SIS is to support the competitive strategy of a company in its industry and its plan for gaining or maintaining competitive advantage, or reducing its competitive disadvantage relative to its rivals. Thus an SIS is any type of information system that helps an organization compete. Perhaps a more accurate term would be *competitive support systems.* However, to be consistent with a popular term, this book uses SIS.

An information system is strategic if it changes the way a firm competes or changes the industry's structure. An SIS provides or contributes to *competitive advantage* if it provides a greater return on investment for a company than its industry's average return. A competitive advantage can increase market share, increase sales, attract new customers, increase customer loyalty, decrease product or service costs in support of a low-cost corporate strategy, or generally improve a company's competitive position in its market. American Airlines' computerized reservation system is a well-known example of competitive advantage from an information technology–based application. For this application, American Airlines' market share and profitability were increased at the expense of competitors.

Industry structure is characterized by the number and distribution of buyers and sellers, product differentiation, entry barriers, vertical integration, diversification, and cost structures. Activities yielding sustained, better than normal return on investment are considered competitive advantages and are therefore strategic in nature. Activities by others that threaten the competitive position of a firm are also strategic because they can alter industry structure. Such activities do not confer advantage and require a response to avoid strategic disadvantage. Obviously, an unutilized competitive advantage is no advantage.

Even though the competitive use of information technology (IT) has been the subject of articles and books since the early 1980s, this particular art remains imprecise and unformed. Most articles about this subject are either prescriptive frameworks or anecdotes, and the anecdotal evidence is often limited in scope.

The lack of empirical evidence is not surprising. The large organizations that have triumphed using SISs are probably happy to brag about it, although the litigation these systems provoke may restrain boasting more than we know. Those organizations that have failed to develop an SIS are understandably less willing to discuss their failures. A corollary problem occurs when these systems are being imitated or are under development—a time when researchers or reporters would love to be observing process and outcome. Then the strategic risks of information leaks are enormous, so few firms are willing to discuss work in progress in detail.

The enormously diverse range of competitive users of IT is another problem. They can involve links with customers, rivals, suppliers, competitors, and partners. They can utilize all types of technology: telecommunications, database, graphics, and expert systems. Their host organizations can range from multinational firms to the corner video store. Another problem is that the frameworks about competitive use of IT have focused on providing tools only for *identifying* arenas where IT can be used strategically, and have not been validated by research. Finally, because most SISs are based on existing transactions processing systems or decision support systems, separating out the specific costs and benefits of the strategic component can be difficult.

Despite the flood of research and testimonials of SIS success, voices also argue for restraint in the strategic use of IT. The most common argument is that organizations must get their non-IT house in order before turning to strategic systems.[2] An SIS can be a boon for healthy firms but a terrible bust for the ill-prepared.

Although the actual extent is unknown, many organizations are pursuing the strategic application of IT. In one 1989 survey of 84 companies, about 70 had installed what they considered to be strategic systems.[3] In some cases these applications were pioneering. In others, they may have been brought about by *competitive necessity* rather than innovation. Because of the anecdotal or case orientation of most reports of SIS use, however, the precise profile of these activities either within or across industries is unclear.

The most visible portion of the SIS iceberg is the small group of major systems that have been eminently successful in providing demonstrable competitive advantage. These star performers include American Airlines' SABRE and United Airlines' APOLLO reservation systems, American Hospital Supply Corporation's ASAP order entry system, McKesson's ECONOMOST order entry system, Federal Express's entire IT infrastructure, Digital Equipment Corporation's XCON configuration system, and Merrill Lynch's Cash Management Account. Some of these, such as American Airlines', have been extensively researched and reported.

What do the "star" anecdotes tell us? American Airlines' SABRE was the first online reservation system to be placed in travel agent offices. The advantages: originally, flight schedules were presented in a way that emphasized AA; a fee was charged for bookings on other airlines; and the information passing through the system could be used to fine-tune fares and schedules. American Hospital Supply Corporation helped their customers automate their inventory and inventory control by installing terminals with direct links to AHSC. In the process they built in nearly insurmountable switching costs for their customers. Merrill Lynch, blessed with excess computer capacity and cursed with a weak securities market, used an SRI International proposed idea for a "do-it-all" financial account (the Cash Management Account) that was sufficiently innovative and difficult to copy that Merrill Lynch had almost no competition for almost five years. So the anecdotes tell us that industry leaders, using IT, locked in large market shares by aggressively pursuing large, innovative SIS projects.

The importance of the current state of an organization and its industry cannot be overemphasized. Organizations without strong information system (IS) operations are unlikely candidates for strategic systems, unless they are new firms being designed from the ground up to be based on IT. As many experts suggest, the "business sense" of IS staff is critically important to the success of these ventures. The support of top management is also essential for the success of these systems. In fact, CEO leadership may be more important than the qualifications of the IS staff.

Strategic partnerships are also becoming a key part of the SIS landscape. Technological advances in database systems, the hardware and software used in networking, the proliferation of open systems and the adoption of standards, and enormous improvements in data communications have made the technical task of *SIS alliances* much simpler. In fact, technology is no longer the serious restraint to SIS development that it once was.

Despite the increasing difficulty of implementing SISs, it is more imperative than ever in the 1990s that organizations do so. As greater numbers of firms in virtually every industry establish such systems, having them will become a strategic necessity to meet the threat of powerful competitors. Even some of the earliest SISs, such as SABRE, were developed in response to such a threat.[4] A corollary to this situation is that in some industries, such as the travel service industry, the development of strategic systems and strategic alliances will seriously threaten the ability of smaller firms to survive. In other words, the entire structure of the industries most heavily influenced by IT may be altered by the introduction of strategic systems to the detriment of certain industry segments.

SISs, under the correct set of circumstances, can provide *sustainable competitive advantage*. Systems almost never yield competitive advantage by themselves. Technology is readily acquired and expertise is readily duplicated. Rather, strategic systems have been shown to provide competitive advantage when they exploit or leverage resource advantages of the host company (such as superior management, patents, and dominant brand name).

In other words, SISs are not an automatic ticket to fame. Systems alone do not confer competitive advantage. Any such advantage is achieved only by having the right business strategy and by excellent execution of key processes. SISs play a strictly ancillary role in this endeavor. It is not the systems that make the difference but the *uses* for which and the methods by which the SISs are developed.

The next section of this chapter describes the structure and plan of the book. The third section tells the story of ASAP, an SIS used by the American Hospital Supply

Corporation to gain a competitive edge. Although ASAP is one of the most often cited and rehashed examples of SIS, it is also the most documented system and lends itself well to historical perspective. ASAP provides the most thorough coverage of the evolution of an SIS, stretching over three decades.

The last section turns attention to the SIS underlying Rosenbluth International Alliance. This case is an example of an SIS developed to exploit a discontinuity: deregulation of air travel in the United States in 1978. It then enabled Rosenbluth Travel to become a major international player through cooperative alliance in the global travel market.

Both cases provide examples for the main SIS issues considered in following chapters of the book.

STRUCTURE AND PLAN OF THE BOOK

The great jazz musician Charlie Mingus once said that to take something simple and make it complex is common, but to take something complex and make it simple, that is creativity. This book attempts to address the multifaceted subject of strategic information system and simplify it. It explores organizational, managerial, economic, and technological aspects and traces pertinent developments end to end: from SIS past roots in conventional transaction processing systems to the impact of new information technologies on strategic information systems.

The book contains 12 chapters. This chapter, Introduction and Overview, introduces the themes that underlie the plan of the book. These themes are illustrated by a description of two functioning SISs. One, the ASAP system, supports the business strategies of the Baxter Healthcare Corporation in the U.S. domestic hospital supplies marketplace. The other plays a critical strategic role in the operation of Rosenbluth International Alliance, a global cooperative alliance of travel agencies.

Chapter 2, Strategic Information Systems Are Conventional Information Systems Used in Innovative Ways, traces the typical history of information systems development in organizations, from *transaction processing systems* (TPSs), to *management information systems* (MISs), to *decision support systems* (DSSs), culminating in *strategic information systems* (SISs). The chapter analyzes the features that are common to all these categories of systems and the features that make SIS unique. It debunks the myth that an SIS is a special higher-level system that can somehow come on the scene only after an organization has developed the other categories of systems.

The subject of information technology and its potential for competitive advantage has been dominated by conceptual frameworks and illustrated by several celebrated SISs such as American Airlines' SABRE. These examples of SISs are considered legendary and overused by practitioners and academics. Chapter 3, Strategic Information Systems Frameworks, reviews the many partial conceptual frameworks that have been suggested to describe or prescribe SIS issues. It acknowledges that while there is no one comprehensive framework, each may shed a light on a specific pertinent SIS concern. After all, as the saying goes, if we all had one standard of beauty, no one would ever marry. . . .

Chapter 4, The Impact of Strategic Information Systems on Industries, Firms, and Strategies, starts by treating the impact of information technology at the industry level. All organizations operate in one or more industries. By the nature of their participation in an industry, they are affected by existing or potential uses of information technology (consider, for example, a bank and ATM technology). The industry is the arena in which comparative advantage is won or lost. The competitive posture and performance of an organization is impacted by the scope, intensity, and form of its interrelationships with external forces that are part of the competitive arena of that organization. The organization can use SISs to give it an edge or defend against an edge gained by one of the forces (e.g., suppliers, customers, competitors). Chapter 4 reviews this impact of information technology at the level of the individual organization. SISs are intended to support corporate (organizational) strategies adopted to reach corporate objectives. The chapter describes common strategies and respective SISs, illustrated by SISs that are being used by companies.

Chapter 5, Impact of Strategic Information Systems on the Internal Structure and Processes of Organizations, treats SISs that enable companies to gain a competitive edge by changing their internal planning and control structure or its processes (e.g., logistics, production, and marketing).

Chapter 6, The Impact of Information Technology on Strategic Alliances, turns attention to SISs that may be shared by two or more companies in a given industry (e.g., banks using an ATM network), or by two or more companies in different industries (e.g., a bank issuing Visa credit cards and an airliner crediting Visa-based purchases with mileage in its frequent-traveler bonus program). The first type SIS supports an intraindustry alliance; the second type SIS supports an interindustry alliance.

In the early 1990s, there is little doubt that information technology will diffuse throughout the world and become the backbone of an increasingly interdependent global economy. Chapter 7, Global Strategic Information Systems, explores how competitive advantage may be obtained in a global marketplace by using SISs. It illustrates how information technology, with its ability to compress time and space, and to share and distribute resources over geographical boundaries, can offer opportunities for organizations to leverage advantage of market size, geographical scope, or market niche.

An SIS can enable an organization to gain a competitive edge, but that can be easily lost unless the advantage is sustainable. Chapter 8, Sustainability of Information Technology–Based Competitive Advantage, attends to this issue and provides examples of both SIS-based short-lived and sustainable advantages. It also expands on the related consideration of SIS, which is a *strategic necessity* (e.g., an ATM), and the pros and cons of an SIS, which supports a leader or a follower in an industry.

SISs are usually big, complex systems that typically keep on adding features (to assure sustainability of a competitive edge). They display risk characteristics common to any large-scale information system project. Chapter 9, Strategic Information Systems Risks, deals with this category of risks. It goes one step further in analyzing the specific *SIS risks* that emanate, paradoxically sometimes, from a successful system that did give a company a significant competitive edge (e.g., a system that may give rise to competitors' claims of unfair practices).

SISs have to be developed, then implemented, then maintained within a company's specific organizational setting that is contingent on its culture, climate, structure, geography, and the like. Chapter 10, Organizational Requirements for Introducing Strategic Information System, attends to these concerns, including the partnership between business managers and information systems professionals and the need for a *SIS champion*.

Chapter 11, Identifying Strategic Information Systems Opportunities, builds on the foundations and lessons from the previous chapters to provide a practical process for identifying opportunities for SISs (or generating SIS ideas).

Chapter 12, New Technologies for Strategic Information Systems, reviews instances of SISs, the information technologies involved, and the degree to which the latter are critical to system success. It then speculates about technology trends over the 1990s with the goal of matching new technologies with SISs that might yield significant competitive advantage.

THE EVOLUTION OF THE ASAP SYSTEM

The Computer is the heart of our success.

Karl D. Bays, Chairman and CEO
of American Hospital Supply
Corporation, 1985

American Hospital Supply Corporation's (later Baxter Healthcare's) Analytic Systems Automatic Purchasing (ASAP) is one of the best-known, most often cited strategic information systems.[5] ASAP, a computerized system for ordering, tracking, and managing hospital supplies, is credited with helping propel American Hospital Supply Corporation (AHSC) from its 1960s position as a medium-sized, regional supplier of generic hospital supplies (gloves, gowns, bandages, and the like) to its 1990s position as market leader in this healthcare segment. The following is the story of the evolution of the ASAP system from 1963 to 1992.

In the 1950s and early 1960s, the typical ordering process between a hospital and any hospital supply firm was the responsibility of an individual salesperson, who either mailed or phoned in the order to the distribution center for delivery. It was a time-consuming, paper-intensive, and expensive process. It was logical that AHSC would computerize the order-entry and billing process at its distribution centers through IBM tab-card machines in 1957. In this sense, AHSC's early initiatives followed a then emerging management practice of reducing costs through selective computerization.

In 1963, the San Francisco office of AHSC was experiencing difficulties in serving Stanford Medical Center with timely and accurate delivery of hospital products. Stanford had adopted a unique numbering system in their product categories to create a common numbering scheme among its ordering clerks, but these categories resulted in inefficiency (i.e., errors) when orders were placed over the telephone with different suppliers. Frank Wolfe, a manager in the AHSC San Francisco office, arrived at a simple solution to improve efficiency: providing prepunched cards for the Stanford purchasing departments—

with the punched holes corresponding to AHSC's numbering scheme—and a handwritten number (with a marker pen) corresponding to the Stanford numbering scheme. The ordering clerks could now thumb through their set of cards and select the ones they wanted (based on the handwritten numbers), and then process these cards through an IBM 1001 Dataphones (at Stanford) attached to an IBM 026 card punch at AHSC's office.

Thus, the availability of prepunched cards from AHSC ensured not only increased efficiency in order processing (fewer errors and lower inventory) but also ensured that the required items were ordered only from AHSC, because the prepunched cards had the AHSC numbering system. The new system was called Tel-American.

The results of experimenting with Tel-American at the San Francisco office diffused through various parts of AHSC, including the corporate management group during 1963–66. During a 1966 corporate strategic planning meeting, the business managers (without any active participation from the information systems managers) decided in favor of allocating IS resources to the leveraging of Tel-American rather than to auto-mating the accounting systems. What started out as a localized experiment for a mar-keting and service problem was formally considered a critical lever for business strategy within three years.

AHSC's corporate Information Systems Division (ISD) was given responsibility for the design, development, and modification of the Tel-American system. The decision was supported by centralized coordination and commitment by senior management. For instance, while the IBM system 1001 was central to the AHSC-Tel-American initiatives, IBM decided in the mid-1970s to discontinue the system 1001. Because AHSC's business strategy was intricately linked to this technology, management decided to acquire a technology unit, TekPro, as a part of its corporate portfolio. The TekPro division devel-oped an information system that could acknowledge the receipt of each line of data from the hospitals, thus ushering in the era of computer-based communications between AHSC and hospitals.

The ASAP system required not only financial resources but also support and com-mitment from senior management. Top management support was essential to ensure continued investment in the information technology infrastructure. AHSC's chairman, Karl Bays, himself participated in regular two-hour monthly meetings with the IS staff to provide encouragement as well as to be informed of the success of the program.

The experimental Tel-American system with handwritten, prepunched cards evolved in 1967 into a system supporting order entry through a touch-tone phone known as ASAP 1. A major limitation of this version was its reliance on prepunched cards, the inability to directly interconnect AHSC, its salespersons and hospital customers, and the lack of printed copies for order verification. Customer requirements in the 1970s led to the next enhancement. ASAP 2 enabled order entry through teletype machines at customer sites (clerks typed in the order and received a printed copy directly from the teletype machine). Customers paid for the teletype machines, while AHSC incurred the telephone charges.

In contrast to ASAP 2's technical improvements, ASAP 3, introduced in 1981, focused on customizing the information system to the specifications and requirements of different hospitals. For instance, hospitals were able to use their internal stock numbers. Similarly, from the output perspective, customers could specify their purchase-order formats and avoid multiplicity of formats. The continuous development of the ASAP system, far ahead of competitive offerings, enabled AHSC to customize inputs and out-puts of order processing and materials management systems. Most hospitals had not computerized their materials management and supply functions by the early 1970s and could not have designed and developed such a system without incurring significant costs. Thus, ASAP 3 capitalized on hospitals' steadily increasing needs to improve their own management of supplies. For a few large customers, AHSC went a step further and put together small teams of sales, distribution, and IS personnel to analyze the hospital's paper flow around materials ordering and receiving.

The first three versions of ASAP were initiated by AHSC, but ASAP 4, introduced in 1983, was a specific response to requests from hospitals to provide computer-to-computer links. This version of ASAP simplified the hospital's purchasing process by eliminating all the manual steps required except the approval of purchases. It also resulted in a closer relationship between AHSC and the hospitals. The customer's internal com-puter system produced recommended orders that, once approved, were automatically transmitted through a high-speed phone connection to AHSC's mainframe. Order con-firmations were sent directly to the customer's computer system to update the hospital's files. Customers did not pay for the use of ASAP or for any necessary software custom-ization.

ASAP 5, which was released in 1985, extended the capabilities of ASAP 3 by using an IBM PC (with modem) as the customer's input and output device. Customers could build and edit order files on the PC instead of online, thus reducing telephone expenses. The PC was equipped with extensive tutorial software, allowing a new user to quickly learn how to enter ASAP orders.

By late 1984, about 50% of AHSC's hospital orders came through ASAP. The ASAP software had been written totally by AHSC. AHSC estimated that until then it had spent about $30 million to build and enhance ASAP. Annual operating costs for the 9000-terminal system were about $3 million. AHSC had also implemented VIP, a system that linked it to its suppliers. Purchase orders, messages about inventory levels, pricing information, and the like were transmitted between AHSC and its suppliers. VIP was not mandatory, but most AHSC suppliers decided to use the system.

In July 1985, Baxter Travenol Laboratories, Inc., a medical products manufacturer, acquired AHSC to form Baxter Healthcare Corporation. Baxter cited AHSC's strengths in distribution, corporate sales program, and information systems as significant factors lead-ing to the merger. The importance of ASAP was further highlighted by noting that AHSC's senior IS executive group was put in charge of Baxter's new IS organization. Subsequent to the acquisition, Baxter continued to emphasize system enhancements. For instance, in 1986, it introduced ASAP 8, with the new distinctive features of electronic invoice and receipt and electronic funds transfer.

By 1986, AHSC's competitors had systems that were fully competitive with, and sometimes superior to, ASAP. Utilization of ASAP had leveled off. By 1988 there were over 50 different order entry/materials management systems in the marketplace. Hospi-tals increasingly demanded all-vendor systems, which were considerably more convenient than separate systems (like ASAP) with individual formats, passwords, and reports. About a decade after the introduction of ASAP 1, and several years after smaller, regional competitors imitated ASAP with their own versions of single-vendor systems, both

Johnson & Johnson and Abbott Laboratories, the two largest competitors of Baxter, introduced their versions of proprietary multivendor systems.

J&J Cooperative Action (COACT) system, first introduced in 1985, was a computer-based logistics system. It featured online order inquiry and consolidated reporting. It brought together 15 J&J companies onto one system. COACT PLUS, introduced shortly thereafter, offered a centralized gateway to J&J products as well as to products from other vendors.

Quik Link, developed jointly by 3M Company and Abbott Laboratories, was released in 1987. The system had the key capabilities of multivendor remote order entry, consolidated product deliveries, and centralized customer service.

By 1988, both Abbott and J&J offered over 30 vendors on each of their systems, significantly broadening their product scope and thus attempting to compete head-on against Baxter. On the customer side, many hospitals considered the option of converting over to COACT or Quik Link or, worse, running all the systems in parallel.

In June 1988, Baxter responded with ASAP Express—its own version of a multivendor system. As a single-vendor order entry system, ASAP had given AHSC (and later Baxter) a distinct competitive advantage. But by 1988, most medical suppliers had developed order entry systems of their own. It was not uncommon to find hospitals using several order entry systems, each requiring a separate phone call and user protocol. This increased the time it took to place orders and has resulted in customer demands for consolidated systems where supplies from all suppliers could be ordered.

ASAP Express used the facilities of both Baxter and the General Electric Information Services Company (GEISCO). The latter provided a worldwide telecommunications network and a clearinghouse. ASAP Express allowed hospitals to enter orders for all participating vendors. Baxter orders would be handled through ASAP, while orders for other vendors would be passed to GEISCO's electronic clearinghouse. All of the vendors participating in ASAP Express had their own computerized order entry systems before. One of the benefits of ASAP Express for Baxter was revenues from participating vendors who pay fees for using the system. In early 1990, Baxter introduced ASAP Express Power Base, an enhanced all-vendor system, linking to 386-type PCs at customers' sites.

Later in 1990, Baxter deployed its *ValueLink* program. ValueLink is a logistics system based on integrated information management that delivers products on a *just-in-time* basis in a ready-to-use package for specified user departments. The system synchronizes the flow of products and information between the customer and Baxter via consolidated purchases and multiple deliveries directly to points of use in the hospital seven days a week, rather than to the central purchasing department. In effect, ValueLink underlies *strategic partnerships* between Baxter and each customer who subscribes to it.

The partnership requires that each hospital commit to a multiyear contract for purchase volume as well as a high share of product flow with fees for value-based services. Baxter, on the other hand, commits to a 100% fill rate and lowered inventory levels in addition to developing customized procedures to ensure delivery to multiple-user departments (i.e., operating rooms, laboratories, and the like). With ValueLink, Baxter took over materials management from the hospital. Before ValueLink, ASAP was dealing with the hospital's purchasing agent, who then distributed supplies to end users. With ValueLink, Baxter went around the purchasing agents and delivers directly to end users.

Lessons from ASAP

The evolution of AHSC's (and later Baxter's) ASAP system illustrates almost all the themes underlying strategic information systems. The following is a list of such themes and the corresponding chapters in this book where the themes are considered.

1. In 1992, half of Baxter sales are still handled by old teletype systems installed in purchasing departments as part of old ASAP versions. Even though the technology cost of PCs is lower than teletypes, it is hard for Baxter to convince purchasing agents to switch to PCs, because of what hospitals see as costs of retraining and changing (chapter ten).

2. The real story of AHSC is how it built on its organizational strengths, made a technological commitment, and provided value to the customer. This approach made it difficult for competitors to gain anything by merely copying the underlying information technology (chapter eight).

3. ASAP is an example of an interorganizational system (AHSC and hospitals). Other IT-based alliances mentioned in the story are Quik Link (Abbott Laboratories and the 3M Company) and ASAP Express (Baxter and GEISCO) (chapter six).

4. It was AHSC's senior management that identified Tel-American as an SIS opportunity in 1966 and not the IS professionals (chapter eleven).

5. The nature of the competition in the hospital supply industry and the impact of ASAP and similar systems can be analyzed by employing Michael Porter's framework for industry and competitive analysis (chapters three and four).

6. Tel-American evolution into ASAP (and the further development of ASAP) was the result of formal planning (chapter ten).

7. ASAP became an important part of AHSC's competitive strategy and differentiated its products (chapter four).

8. The issue of whether ASAP's technical features were easy to replicate by AHSC's rivals was an important concern for ASAP's developers (chapter nine).

9. ASAP supported competitive advantage but did not itself provide it. Without a broad product line and a nationwide distribution network, it is unlikely that AHSC would have been so successful with ASAP. In other words, AHSC used information technology to leverage other organizational assets it had (chapter eight).

10. Tel-American, which later evolved into ASAP, started as a conventional order entry transactions processing system, not as a preplanned strategic information system to which it later evolved (chapter two).

11. New information technologies (such as PCs and telecommunications) prompted AHSC (and Baxter) to enhance ASAP and come out with new versions of the system (chapter twelve).

12. By the mid-1980s, with the proliferation of competing single-vendor ASAP-like systems, it seemed that a competitive advantage had become a competitive necessity (chapter eight).

13. The involvement of GEISCO and other players, the existing expertise of Baxter, plus a phased rollout of ASAP Express reduced the system's technical risks of failure (chapter nine).

14. AHSC's senior management support and involvement in the development of Tel-American and ASAP systems was crucial to their success (chapter ten).

15. First mover advantages generally accrue owing to technological leadership and preemption. AHSC succeeded in obtaining acceptance from approximately 200 hospitals within the first few years of ASAP 1's introduction and over 500 hospitals by the mid-1970s (chapter eight).

16. In 1978, a suit was filed in the Western District of Michigan Federal Court by White and White, Inc., a local competitor, charging AHSC with unfair trade practices. The suit was initially decided in favor of the plaintiffs but was reversed on appeal in 1983. This is one example of the legal risks facing successful strategic information systems that become a threat to industry rivals (chapter nine).

17. Baxter was about half the size of AHSC before its leveraged buyout of AHSC in 1985. Before 1985, AHSC was a distributer of hospital supplies, with Johnson & Johnson its largest customer and Abbott Laboratories its third-largest customer. At that time, both benefited from the ASAP system. All that changed in 1985, because the new Baxter Healthcare Corporation, like J&J and Abbott Laboratories, was also a manufacturer of hospital supplies (chapter five).

18. ASAP created high barriers to entry because of the complexity of its software and the company's ability to introduce value-added information services to its customers (chapter four).

19. ASAP created high switching costs for hospital customers and locked them into AHSC as increased operational dependence and normal human inertia made switching to competitors unattractive (chapter four).

20. From a business transformation point of view, the critical turning point was the 1966 decision of AHSC's corporate management to shift order entry out of AHSC's distribution center into the purchasing department of the customer (chapter five).

21. AHSC responded with ASAP to the needs of a few, *leading-edge* customers in the beginning, but this service level requirement rapidly diffused throughout the industry and became a *necessary* service for all customers by the early 1980s (chapter eight).

22. The feeling among AHSC management was that ASAP's technology could be imitated by competitors. However, it was the one-stop *shopping approach* (AHSC being the hospital's *prime vendor*), supported by AHSC's broad product line, that could not. Thus, AHSC's two-pronged strategy rested on the company's ability to leverage their extensive product scope and the ASAP platform to market the concept of *prime vendor* to the hospitals. By the late 1980s, of about 6,900 hospitals nationwide, 5,500 were using ASAP (chapter eight).

23. The alliance between Baxter and GEISCO made the ASAP Express system accessible to customers worldwide (chapter seven).

ROSENBLUTH TRAVEL

Rosenbluth Travel (RT), based in Philadelphia, was in 1992 one of the five largest travel agencies in the United States. Since 1980 it has grown from a regional agency with $40 million in annual sales to an international agency with sales of over $1.3 billion in 1991.[6]

Prior to deregulation of the airline industry in 1978, there was little that travel agents could do for corporate accounts except deliver tickets. Fare and route structures were simple and fixed. After deregulation fares became volatile and carriers were free to add or drop routes. In this increasingly dynamic environment, travel agents began to function as information brokers, getting their corporate clients the best fares for the most convenient flights. RT's corporate strategy focused on capturing a substantial share of corporate travel through innovation and superior service based on the use of information technology (IT). By exploiting its information systems, RT sought to achieve better rates for its corporate accounts in a market that has become more competitive and price-sensitive.

IT has been critical to RT's strategy. IT-based devices allowed RT to attract customers and provide high-quality service. RT has developed pioneering applications to produce an integrated IT infrastructure. By continuously enhancing and innovating applications, RT made it harder for competitors to replicate the systems. Thus, REDOUT enables agents to sell flights based on costs, instead of relying on the computerized reservation system's (CRS) display based on departure times. PRECISION introduced scripts into the CRS, thereby improving the agents' service, guiding them through the sales process, and reducing opportunities to err. VISION automatically captures information at the time reservations are ticketed and provides travel patterns throughout the United States.

By the late 1980s, RT was experiencing pressures by major corporate clients to offer global service. Global travel was growing in response to changes in global business. Like other agencies, RT felt that it was necessary to follow their customers who were going global to avoid losing these accounts. International travelers are often senior managers and demanding customers. They require a local presence where they travel for making itinerary changes, handling emergencies, and providing local expertise. The ability to provide this support became a factor in capturing or retaining large domestic corporate clients.

Global support required that an agency be present in all major foreign markets, but this was not consistent with RT's limited financial and managerial resources. The cost and time involved in a global acquisition strategy were prohibitive for RT. Moreover, differences in local markets (culture, language, regulations, and the like) required reliance on local agencies for local support. RT's challenge was to develop an organization coordinating travel management of global accounts, based on travel management in autonomous, heterogeneous markets that needed to remain so and were difficult to integrate. RT's response was the Rosenbluth International Alliance (RIA).

RIA is an alliance of 34 partners in 37 countries (in 1991) operating close to 1,500 offices. RT owns only 500 of these, in the United States. The RIA has local presence in all major travel markets around the world and has gross annual sales of over $5 billion. RIA is structured as an alliance of independent organizations bound by common interest.

Each member retains its own identity and autonomy. Each had to possess a service orientation and culture compatible with RT. They also had to demonstrate an IS capability that would support RT's view of the role of IT in global travel management. The RIA is in effect a *global virtual corporation.*

The key to RIA global travel support is the RIA desk maintained by each RIA member. The agent in charge of the desk has online access to the local member's resources and to the traveler's itinerary (stored in the home country's database), as well as information on the traveler's individual preferences and his or her corporation's travel policies. Moreover, the agent has online access to any other RIA member and to RIA proprietary databases such as information on hotels and special rates. The RIA desk provides complete support from changing itineraries to renting a car.

Perhaps the most important service of the RIA is the ability to support worldwide consolidated travel reporting. Such reporting allows global clients to use their global travel volume in negotiating better fares. This has been a strong driver for corporate customers to consolidate their travel through a single agency (like RT) in a given market that can offer this facility.

IT has played a critical role in the success of the RIA. IT enables global access to client itineraries and records and supports the global consolidation of travel information. There is no massive integrated infrastructure. The RIA is exploiting existing systems, such as various CRSs and the members' own fragmented systems. Their success is in linking together these islands of technology to offer integrated services.

The basic infrastructure for the RIA is the APOLLO computerized reservation system, offered by Covia (a subsidiary of United Airlines) in the United States, Mexico, and Japan; by Gemini in Canada; and by Galileo in the rest of the world. All RIA members have access to the APOLLO CRS for RIA business. Several proprietary applications have been built on the APOLLO system (for example, a program that gives RIA members access to preferred rates that have been negotiated with hotels across the world). The major CRSs are accessed through flexible workstations programmed to customize the user dialog with the CRS and RIA's proprietary applications. With this capability, a traveler originating in Los Angeles but needing service in Tel Aviv can go to the RIA partner in Israel. The Israeli agent can display the itinerary as well as information on the client's travel policies and special rates, and the traveler's preferences. If the traveler in Israel makes changes, a record of that transaction is automatically routed to RT in Los Angeles for consolidated reporting.

Lessons from RIA

Rosenbluth International Alliance's story demonstrates some of the major themes underlying strategic information systems. The following is a list of such themes and the corresponding chapters in this book where the themes are considered.

1. RIA is based on several SIS alliances. One of them is the SIS alliance between RIA members offering the online data and information linkages among members.

Another is the SIS allowing linkages between RIA and the APOLLO CRS offered by Covia, Gemini, and Galileo (chapter six).

2. The RIA was formed and structured to implement Hal Rosenbluth's (CEO of RT) vision in the global travel arena (chapter ten).

3. The implementation and functioning of the RIA's SISs would not have been possible without the support and involvement of the management of RT and other RIA members (chapter ten).

4. By continuously cascading new IS applications, RIA has made it difficult for competitors to replicate the system and erode RIA's competitive advantage (chapter eight).

5. RIA's IT infrastructure has changed the internal structure and processes of its RIA members (chapter five).

6. RIA enables even a relatively small local agency to protect its existing relationships with a corporate client who is going global (chapter four).

7. The SISs underlying RIA are prime examples of global SISs (chapter seven).

8. One important source of stability of the RIA is that members are in noncompeting areas. However, there is a risk that this may change, particularly if Europe becomes more unified in the future, possibly forcing members into direct competition (chapter nine).

REFERENCES

1. Johnson, H. R. and Carrico, S. R., "Developing Capabilities to Use Information Strategically," *MIS Quarterly,* Mar. 1988.

2. Warner, T., "Information Technology as a Competitive Burden," *Sloan Management Review,* Fall 1987.

3. King, W. R., Grover, V., and Hufnagel, E. H., "Using Information and Information Technology for Sustainable Competitive Advantage: Some Empirical Evidence," *Information and Management,* 17, 1989.

4. Copeland, D. G. and McKenney, J. L., "Airline Reservations Systems: Lessons from History," *MIS Quarterly,* Sept. 1988.

5. Venkatraman, N., and Short, J. E., "Baxter Healthcare: Evolution from ASAP to ValueLink in the Hospital Supplies Marketplace," *Proceedings of the Twenty-Fifth Annual Hawaii International Conference on System Sciences,* IEEE Computer Society Press, California, 1992; Venkatraman N. and Short, J. E. "Strategies for Electronic Integration: From Order-Entry to Value-Added Partnerships at Baxter," *CISR Working Paper no. 210,* Sloan School of Management, Massachusetts Institute of Technology, June 1990; Vitale, M. R., *American Hospital Supply Corporation (A): the ASAP System,* Harvard Business School Case 9-186-005, Harvard Business School, 1985; Vitale, M. R., *Baxter Healthcare Corporation: ASAP Express,* Harvard Business School Case 9-188-080, Harvard Business School, 1988.

6. Clemons, E. K., Row, M. C., and Miller, D. B., "Rosenbluth International Alliance: Information Technology and the Global Virtual Corporation," *Proceedings of the Twenty-Fifth Annual Hawaii International Conference on System Sciences,* IEEE Computer Society Press, Los Alamitos, California, 1992.

2

Strategic Information Systems Are Conventional Information Systems Used in Innovative Ways

It's déjà vu all over again.

—Attributed to Yogi Berra.

INTRODUCTION

The development of information systems is often viewed as an evolution from the simple to the more complex. In the 1950s, when computer technology was in its infancy, most viewed computers as giant calculating machines used by scientists to find solutions to equations that would have taken a human many years to solve. As these machines gradually became more sophisticated, their commercial use became cost-effective. As expected, the first applications of computers in industry were for tasks like payroll or general ledger. These tasks were routine, well understood, and involved a degree of number crunching. In the history of computers, the late 1960s could be described as the era of mainframe. Businesses with highly data-driven tasks (i.e., banks) operated large, centralized computer systems that typically ran batch jobs to process the daily transactions of their business. This was the birth of *transaction processing systems* (TPSs). At that time, the efforts in computing were toward making computers work, rather than making a system work. Among the problems of that period were huge maintenance costs, duplication of data, and user dissatisfaction.[1]

With the emergence of minicomputers in the 1970s, online systems began to offer solutions to the problems of batch systems. Database management and high-order programming languages became widespread. Minis were cheap and convenient, and online systems made accurate and timely information readily available to managers. Comprehensive data and reports based on huge databases that in the past would not have been possible were now available. A higher level of decision capability could be managed by computers. The systems that emerged were *management information systems* (MISs). The arrival of networking technology made it possible for data from several systems to be merged or shared. A trend toward distributed processing for TPS activities and centralized MIS activities took place. The proliferation of personal computers and friendly PC software in the 1980s and the ability to link remote data to a central location and streamline it quickly into meaningful reports offered great advantages to decision makers in the form of *decision support systems* (DSSs).

In the late 1980s there were growing numbers of cases in which information technology has had successful strategic impact on organizations. For this reason, corporate executives have increased interest in what is termed *strategic information systems* (SISs).

This chapter investigates the attributes of TPS, MIS, DSS, and SIS. Similarities and differences among all four will be discussed, and arguments will be given as to why SISs are special forms of TPS, MIS, and DSS but not distinct, separate systems.

TYPES OF INFORMATION SYSTEMS

In the introduction, we described the emergence of four types of information systems. A framework developed by Robert Anthony of the Harvard Business School to provide a view of organizations through their hierarchy of decision making can provide a useful anchor for categorizing information systems.[2] Anthony divided a firm's activities into three control levels: strategic planning, management control, and operational control. From Henry Fayol's five managerial functions, a notion of how the levels of managerial control differ can be grasped.[3] According to Fayol, all managers perform the following five functions:

1. *Planning* what is to be done.
2. *Organizing* the appropriate structure to accomplish the plan.
3. *Staffing* the organization with appropriate personnel and coordinating their activities.
4. *Directing* (commanding) the staff toward the accomplishment of the plans.
5. *Controlling* the activities so that the objectives can be met.

These functions are performed at each level of Anthony's framework. But the scope of each function at the different levels varies considerably. For example, the planning activity at the *strategic level* would have a long-range focus. Strategic goals for the organization would be set for the present as well as the future. Additionally, this planning activity would broadly examine factors external to the firm. The firm's competitors as well as the political and social environment would be examined before setting the firm's long-range strategic goals. At the *management control level*, planning would be medium-range. This would involve gaining the resources and planning their use for meeting the goals set in the organization's long-range strategic plan. At the *operational control level*, planning would deal with the short-range goals of the organization. This involves decisions like What date should our shipment of widgets be manufactured to meet the delivery deadline? Table 2.1 lists Anthony's levels and types of management functions associated with each level.

TABLE 2.1 Management functions at various managerial levels

Management Function	Managerial Levels		
	Strategic Planning	Management Control	Operational Control
Planning	Long-range	Medium-range	Short-range
Organizing	General framework	Departmental level	Small unit level
Staffing	Key persons	Medium-level personnel	Operational personnel
Directing	General and long-range directives	Tactics and procedures	Daily and routine activities
Controlling	Aggregate level	Periodic control and exceptions	Regular and continuous supervision

SOURCE: N. Ahituv and S. Neumann. *Principles of Information Systems for Management,* 3rd ed. Copyright ©
1990, Wm. C. Brown Communications, Inc. Dubuque, Iowa. All Rights Reserved, Reprinted by permission.

An example of the strategic planning level in a university might be in enrollment decisions. In making decisions about enrollment, the strategic planning office for a university might decide how many students to admit in each field of study, how admittance might look for future years, and perhaps what budget will be available for recruitment and scholarships. The strategic planning level controls the long-term activities and decisions of the university. These tasks are nonredundant, long-range, typically involve senior management, and are not well understood or well structured. This clearly sounds like the mission of software supporting a DSS. For example, the Interactive Financial Planning System (IFPS) software package allows ad hoc financial modeling and what-if analysis in a relatively easy manner. The system aids management in providing a simple technique to model financial solutions to long-range corporate goals.[4]

The management control level for university enrollment would have a different role than that of strategic planning. Instead of setting the goals of the organization, they would initiate procedures to ensure that the goals are met. In this example, these activities might include developing registration procedures, establishing eligibility criteria, and staffing the registration office with qualified personnel. The management control level controls the university's medium-term activities. Mid-level managers might perform these tasks to meet the goals of the strategic planning level. They are more frequent than decisions faced at the strategic planning level but not highly redundant. These decisions have a higher degree of structure and can be classified as MISs. For example, an inventory management system that tracks distribution of merchandise and reorders items is a MIS. The functions performed by the system have a well-defined structure but are not highly redundant.

At the operational control level of university enrollment, the actual activity of accepting or rejecting applicants would be controlled. The operational control level represents the lowest level where the goals of an organization are implemented. This level controls the short-term activities of the organization. These tasks are highly redundant, highly structured, and well understood. The processing of deposits and withdrawals at banks is another example of an activity controlled by the operational control level. Each transaction uses exactly the same type of information, and the processes followed to perform the transactions are identical. The transactions are highly repetitive, and the decision process is highly defined. Systems of this type are TPSs.

Anthony's three levels can be summarized as follows:

1. *Strategic Planning*—Deciding on objectives of the organization, changes in these objectives, the resources used to attain these objectives, and the policies that are to govern the acquisition, use, and disposition of these resources.

2. *Management Control*—Assuring that resources are obtained and used effectively and efficiently in the accomplishment of the organization's objectives.

3. *Operational Control*—Assuring that specific tasks are carried out effectively and efficiently.

To draw an analogy from the military: while the top-level managers are involved with wars (strategy) and the middle-level managers are engaged in battles (tactics), the low-level managers are controlling the organizational skirmishes, patrols, raids, ambushes, recruiting, and training.

As yet, we have not discussed SISs. What are the characteristics of SISs, and where do they fit in Anthony's model? Perhaps the most heralded SIS is American Airlines' SABRE system.[5] Taking SABRE as a model SIS, one might describe an SIS as a well-structured, highly redundant, and well-understood system. In short, an SIS is a TPS! The same impression is evident when one reviews the historical development and attributes of the ASAP system described in chapter one.

The point to be made here is that an SIS is not an information system distinct from TPS, MIS, or DSS but a special case of these systems (if it walks like a duck and quacks like a duck and looks like a duck, it probably is a duck). Perhaps it is better to define information systems as strategic if they *change the way a firm competes,* whatever their operational characteristics are.

STRATEGIC INFORMATION SYSTEMS

The four systems discussed above are sequential in their emergence in computing history; however, it would be wrong to describe them as wholly evolutionary. The emergence of TPSs and large databases perhaps made it possible for users to conceive of MISs. Having access to huge amounts of data in report form would naturally lead users to ask for their own "tailored" reports and wish for the ability to perform specific queries of the data. This is exactly what happened in the case of CIGNA risk information services.[6]

The CIGNA Corporation was formed in 1982, through the merger of the Connecticut General Corporation and the INA Corporation. In just four years, CIGNA Corporation grew to be one of the largest insurance and financial services companies in the United States. CIGNA's primary sources of revenue came from Employee Benefits and Health Care Services, the Individual Financial Group, the Investment Group, and Property and Casualty. In 1986, CIGNA had 50,000 employees and $50 billion in assets.

The property and casualty area of CIGNA's business included a Special Risk Facilities (SRF) Group responsible for handling all large commercial customers. These firms were typically Fortune 500 companies, such as Ford, ITT, Monsanto, United Technologies, and General Dynamics.

The property and casualty business was highly cyclic. During good periods, new competitors were motivated to enter the market. This caused downward pressures on prices that, in turn, made the competition for business more aggressive. As a result, insurers assumed greater underwriting risk, which caused higher loss ratios and underwriting losses, which, in turn, made the industry less attractive to competing insurers. Eventually, the cycle would recur. As part of managing the risk cycle for property and casualty business, insurance brokers began to offer automated risk management services. By 1980 eight independent firms offered these services. The CIGNA Corporation felt that if they did not act, these systems could impact CIGNA's profitability.

In 1981 CIGNAs SRF group launched SATRA, its first information system to support risk-management services. SATRA was a batch system that produced large quarterly reports for CIGNA customers. It really just stripped desired data off a giant database and provided it to customers. SATRA was a typical TPS. While containing a lot of information on risks, it merely printed standardized reports for customers at the end of each financial quarter. It did not enhance the information with graphics, sorting, or error-checking capability. SATRA merely provided customer information in a noninteractive style. As a result of the voluminous data, customers began to ask for customized, streamlined reports. CIGNA found it increasingly hard to keep up with requests and decided to replace SATRA with CIGNA's Risk Information System (CRIS). CRIS provided CIGNA customers online access to the CIGNA database. Customers were allowed to query the database and tailor their own reports. In this sense CRIS can be categorized as an MIS. CRIS supported midlevel management decision making in that it allowed customers to query the database on a real-time basis and customize CRIS to support their repetitive yet individual decision needs.

CRIS is also an SIS. It did not evolve from an MIS to an SIS. It is actually an *MIS with strategic significance.* CRIS had the characteristics of an MIS, but with the additional feature of changing the way CIGNA competed in the risk-management business. In the past, insurance brokers acted as the go-between for customers and insurance carriers. The automated system allowed customers online access to data that was previously available only through brokers. This reduction in broker power pushed many of them out of the risk-management services business. By computerizing their services, CIGNA also built a significant barrier to new entrants into the business. In the past, risk management was cyclic and always saw a period of new entrants into the business. The capital required to build a large computer database and provide customers online access to it discouraged entry of other insurers. CRIS thus helped CIGNA smooth the low part of the insurance business cycle. Lastly, their existing competition, other firms offering risk management services, were behind in what they could offer customers, namely, quick access to accurate and updated information about their risk exposures.

The ASAP system provides a good example of a *strategic TPS.*[7] As described in chapter one, this system provided hospital staff with terminals and a simple system to order hospital supplies directly from the vendor. It made ordering of supplies easy and immediate. By offering a superior means for customers to order supplies, they were much more likely to order on ASAP than by other means. As ASAP offered only the vendor's products, this gave them a tremendous advantage over their competitors.

Figure 2.1 illustrates Anthony's framework, information systems associated with different levels of the organization, and how strategic information systems can play a role in supporting managers' decisions at all levels.

CIGNA's CRIS is an example of an MIS that is also strategic. Nonstrategic MISs include inventory management systems, Materials Requirements Planning (MRP) systems, and Just-in-Time (JIT) systems. An MRP is an information system that aids a decision maker in materials planning. Based on sales forecasts and supplies, raw material forecasts can be generated. These systems and JIT systems have saved manufacturers a great deal of money. The idea behind JIT is that by planning resources carefully, a manufacturer can eliminate storage of items along the product life cycle. Money is saved because materials and inventories are stored by suppliers, and the cost of storage by the manufacturer is greatly reduced. The decisions made at the management control level are more structured than those made at the strategic planning level. They also have a short time horizon and are more tactical in nature.

SABRE and ASAP are classic examples of TPSs that have proven to be highly strategic. An ATM or software used for producing a company payroll are also examples of TPSs. These systems address simple, highly redundant, well-defined tasks. Their aim is to support the operations level of an organization.

WHY SIS IS UNIQUE

Figure 2.1 gives a sense of how DSS, MIS, and TPS differ, and that SISs are represented across these systems. Four additional aspects of strategic information systems set them apart from other types of information systems:

- They change the way a firm competes.
- They have external focus.
- They are associated with a higher project risk.
- They are innovative.

As already mentioned, a system is strategic if it changes the way a firm competes. Consider how AHSC processed customer orders before ASAP was installed. It would hardly be classified as strategic because all hospital supply firms would have a similar system. ASAP expedited and simplified the ordering process and locked in customers,

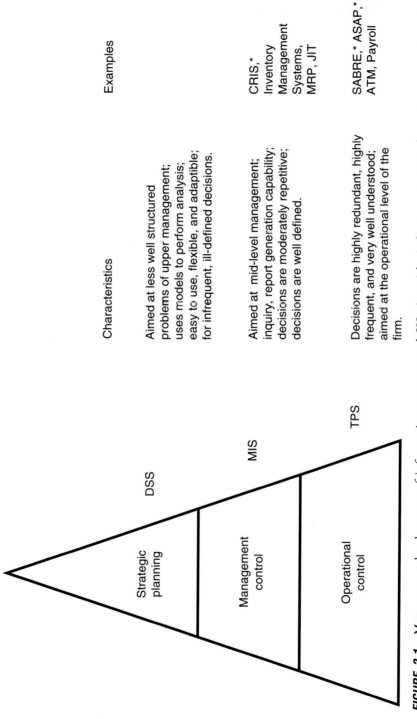

	Characteristics	Examples
DSS Strategic planning	Aimed at less well structured problems of upper management; uses models to perform analysis; easy to use, flexible, and adaptible; for infrequent, ill-defined decisions.	
MIS Management control	Aimed at mid-level management; inquiry, report generation capability; decisions are moderately repetitive; decisions are well defined.	CRIS,* Inventory Management Systems, MRP, JIT
TPS Operational control	Decisions are highly redundant, highly frequent, and very well understood; aimed at the operational level of the firm.	SABRE,* ASAP,* ATM, Payroll

FIGURE 2.1 Management levels, types of information systems, and SISs (asterisks indicate strategic information systems)

giving AHSC a tremendous advantage over rivals using manual or conventionally computerized TPSs.

A second distinguishing factor is that SISs have an external, broader focus. Whereas
payroll is directed at an internal business function, order processing is directed at a firm's
relationship with external customers. ASAP certainly made the internal processes involved in order processing easier because of the degree of automation. However, where it
proved to have significant impact was in electronically linking customers to AHSC.

SISs are also unique in that the risks associated with them are significantly higher
than those associated with development of internal systems. The losses associated with the
development of a system internal to the firm are monetary. They can be quantified in
terms of equipment purchased, person-hours invested, or salaries. The losses associated
with SIS development include these, in addition to jeopardizing a firm's competitive place
in the market. Ways in which this could happen are in creating systems that are easy to
replicate, creating lower entry barriers, inviting litigation, draining the resources of the
firm, or producing an advantage that is not sustainable. These risks and others are
discussed in chapter nine.

Lastly, SISs are in some sense innovative. They offer a change to a process or product
that distinguishes a firm from its competitors. Although ASAP ostensibly automated a
well-defined activity that all hospital supply firms performed, it was strategically innovative in that it linked customers to a specific supplier.

MISCONCEPTIONS ABOUT SIS

James Senn of Georgia State University dispelled several myths about strategic information systems.[8] First, strategic systems need not be the system of preference. Many times
the discussion of strategic systems leads the reader to believe that they are separate,
distinct entities from TPS, MIS, and DSS. From the examples presented in this chapter,
we hope this interpretation is refuted. ASAP and SABRE are clear examples of highly
strategic TPSs. ASAP performed simple order entry and processing. However, technology
made it easier for customers to place an order and provided quick, accurate delivery of
orders. ASAP was a strategic system because it captured more orders for AHSC at the
expense of competitors. The importance of being classified as strategic is not so much with
what type of information system is built but with how the system is used. It is the *use*,
not the system type, that makes an information system *strategic*. It seems that systems
labeled "strategic" are simpler than they are claimed to be. One is reminded of the story
about the football player who roughed the passer on fourth down at the five-yard line,
awarding the opposing team the ball half the distance to the goal line with four more
downs. As he trotted to the sideline, his coach asked him, "What happened?" Answered
the player, "Didn't you see?"

Another misconception about strategic systems is that they are carefully, deliberately
planned, or that they are accidents that just instantaneously occur. In reality, strategic
systems evolve over time. It is true that the king of strategic systems, American Airlines'
SABRE system, was originally planned to do inventory (passenger seat) management.

Max Hopper, who joined American Airlines in 1972 as director of SABRE, had little hint at the early stages that it would grow to earn more revenues than American Airlines itself.[9] As it happened, SABRE evolved to its present state over a long time. In fact, Hopper speculated in 1991 that the age of mega-impact systems like SABRE was rapidly closing, and that the strategic systems of the future would rely on more than automating existing processes. Hopper predicts that the strategic systems of the future will focus on exploitation of arising technology. Advances in technology will make it possible to solve existing problems not answered by strategic systems. The future of strategic systems is perhaps in streamlining and improving the operational-level functions of a firm. The future may thus see the development of SISs that will be more deliberate in nature.

A third fiction is that an SIS, once implemented, can offer sustained competitive advantage. It is hard to think of highly successful systems that a firm's competitors will not try to imitate. For example, when ATMs were introduced, virtually all banks adopted them. When certain banks became allies to provide a nationwide network of ATMs to customers, all banks followed suit either by forming alliances with other banks or by buying into an existing network. In fact, an ATM is no longer of strategic significance but, rather, a necessity for doing business. Federal Express invented the overnight delivery of packages through a hub-and-spoke network of airport terminals. Information systems helped them and their customers track packages and move them faster than the regular mail. Shortly after this business proved to be lucrative, many other air freight companies were formed. Airborne, Emery, and United Parcel Service became some of Federal Express's larger competitors. As a result, Federal Express is constantly innovating to try to sustain its advantage over other companies. Two steps that a company can take toward attaining a sustained competitive advantage are making additional innovations that competitors cannot duplicate, and locking in customers so they cannot switch to a competitor's system. In not being able to duplicate an innovation, one might think of patent laws or proprietary information. In locking in customers, one might think of supplying terminals, software, and training to customers, thereby making it too expensive and time-consuming for them to switch to a new system. However, these efforts are not easy to implement, making the introduction of strategic systems a risky project. Chapter eight elaborates on SISs and sustainable advantages.

Indeed, the plethora of cases reporting tremendously successful SISs may cause one to believe that SISs are risk-free tickets to competitive advantage. However, as mentioned earlier, the risks associated with systems development are magnified when the system is strategic. A case in point is a manufacturer of heating, ventilation, and cooling (HVAC) equipment that developed a system to support users in determining their specific HVAC requirements. Software, hardware, and databases were provided to customers. Unfortunately, a competitor soon introduced a similar system that used a telecommunications link to the manufacturer's mainframe. The competitor's system had a quicker response time and offered customers additional features. Thus, the development of the HVAC system *created* instead of *discouraged* competition. Other risks that can be triggered by an SIS include awakening competitors in the industry, creating a new basis for competition where competitors can do better, raising the cost of doing business for everyone, and failing.

Another common misconception is that ideas for strategic systems arise only within the information systems group. However, because strategic systems typically affect the relationship of the firm to external entities (i.e., customer or suppliers), one would expect ideas for strategic systems to arise from these areas. In reality, general managers and staff members are the source of most ideas for competitive systems. In fact, the idea for American Airlines' SABRE system came from the chief executive officer and the marketing department. The information systems group often acts in a support capacity to the rest of the firm. As such, they lack contact with customers or suppliers. They function internally in the firm's day-to-day operations. For this reason, IS staff members lack the global insight to organizational goals. Additionally, there is a tendency for IS management to view information technology as being of supportive, not strategic, importance.

Lastly, there is a misconception that strategic advantages can be attained only by large, spectacular innovations. As Lao Tsu said, a journey of a thousand leagues begins with a single step. Often careful examination of a process can yield ideas to add efficiency. Small efficiencies over millions of operations can lead to a great cost savings. For example, the introduction of JIT to hospital supply rooms is proving to offer great cost savings. Another example is Sears's collection of sales information on customers to determine when product warranties are due to expire. Telemarketers call these customers and sell them follow-up maintenance warranties.

SUMMARY

This chapter has provided an in-depth discussion of types of information systems and their characteristics. The idea that strategic systems are actually traditional information systems (TPS, MIS, DSS) with strategic value has been supported. In fact, all the traditional information systems used by organizations support strategic objectives. Ways that make strategic systems unique have also been explored. Strategic systems change the way firms compete and make a strategic difference in their competitive position. They are externally focused, can be very risky, and involve some degree of innovation.

Implications for development of strategic information systems involve careful examination of business and industry processes before investing in a strategic system. The goals and strategies of the corporation must be well understood, and risks associated with the introduction of an innovating information system must be assessed.

REFERENCES

1. Somogyi, E. K., and Gailliers, R. D., "From Data Processing to Strategic Information Systems—A Historical Perspective," in *Towards Strategic Information Systems,* Cambridge, Mass.: Abacus Press, 1987.
2. Anthony, R. N., *Planning and Control Systems: A Framework for Analysis,* Boston: Harvard University Press, 1965.

3. Fayol, H., *General and Industrial Management,* trans. C. Storrs. London: Sir Isaac Pitman & Sons, 1949.

4. Carlson, E. D., and Sprague, R. H., *Building Effective Decision Support Systems,* Englewood Cliffs, N.J.: Prentice-Hall, 1982.

5. Copeland, D. G., and McKenney, J. L., "Airline Reservation Systems: Lessons From History," *MIS Quarterly,* Sept. 1988.

6. Ives, B., *CIGNA Risk Information Services,* Harvard Business School Case 9-188-034, 1987, Harvard Business School, 1987.

7. Vitale, M. R., *American Hospital Supply Corporation (A): The ASAP System,* Harvard Business School Case 9-186-005, Harvard Business School, 1985.

8. Senn, J. A., "Debunking the Myths of Strategic Information Systems," *Business,* Oct. 1989.

9. Hopper, M., "In Depth Interview," *Computerworld,* Aug. 5, 1991.

3

Strategic Information Systems Frameworks

There are two classes of systems in the world;
those that divide the systems of the world
into two classes and those that do not.

WHAT ARE FRAMEWORKS FOR SIS?

The previous chapter made the point that in terms of their *use*, strategic information systems (SISs) can be considered a unique type of information system. Some scholars have suggested that a new conceptual foundation for SISs is required that goes beyond Robert Anthony's conventional framework of three management control levels. Many practitioners and academics have heeded this call by devising various frameworks for SISs. This chapter discusses several of these frameworks.

To use or discuss SIS frameworks, some important terms must first be defined. One definition of SIS focuses on the *use* of information and information technology: the primary function of an SIS is to "support or shape" the competitive strategy of the enterprise, its plan for gaining or maintaining "competitive advantage or reducing the advantage of its rivals."[1] Thus an SIS is any single type or hybrid information system—Transaction Processing System (TPS), Management Information System (MIS), Decision Support System (DSS)—that helps an organization compete. Perhaps a more accurate term would be *Competitive Information Systems* or *Competition Support Systems* (CSS). But to be consistent with the literature, this chapter uses the term SIS.

One common type of SIS crosses the borders of different organizations. These are called *Interorganizational Systems* (IOSs). Confusion about IOSs led to a medley of interpretations. A simple definition characterizes an IOS as "an automated information system shared by two or more companies."[2] Many of the frameworks described in this chapter deal exclusively or in part with IOSs. Chapter six is devoted to an expanded treatment of IOSs.

An additional definition may be helpful in reading this chapter. *Information technology* (IT) is composed of *information* that a business creates and uses as well as the wide spectrum of *technologies* that process this information.[3]

WHAT GENERAL FUNCTIONS DO FRAMEWORKS PERFORM?

Because issues in SIS are complex and dynamic, a structure is needed to analyze the issues. Frameworks provide that structure. They help us understand and classify the relation between competitive strategy and information technology. The power of frameworks is that they provide a shorthand language for describing the relation. They highlight important dimensions as well as suggest which dimensions are unimportant. Frameworks are *not* theories; they are only a classification language. As such, they are not subject to empirical verification. Michael Treacy of MIT stated that a "framework is not used because it is "true"; it is used because it is more powerful than competing language systems for describing elements of the research."[4] Some frameworks classify competitive uses for particular technologies. Most are used to assess the impact of IT or to search for SIS opportunities. Frameworks are also used as pedagogic tools to reorient thinking and raise awareness of the IT strategy relationship.

Despite the large number of frameworks cited in the literature, one study found that 55% of respondents did not use a regular or formal process of identifying IT opportunities.[5] One reason may be the overabundance of frameworks. To help readers deal with the *framework overload,* this chapter summarizes the more salient frameworks (in the land of the blind, the one-eyed man is king . . .).

WHAT ARE THE LIMITATIONS OF FRAMEWORKS FOR SIS?

Treacy has captured the major drawback of frameworks:

> As descriptive structures, these categorization schemes are useful and valuable. As a basis for making decisions about opportunities for new systems, they are badly flawed. Description does not beget prescription. Categories do not equate to opportunities. Only if one assumes that the salient dimensions used to differentiate systems are also the critical features for explaining systems success can one make that leap in logic. Yet such simple facts are often overlooked and many researchers have come to believe that the work is complete when a satisfactory framework has been developed. Instead, it is just the beginning.[6]

This caveat is especially important to keep in mind when viewing frameworks that help managers search for SIS opportunities.

Another problem with frameworks is their attempt to categorize a moving target. Technology is dynamic—never static—and competition is turbulent. Many frameworks fail to capture the dynamism between competition and technology.

Another set of factors that have caught managers by surprise are the inherent risks of SIS. It is noteworthy that only one of the frameworks presented here explicitly considers these risks—some subsume the risks within other dimensions. There are two general types of risks: risk of failure and risk of success; these are outlined later in this chapter.

Frameworks may also fail in "their lack of articulation of the fundamental logic and rationale for exploiting IT capabilities as well as the complexities of the organizational transformation required to leverage technological capabilities."[7] Because of their elegant simplicity, frameworks necessarily leave out many vital factors, complexities, and rationale to implement SISs. A framework, like a prescription drug, is useful for its intended purpose but may be harmful if used excessively or in the wrong context, or if it is abused.

HOW DO WE ASSESS A FRAMEWORK?

Three principles proposed to assess SIS frameworks state that they must

1. provide for intentional actions of people who devise and act on a strategy;
2. pay attention to product quality, customer service, employee commitment, competition, and other fundamental factors; and
3. allow management to make timely decisions and to act decisively.[8]

The principles attempt to account for the complexities inherent in developing and executing a competitive strategy. The first principle, the *principle of persons,* suggests that people who devise and act on the strategy have their own agendas. The second principle, the *principle of factors,* makes a distinction about the factors affected by the strategy. The third principle, the *principle of timely decisions,* states that a framework is not useful unless it provides an enduring guide to action and decision making. Few if any of the frameworks that follow abide by all three principles. Some may exhibit strength in one or two principles but neglect the third. This is not to be interpreted as a sign of a weak framework. A single framework cannot be everything to everybody. But assessment using these three principles informs about areas of emphasis. An astute manager uses a combination of frameworks as a hedge against *framework failure.* In this chapter, frameworks are also assessed in terms of specific uses, scope, advantages, and disadvantages.

FRAMEWORK FOR FRAMEWORKS

This chapter classifies frameworks into four simple categories: (1) foundation frameworks, (2) SIS opportunity-seeking frameworks, (3) strategic impact/value frameworks, and (4) contingency factors frameworks. The majority of the frameworks are based on the work of Michael Porter and Gregory Parsons. These *foundation frameworks* are presented first. Many frameworks have two general purposes: the first is to search for SIS opportunities; the second is to assess the impact or value of existing or potential SISs. Some of the frameworks can be used in either mode; however, they are classified according to their most obvious use. Finally, a few frameworks do not fall within the first three categories. These contingency factors frameworks are included in the fourth category.

THE FRAMEWORKS

A detailed description of each framework is beyond the scope of this chapter, but references are often given so that readers may investigate on a deeper level. This chapter focuses on the specific use of each framework, its strengths, and its weaknesses as well as its scope.

FOUNDATION FRAMEWORKS

A search of the literature reveals that almost every framework in this category has been derived either explicitly or implicitly from the seminal work of Michael Porter of the Harvard Business School.

Porter's Five Forces

Porter maintained that in every industry, competition depends on the collective strength of five basic forces (Figure 3.1). Interacting with these forces are the generic corporate strategies (see below). Porter's *industry and competitive analysis* (ICA) framework provides managers with a structure to facilitate strategic planning.[9] IT can be a powerful agent to change the balance of power in and between these forces. One key element in several of the forces is knowledge; better information begets greater negotiation power.

Threat of new entrants is deterred by barriers to entry into the industry. Barriers are structural characteristics of the industry. There are many types of barriers: switching costs, economies of scale, high investment in IT, economies of experience, access to distribution

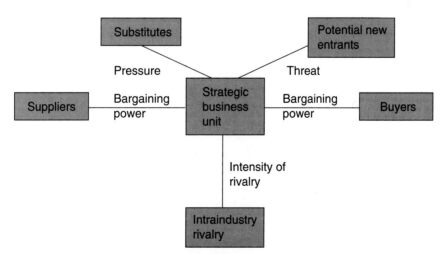

FIGURE 3.1   Forces in the competitive arena

channels, and government policy. New entrants can increase overall capacity in the industry, thereby reducing prices and incumbents' cost advantages. IT can help create or raise barriers to entry by increasing mandatory investments in hardware and software, facilitating control over databases, or locking in customers to existing distribution channels.

Intensity of rivalry depends on factors beyond the control of the individual firm, such as degree of concentration, diversity, or dependency; rate of industry growth; or switching costs. It is critical to understand the strategies of one's rivals in detail. For instance, Ford's strategy depends on the strategies of Toyota, Nissan, GM, and Volkswagen, and vice versa. Because of these interdependencies, signaling of intentions is important in understanding rivalry. IT can also be used to create alliances between rivals, such as ATM networks.

Threat of substitute products may arise from products and services in other industries. For example, the products of stock brokers and insurance companies now compete against banks for the investment dollar. This force directs managers' attention to the various ways a customer's dollar can be spent for the same function. Substitute products can eliminate an industry. For example, the automobile eliminated the horse with buggy, and the silicon chip eliminated electromechanical adding machines. The life cycle of products can be reduced through the use of technology, such as Computer-Aided Design (CAD). IT has also provided the basis for creating new information-intensive products.

Bargaining power of buyers drives prices down and the quality of products up. Buyer power depends on the level of switching costs, the competitive position of the buyer in the industry (size, volume), whether the buyer can purchase a commodity product, or whether the buyer poses a serious threat of backward integration (i.e., buying out or merging with its suppliers). Electronic bulletin boards can increase the number of buyers, thereby reducing the influence of any individual buyer. Installing computer terminals at the buyers' site is one way to raise the buyers' cost of switching to other suppliers.

Bargaining power of suppliers is in some ways the antithesis of buyer power. The threat of forward integration (i.e., buying out or merging with its customers) is one determinant of supplier power. Influential suppliers drive prices up and reduce the quality and quantity of products and services. Supplier power also depends on size, volume, and concentration relative to other firms in the industry. A differentiated product and availability of industry information to buyers also impacts suppliers' power.

Porter's ICA framework leaves the definition of "industry" up to the manager. The framework does not help determine the scope of the industry or likely reactions of buyers, suppliers, or rivals. How can managers be vigilant about new entrants or substitute products if they do not know from which industry they may emerge?

The ICA framework is deceptive in its simplicity. Analysis of competitive forces in practice is complex and time-consuming. This violates the third framework assessment principle of timely decision making.

Porter's framework has been criticized as being grossly incomplete. This framework ignores the role of other external entities and social factors such as the government, consumer activists, employees, and pollution, to name a few. A *Strategic Forces* framework addresses these criticisms by augmenting Porter's ICA framework with seven other forces: technology, converging industries, global competition, knowledge as capital, demographics, government regulations, and important items in the environment.[10] This last force, environmental factors, functions as a catchall category but makes the framework useful for specific firms, because items in the environment are evaluated according to individual circumstances. These seven additional forces are intended to help managers identify changes among an organization's internal and external relationships. Because of its emphasis on various fundamental factors, the Strategic Forces framework is the best example of a framework exhibiting strength in the second assessment principle.

IOS Framework

Cash and Konsynski of the Harvard Business School used Porter's five forces to outline uses of an interorganizational system (IOS) for competitive advantage.[11] Use varies depending on the involvement of the organization. There are two types of entities involved with an IOS: *participants* and *facilitators.* An IOS participant is an organization that develops, operates, or uses an IOS to exchange information that supports a primary business process. Participants can be competitors, organizations in a buyer-supplier chain, or a combination of these. For example, Bank of America participates in several automated teller machine (ATM) networks. Travel agents are participants in airline reservation systems. An IOS facilitator is an organization that aids in the development, operation, or use of a network for exchange of information among participants. The supporting products or services are a part of the primary business of the facilitator. For example, CompuServe operates a network for various information services including home banking, database retrieval, and electronic communications. Eastman Kodak developed a system that allows film-developing laboratories to obtain information about Kodak and order its products.

The IOS framework helps managers in planning decisions related to IOS and highlights areas impacted by an IOS. The framework acts as a general guidepost in directing managers' attention to potential uses of an IOS. Analysis of an IOS adds another level of complexity to Porter's framework and increases the time frame for decisions:

1. *New entrants:* IOSs provide entry barriers, greater economies of scale, switching costs, product differentiation, limited access to distribution channels, and control over market access.
2. *Buyers:* IOSs are used to influence buyers, differentiate products, and raise switching costs.
3. *Suppliers:* IOSs reduce switching costs, encourage competition, and increase the threat of backward integration.
4. *Substitute products:* IOSs improve price and performance as well as redefine products and services.
5. *Rivals:* IOSs improve cost effectiveness, control market access, and differentiate product and company.

Porter's Generic Corporate Strategies

Porter suggests three *generic corporate strategies:* cost leadership, differentiation of products or services, and focus.[12] Focus strategy is used with either cost leadership or differentiation in a narrow market segment. These generic strategies are logical approaches to obtain competitive advantage. Specific actions to implement these strategies differ from firm to firm and from industry to industry. SISs impact an organization's execution of competitive strategy in various ways.

Cost Leadership.   A firm with the lowest production costs in the industry can price its offerings below competitors'. IT can enhance or make it possible for a firm to achieve cost leadership. For example, material requirement planning (MRP) systems help drive down the costs of inventory and stock control. Computer-aided design (CAD) and computer-aided engineering (CAE) systems reduce the cost of design and engineering operations.

Differentiation.   If a product or service is perceived as unique, the firm can extract an above-average profit. The opportunities are greater when there is a large portion of information content in the product or process. For instance, a builder of standardized houses in Tampa, Florida, used a CAD system to redirect its business toward customized housing and as one element in differentiating its product (house plans) from the competition in the housing industry. Its house plans commanded a premium price.

Focus (niche).   Porter suggested that the preceding two strategies could have either a narrow scope (focusing in a narrow segment of the industry) or a broad scope (participating in a large range in the industry). Attention to a specific market segment is a *niche* strategy. Analysis of public or private databases can facilitate discovery of niche opportunities. For example, a greeting card company can determine what color cards are popular in a specific city and allocate resources to respond quickly to changing trends.

According to Porter, explicit choice of a specific generic strategy is important because cost leadership and differentiation are mutually exclusive. Differentiation is expensive. Those who attempt to follow both end up in a failure mode called *stuck in the middle.* A study of the 64 largest U.S. manufacturing firms found that skills and resources needed for a cost-leadership strategy were incompatible with the skills and resources required for a differentiation strategy.[13]

It has been suggested that Porter's strategies are too rationalistic and formal to be even close to the reality of business practice in small- and medium-sized companies.[14] Charles Wiseman of Columbia University expanded Porter's choices by adding strategies of *alliance, growth,* and *innovation.* Practitioners and academics have suggested other corporate competitive strategies.

Porter claims that merely following a generic strategy is inadequate. The firm must also gain a *sustainable competitive advantage.* There is considerable debate about whether and when advantage is sustainable. (Chapter eight focuses on this subject.) Nonetheless, this chapter is concerned with frameworks to seek opportunities and assess the value of competitive advantage, sustainable or otherwise.

Parsons's Trilevel Framework

Gregory Parsons, while at the Harvard Business School, identified three levels of interaction where IT can be used as a competitive tool: the industry level, the firm level, and the strategy level.[15] Parsons based his framework on Porter's five forces and generic strategies. At the firm level, specific competitive forces (discussed above) shape the impact of IT on the competing firm. At the strategy level, IT supports the execution of generic corporate strategies (also discussed above).

At the industry level, IT impacts the nature of the industry's products and services, the product life cycle, and the speed of product distribution. In markets, IT impacts overall demand, degree of segmentation, and geographic distribution possibilities. IT can impact the economics of production via factors like economies of scale, the value-added stream, and the flexibility versus standardization trade-off. Many industries have been altered because of IT. Examples include banking, publishing, distribution chains, manufacturing, retailing, health care organizations, and airlines. More recently, public-sector and not-for-profit organizations have been affected by IT.

Parsons's taxonomy is one of the earliest examples of an impact framework. His framework helped shift the focus from technology to the firm's strategy. The value in this framework is its emphasis on linking IT to strategy at a preliminary stage of analysis. Because of its wide scope, Parsons's framework provides a background for further analysis of IT opportunities and threats. The next chapter further elaborates on this framework.

SIS OPPORTUNITY-SEEKING/IDENTIFYING FRAMEWORKS

These frameworks are useful as analytical tools which can help managers discover firm-specific opportunities for IT.

The Value Chain

The *value chain* is an analytical framework to examine value-adding activities in the individual firm and between firms. It was developed by Porter[16,17] and later adapted by Porter and Millar[18] in an IT context. The assumption of the value chain is that competitive advantage arises from the value created for the customer that exceeds the cost of creating the value. The more a firm understands its own value chain as well as the value chain of the customer, the greater the ability to create value for that customer. Value activities consist of primary and support activities. Primary activities involve the production and delivery of the product or service plus after-sale support:

> *Inbound logistics*—expediting raw materials to production
> IT examples: automated warehousing, just-in-time inventory
> *Operations*—transforming inputs into finished products
> IT examples: flexible manufacturing, robotics
> *Outbound logistics*—storing and distributing finished products
> IT examples: automated order processing, electronic bills of lading
> *Marketing and sales*—promotion and sale of products
> IT examples: telemarketing, portable computers for salespersons

Service—postsale service to maintain and enhance product

IT examples: remote servicing, computer scheduling of repair technicians, automated help desks

Support activities provide the infrastructure for primary activities:

Firm infrastructure—support of entire value chain, includes general management, legal services, finance, and public relations

IT examples: planning models, decision support tools

Human resources management—recruiting, hiring, training, development

IT examples: automated personnel scheduling, computerized training tools

Technology development—improving products or processes, R&D

IT examples: CAD, CAE

Procurement—purchasing inputs

IT example: online procurement systems, inventory locator system

One important concept in the value chain framework is linkages. A firm's value chain is a link in the collective value chains in the industry, called the *value system.* Suppliers' value chains are *upstream,* while customers' value chains are *downstream.* Managers can use the value chain in conjunction with generic corporate strategies to analyze where and how to add value to products and services (Figure 3.2). This analysis could be used throughout the value system.

Every value activity has both a physical and an informational content. This dichotomy brought attention to the information provided by technology and not just the technology.[19] The *information intensity* framework described below provides a detailed description of this dichotomy. Furthermore, IT can be used to shape the products *and* the processes. To identify SIS applications, managers can investigate the linkages and the points where IT can transform the product or process and add value to it.

The value chain framework has been characterized as simple yet powerful. It is based on the theory of industrial economics. It directs managers' attention to customers—after all, it is the customer who generates revenues. Yet it does not confine an analysis to customers. The value chain has been criticized as shortsighted and as more useful at the operational rather than the strategic level. Other critics suggested that value chain anal-

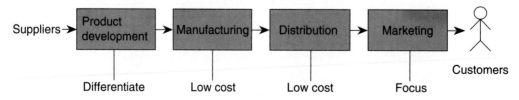

FIGURE 3.2   Where and how can value be added?

ysis provided only a simple checklist or prompts for IT applications.[20] This framework cannot prescribe particular technologies or applications but helps in appraising particular areas of opportunity.

Strategic Thrusts

Five basic mechanisms that an organization adopts to compete—differentiation, cost, innovation, growth, and alliance—are what Wiseman called *strategic thrusts*.[21] He characterized thrusts as transformations that affect the state of an organization. A thrust can be identified as a strategy or a strategy may be supported by one or more thrusts. A thrust manifests polarity, for example, differentiation may be used *offensively* or *defensively*. Thrusts also exhibit degree relations such as intensity (minor, major) or duration (long-term versus short-term). Differentiation thrusts distinguish a firm's products or services from its competitors'. Cost thrusts achieve advantage by reducing one's own costs or increasing the costs of one's competitors. Innovation thrusts are changes in the products or processes that affect the entire industry. Growth thrusts are achieved via increased volume, geographic expansion, diversification of products, or backward/forward integration. Alliance thrusts revolve around joint ventures or agreements formed between organizations.

Strategic Option Generator (SOG)

An important framework used by practitioners is Wiseman's SOG.[22] Wiseman cautions that the SOG must be used with knowledge of the strategic thrusts framework. Wiseman suggested that the SOG not be used as a "rigid scheme for classifying strategic uses of information technology" but rather as a procedure for identifying SIS opportunities. This framework attempts to capture the moves open to an organization in search of competitive advantage.

The framework focuses on how information technology is related to the five strategic thrusts and two types of strategic targets that can be impacted by them. Targets are either those that pertain to the SIS or those that play a role in the competitive arena. Competitive *arena targets* are supplier, channel, customer, and rival. *SIS targets* are the organization (enterprise) using the SIS, supplier, channel, customer, and rival. Specifying the targets helps differentiate among the different influences exerted by the targets and the effects of strategic thrusts on those targets. Enterprise targets include functional units or business units in the product network. Supplier targets are the suppliers to the enterprise. Organizations involved in the distribution channels are channel targets. Customer targets are self-explanatory. Rival targets are potential, indirect, or direct competitors. Each of these targets can be examined in the context of each strategic thrust. For example, the relationship between the differentiation thrust and channels in the competitive arena is one potential area of analysis.

Because of this focus on targets, the SOG was examined empirically and found to be effective in generating SIS ideas.[23] An early version of the SOG was used at GTE to generate 300 ideas for strategic applications. Six of these ideas were considered strategically important.[24] Likewise, firms can take a subset of the SOG and use it to develop

SIS ideas relevant to their own circumstances. For instance, a firm considering a joint venture with a competitor may want to analyze the effect of the alliance thrust in terms of the effect on its customers. Another possible adaptation might be to list important stakeholders as those targets who may be affected by or influence the success of a chosen thrust.

Because thrusts are not mutually exclusive, one problem may arise when they are used in combination. For example, innovation and differentiation may be used together as well as growth and cost or growth and alliance. Such combinations can make SIS analysis increasingly complex.

IOS Opportunities

The best-known examples of using IT for competitive advantage have revolved around systems that link together different organizations (IOS). To appreciate the strategic opportunities for IOS, Johnston and Vitale developed a framework to categorize IOS based on three criteria: *business purpose, relationship* between sponsoring organization and other participants, and *information function* of the system.[25]

The framework takes the form of a decision tree. Four questions are sequentially addressed to map a path through the tree: why? who? what? and how? The first question—*why*—is designed to determine the business purpose. Gaining advantage over competitors is a basic business purpose. When discussing business purpose, knowledge of the competitive dynamics in the industry is valuable. In the framework, a firm can make a choice to leverage the present business or enter a new one.

The next question—*who*—deals with the relationships with other participants (i.e., who is involved with the IOS?). Four entities commonly associated with IOSs are listed in the framework: customers, dealers, suppliers, and competitors. IOSs usually change the balance of power between entities. For a sponsor of the IOS to gain competitive advantage, the IOS needs to provide incentives and benefits for each participant. Thus, thorough knowledge of the relationships between sponsors and participants is important.

The third question—*what*—addresses the information function of the IOS. Function is a measure of the number and kinds of capabilities allowed to participants. For example, some participants can enter, store, and manipulate data; others are limited in their access to information. The function can have three forms: boundary, shared, or internal. The most common type of IOS handles *boundary* transactions such as order entry or electronic shopping. *Shared* access allows participants to retrieve and analyze information from the sponsoring organization's database. This shared function is found in the freight-tracking systems used by freight carriers like Consolidated Freightways. Customers can access the carrier's database to check on the progress and location of their shipment. Some IOSs help participants with *internal* or *back office* operations. For example, one IOS allows individual pharmacies to manage their drug inventories. Participating pharmacies can enter, store, and manipulate data without transmitting it to the IOS sponsoring organization.

The last question—*how*—focuses on specific improvements that can be considered in the IOS analysis. This last decision is a consequence of the path taken. For example, if the path through the tree (1) leverages the present business (why), (2) is concerned with suppliers (who), and (3) functions as a boundary system (what), then several possible IOS improvements can be examined. The framework lists five areas of improvement borrowed directly from the *Causal Model of Competitive Advantage* (described later): search-related costs, unique product features, switching costs, internal efficiency, and interorganizational efficiency.

This framework is complex because there is a large number of search combinations. Judgment is advised in searching for opportunities that fit with the interests and capabilities of the organization. This framework helps clarify the objectives of the IOS as well as the costs and benefits to all IOS participants. Moreover, the framework allows managers to focus on the relationships between the participants. This focus strengthens the framework in the first assessment principle (persons).

Levels of IOS

Barrett and Konsynski developed a five-level classification scheme for IOS nodes.[26] An IOS node is the role of an organization in an IOS. This framework for IOS is useful for understanding the numerous types of IOS and the various ways that organizations participate in them. The *sponsoring* organization of the IOS must be especially cognizant of the level of each *participant* because that level determines the degree of security, availability of information, and privacy required in the IOS.

Level 1 Remote I/O node
Level 2 Application processing node
Level 3 Multiparticipant exchange node
Level 4 Network control node
Level 5 Integrating network node

At Level 1, the firm serves as a remote node for one of the higher-level nodes. A travel agent connected to an airline reservation system would function at Level 1. Level 2 describes an organization that does application processing in an IOS. For example, a supplier firm processes orders from electronically linked customers. A multiparticipant exchange node describes an organization that functions as one of several points in a network where information is exchanged among participants. The fourth level differs from the third in that, at Level 4, the organization controls the network. The highest level is usually a data communication or data processing utility that integrates any number of lower-level participants and applications in real time. An example of an organization at Level 5 is CIRRUS, which runs a nationwide ATM network.

Strategic Opportunities Framework

The Strategic Opportunities framework challenges the assumption that SIS opportunities are only external to the organization.[27] The framework suggests two areas that managers should focus on: (1) external versus internal, and (2) traditional business versus business

	External operations	Internal operations
IT-intensive products and services	Gannett-USA Today	Digital Equipment Corporation
Traditional products and processes	American Hospital Supply Corporation	United Airlines

FIGURE 3.3   Strategic opportunities framework

transformed by IT. The framework stresses the role of top management vision and support as a prerequisite for a successful SIS. Figure 3.3 illustrates the framework and provides examples of now classic cases of companies that implemented SISs. The major contribution of this framework is in providing the external/internal dimension. Other frameworks have subsequently incorporated this dimension.

The scope of this framework is so broad that the three framework assessment principles do not apply to it. It is perhaps too general to help a specific firm pinpoint opportunities and may require modification for use. For example, a building firm in the United Kingdom expanded the *Internal Operations* column into *back office* and *front office* systems and rephrased the vertical dimension of the matrix in terms of old technology and new technology. Within each of the six cells, it listed the general types of systems that provide opportunities.

SIS Support Mechanisms

The underlying assumption of the *SIS Support Mechanisms* framework is that investment in information systems is intended to gain a competitive edge. This framework expands the internal versus external dimension of the Strategic Opportunities Framework.[28] It sorts out the mechanisms to support each of the two types of SIS systems (internal and external) and provides prescriptions for applications. External systems directly benefit the corporation's customer, whereas internal systems directly benefit the corporation. For each category of system there are several mechanisms and exemplar systems, as follows:

External Systems

Mechanism 1 Service delivery (in-home electronic shopping)
Mechanism 2 Product delivery (portable insurance selling)

Mechanism 3 Distribution channel delivery (automated teller machines)

Mechanism 4 Other concepts delivery (direct physicians' electronic claims processing)

Internal Systems

Mechanism 1 information intelligence delivery (integration of internal and external marketing information)

Mechanism 2 Product cost delivery (integrated manufacturing distribution system with feedback and controls)

Mechanism 3 Service cost delivery (IT for labor substitution)

Mechanism 4 Organizational delivery (office functions automation)

This framework is useful in describing generic areas for SIS. It can be pointed out that strategic systems benefiting customers are generally found in the service industries, while those benefiting the corporation are in the industrial sector. The drawback of the framework is that the mechanisms it describes do not identify specific processes, interactions, or relationships on which to focus an information system to gain competitive advantage. The mechanisms represent only generic areas in which information systems could be deployed. This framework does pay attention to a few important factors, thus meeting the second framework assessment principle of fundamental factors.

The Customer Resource Life Cycle Model

The *Customer Resource Life Cycle* model (CRLC) is a simple but elegant framework that focuses on the relationship or linkages between a company and its customers.[29] The framework is based on four major stages, each comprising several steps, as follows:

The Requirements Stage

1. *Establish* requirements by customers (determine how much of a resource is needed by them)
2. *Specify* (determine a resource's attributes)

The Acquisition Stage

3. *Select* source (determine where customers will buy a resource)
4. *Order* (order a quantity of a resource from a supplier)
5. *Authorize* and pay for (transfer funds or extend credit)
6. *Acquire* (take possession of a resource)
7. *Test and accept* (ensure that a resource meets specifications)

The Stewardship Stage

8. *Integrate* (add to an existing inventory)
9. *Monitor* (control access and use of a resource)

10. *Upgrade* (upgrade a resource if conditions change)
11. *Maintain* (repair a resource, if necessary)

The Retirement Stage

12. *Transfer or dispose* (move or dispose of inventory as necessary)
13. *Account* for (monitor where and how much is spent on a resource)

The CRLC is one of the more useful frameworks available. It allows managers to adopt the customer's perspective in evaluating IT to differentiate offerings. The assumption is that a customer's consumption of products and services (resources) go through this life cycle. The 13-step resource life cycle provides a structure for identifying new IT-based opportunities. This framework views each step as a point of opportunity for competitive advantage and provides detailed guidance for managers. Examples of applications for the various steps are found throughout the literature. Toll-free telephone numbers for customer service and maintenance are one example of using IT in the *maintain* step. In the *dispose* step, a common example of using IT is the quick check-out systems used in hotels and car rental agencies. Some applications cover two or more steps.

The CRLC framework has little prescriptive power. As a descriptive device, it is best viewed as a framework to search for strategic opportunities at a detailed level. Its strength lies in its application to competitive marketing strategies, but a firm should not limit its search to a single relationship (i.e., between customer and company). Adaptation to other relationships between a company and external entities might prove valuable.

Runge's Adaptation of the CRLC

Runge's adaptation of the CRLC is an example of an information technology–fitting framework.[30] This framework was used to analyze telecommunications-based information system (TBIS) links to customers. Runge found that 12 steps, similar to the 13 steps of the CRLC, were important. The 12 steps are divided among the four stages as follows:

Requirements Stage

1. *Establish* requirements
2. *Acquire* information

Acquisition Stage

3. *Specify*
4. *Select* a source
5. *Order*
6. *Authorize and pay*
7. *Acquire*

Stewardship Stage

8. *Monitor*
9. *Manage*
10. *Support*

Retirement Stage

11. *Terminate use*
12. *Account for*

For each of the 12 steps there are three possible types of links: internal, link-up, and lock-in. *Lock-in* between a supplier firm and its customer is the supplier's ultimate goal. Lock-in of customers can be achieved by differentiating the supplier from rivals or raising customers' costs of switching to other suppliers. Firms can accomplish this goal through electronic linkages. Lock-in is not a one-move strategy but evolves through a series of moves beginning with *internal* routines that add value for the customer and then progressing to a basic electronic *link-up* with the customer. *Internal* routines impact functions that involve customer interactions with the firm. Internal routines usually do not involve physical (electronic) links with customers. Link-up, however, does include electronic ties to customers such as the placement of terminals on the customer's site.

Runge suggested that this framework is best used in a specific sequence of steps. First, plot the customer interactions with the supplier firm. Then look at each interaction and ask whether TBIS can add value, simplify, or improve that interaction. Look for latent opportunities in internal, link-up, and lock-in dimensions within the current information system. Finally, search for opportunities to achieve lock-in either immediately or incrementally from internal routines through link-up.

5-Phase Planning and 7-Step Idea-Generation Frameworks

Although the next two frameworks are not aimed specifically at generating SIS opportunities, they are both useful in creating an organizational mindset that leads to opportunity identification.[31] Both the 5-phase and 7-step frameworks can be synthesized into two activities: educating executives about SIS and generating SIS ideas. Within each step, other frameworks can be used to complete the step. For example, during the *tutorial step,* the SOG framework can be used to introduce the concepts of strategic thrusts. Later, in the *opportunity identification step,* the CRLC framework might be used. Because they lend structure to SIS idea-generation and planning, the 5-phase and 7-step frameworks help reduce wasted effort and promote timely decisions. The framework assessment principle of timely decisions applies to both these frameworks.

The 5-phase framework is a planning tool that educates executives about SIS and includes the following phases:

Phase 1: Introduce the chief information officer (CIO) to SIS concepts (gain approval to proceed with idea-generation meeting for entire IS group)

Phase 2: Idea-generation meeting for IS middle management (test SIS idea-generation methodology; identify significant SIS ideas for executive consideration)

Phase 3: Conduct SIS idea-generation meeting for senior IS executives (identify SIS ideas and evaluate these together with previous ideas)

Phase 4: Introduce SIS concept to CEO (gain approval to proceed with SIS idea-generation meeting for business planners)

Phase 5: Conduct SIS idea-generation meeting for corporate business planners (identify SIS ideas and evaluate those ideas together with previous ideas)

The 7-step framework details procedures to generate SIS ideas. The steps are as follows:

Step 1: Present tutorial on SIS and competitive strategy (i.e., introduce the concepts of strategic targets and competitive strategy)

Step 2: Apply SIS concepts to actual cases (raise consciousness about SIS possibilities via good examples)

Step 3: Review company's competitive position (gain understanding of the competitive position and strategies of the organization)

Step 4: Brainstorm for SIS opportunities (generate SIS ideas in small groups)

Step 5: Discuss SIS opportunities (eliminate duplication and condense ideas)

Step 6: Evaluate remaining SIS ideas (assess competitive significance of ideas)

Step 7: Detail SIS blockbusters (detail each SIS blockbuster idea, its competitive advantage, and implementation issues)

Information in Pricing Framework

This framework classifies pricing systems along two interacting dimensions: pricing decision type and information attributes.[32] The *pricing decision type* is divided according to Anthony's three levels of planning and control: strategic planning, management control, and operational control. Pricing decisions on the strategic level pertain to choosing the pricing strategy. Management control level decisions have to do with (1) setting a basic price, and (2) determining the price structure. On the operational level, the pricing decisions are concerned with pricing administration.

Information attribute categories, the second dimension of pricing systems, are based on a three-part classification: (1) timeliness, (2) content, and (3) format of information.[33] *Timeliness* is characterized by age of information, response time, and frequency of update. *Content* attribute is composed of accuracy, level of detail, completeness, and relevance of information. *Format of information* includes ordering, access, graphic design, and the medium of display (e.g., screen, voice, hard copy).

Case examples of IS are used to illustrate the various relationships among attributes and decision types. Some systems span all three attributes within a decision level. For example, frequent-flyer promotions deal with price administration decisions but must include all three types of information attributes. They must respond to price changes by competitors within hours (response time), know which routes are affected (relevance), and know how to target (medium) and which market segment (ordering) to target. Other case examples are confined to a simpler relationship between pricing decision and information attribute. A real estate example illustrates the relationship between format and setting the right price. Real estate appraisers are highly concerned about setting the right price on a property and must use various sources of information to help set that price. Sources like tax records, county assessor files, and listing books are difficult to use. To expedite the process, most appraisers download information from electronic databases that have a format they understand.

Pricing is an information-intensive activity; thus, IS can provide support for this activity in various ways. This framework aids identification of opportunities to improve the pricing activity. Competitive advantage can be gained if response is improved at all levels of the pricing decision process. Managers must have solid knowledge of the firm's pricing practices and strategy before using this framework. A knowledge of IS technology is also advised. Such widespread knowledge requirements imply that a team approach is appropriate. A problem with this framework is that applications often span several information attributes as well as several levels of pricing decisions, making it difficult to categorize a system exactly.

Marketing Opportunities Framework

Another framework that aids in searching for marketing opportunities, besides the CRLC, is the *Marketing Opportunities Search* (MOS) framework.[34] There are six crucial factors in IT support of marketing. Each one suggests a direction that an information system development could take. The six factors with suggestions for IT opportunities are as follows:

1. *Perceived product differentiation by customers* (if low, use product information; if high, use market analysis)
2. *Distribution channel structure* (if direct, use sales support or retail alliances; if dedicated, use sales support; if shared, use service provision)
3. *Relationship between customer need and product* (if unclear, use consumer guidance)
4. *Frequency of customer's purchase decision* (if high, use fastest service provision; if low, use customer tracking)
5. *Frequency of delivery within contract* (if high, build partnership with customer, e.g., electronic linkage)
6. *Buyer access to IT resources* (if poor, provide consumer guidance; if good, build partnership with customer)

The strength of this framework is that managers can ask application-specific questions. It is therefore more pragmatic than the general frameworks that characterize so much of the SIS field. Firms can use the framework as a shell and brainstorm for additional ideas for IT support in marketing. The second framework assessment principle, the principle of fundamental factors, is relevant to the MOS framework.

Information Weapon Framework

This three-dimensional framework is used for searching out competitive advantage. The first dimension pertains to three information strategies: technological innovation, information services, and productivity.[35] *Technological innovation* can support a product differentiation strategy but requires input from product managers, marketers, and strategic planners. Technological innovation can range from a revolutionary new product to a simple idea like placing a computer terminal on the customer's site. *Information services* can be internal or external. Decision support systems and risk analysis software packages are two examples of internal information services. External information services include marketing databases and customer demographics systems. *Productivity* supports a low-cost strategy. Automation of labor-intensive processes, information centers, and end-user computing can be used as examples of this category.

The second dimension emphasizes the internal and the external application. The internal/external dimension focuses on looking for competitive opportunities in productivity, innovation, and information services within the firm or for external entities.

The third dimension of the framework views competitive advantage from the perspective of either a leader or a follower. A leader engenders greater risk by being a first mover in introducing an SIS. However, the leader may in the process create well-entrenched gains. Followers can learn from a leader's mistakes and can perhaps improve or alter products for greater differentiation and strategic success.

This framework has little prescriptive power and is best used as another classification scheme for potential SIS. The strength of this framework, unlike others presented here, is that it has more than two dimensions. Cognitive limitations prevent us from thinking about more than a few items at one time. This framework stretches these limitations by classifying 12 ($3 \times 2 \times 2$) areas of potential opportunity.

STRATEGIC IMPACT/VALUE FRAMEWORKS

The value of an advantage or strategy refers to how much it is worth to possess the advantage or follow the strategy. The frameworks in this category help assess the value of following a particular course of action. Some of these frameworks highlight the potential impact of an SIS.

Strategic Impact Grid

The Strategic Grid framework (Figure 3.4) classifies firms according to two dimensions: strategic impact of existing IT applications and those under development.[36] Each quadrant has a different implication for IT decisions.

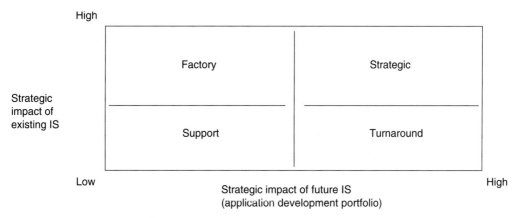

FIGURE 3.4 Strategic grid

Support.   Information technology resources are important for supporting backbone applications like accounting or payroll, but operations are not dependent on the smooth functioning of IS. Applications portfolios do not include systems crucial for strategic success.

Factory.   Smooth functioning of automated systems is vital to daily operations. In some cases, a one-hour interruption can cause serious harm. Applications portfolios focus on repair, maintenance, continuous process, and update programs. Railroads are usually in this category.

Turnaround.   An organization in this quadrant is in the process of revitalizing the business through a new information system. Applications in development are vital for strategic success.

Strategic.   IS is critical to the survival and competitive position of the organization. Applications portfolios contain systems that are also vital. Banks typically belong to this category.

The strategic grid is useful in highlighting varying levels of attention needed in managing current as well as future information systems. Structures and processes in managing IS vary according to how critical IS is to the firm. This framework does *not* identify specific structures or processes that should accompany a shift in IS importance to the firm, but many subsequent textbooks and articles have used the strategic grid as a guide to discuss this issue.

Corporations can use the strategic grid to compare several business units or divisions. Below the firm or business unit level, the framework becomes less useful. The strategic grid can also map the temporal shift in position on the grid, for example, from support to factory. Prior to banking deregulation, many banks fell into the factory quadrant with day-to-day applications important for the functioning of the bank. After deregulation, several banks were forerunners in bringing new information-intensive products to the market. Thus, they passed through the turnaround quadrant and found themselves in the strategic quadrant. The matrix does not suggest whether that shift between quadrants is appropriate. The strategic grid may not be helpful in identifying SIS opportunities because that type of analysis precedes current and planned applications. None of the framework assessment principles apply to the framework.

Impact-Value Framework

This framework expands the Strategic Impact Grid to account for two interacting dimensions of IT: impact and value.[37] The *impact* dimension is segregated into (1) time, (2) geography, and (3) relationships. Three different types of business value—(1) efficiency, (2) effectiveness, and (3) innovation—make up the *value* dimension. This framework can be used as an information technology–fitting scheme that helps organize and analyze Communications-Intensive Information System (CIIS) applications.

This framework is valuable because it emphasizes elements that other frameworks overlook. The framework meets with all three of the framework assessment principles: persons, fundamental factors, and timely decisions. Each intersection of the *impact* and *value* categories describes how impact is translated into value. *Efficiency* (i.e., increased productivity) has been the focus of traditional IS applications like payroll. *Effectiveness* is improved with applications that result in better communication systems. *Innovation* applications enhance the quality of products and services. CIIS applications result in *time compression* (i.e., the time to perform a process is reduced). Limitations of *geography* are reduced by communications technology. Organizational *relationships,* both external and internal, are altered by information technology. A description of the *impact-value* interactions follows.

Using Time Compression with:

Efficiency = Accelerate Business Process.
A CIIS can reduce the time required to perform a process—especially one that involves heavy information exchange. Opportunities may be found in labor-intensive or time-critical processes.

Effectiveness = Reduce Information Float.
Decision making can be improved by making data rapidly available to managers. Opportunities may be found when data arrive from multiple sources.

Innovation = Create Service Excellence.
CIIS can change perceptions of customers regarding response rates. Opportunities can be found wherever customers interact with the firm.

Overcoming Geographical Restrictions with:

Efficiency = Recapture Scale.   CIIS allows geographically dispersed units to operate as efficiently as a single large organization. Opportunities may be found in remote units, especially where processes require special skills or when they experience variations in volume.

Effectiveness = Ensure Global Management Control.   CIISs give managers rapid information about dispersed units and help consistency and quality of control. Opportunities can be found when there is interdependent contribution of organizational entities and where local needs must be balanced against corporate needs.

Innovation = Penetrate New Markets.   CIISs help penetrate new markets by allowing firms to open a field office with skeleton staff, create a logical or electronic presence, or expand the window of operations across time zones. Opportunities are found when customers require global reporting or when physical presence is not economical.

Restructuring Business Relationships with:

Efficiency = Bypass Intermediaries.   CIISs can help reduce management layers. Opportunities may be found when the cost of "expeditors" or liaisons is high.

Effectiveness = Replicate Scarce Knowledge.   CIISs can help distribute knowledge in organizations. This changes the power structure and culture of the organization. Opportunities can be found where dispersed units or individuals require scarce knowledge to service local markets.

Innovation = Build Umbilical Cords to Customers.   CIISs can be used as electronic ties between customers and organizations.

Risk-Assessment Framework

Using Porter's five forces (ICA) framework, this framework classifies the various risks of SIS success.[38] An organization must be prepared to stay the course with continued investments in information systems to remain competitive. A company may become vulnerable to competitors that have underutilized IT resources. Raising entry barriers can also raise the exit barriers. Legal problems may arise from very successful SISs when competitors claim unfair practices and lobby for government regulation. Increased dependencies on SISs may open up vulnerabilities to software and hardware suppliers.

To assess such risks, Michael Vitale, while at the Harvard Business School, developed a quadripartite framework based on the *strategic impact grid.* The current impact of IS is mapped against the future competitive importance of IS (Figure 3.5).

This risk-assessment framework is intended to help managers focus on the options and consequences of SIS choices. For example, a successful proprietary system that moves

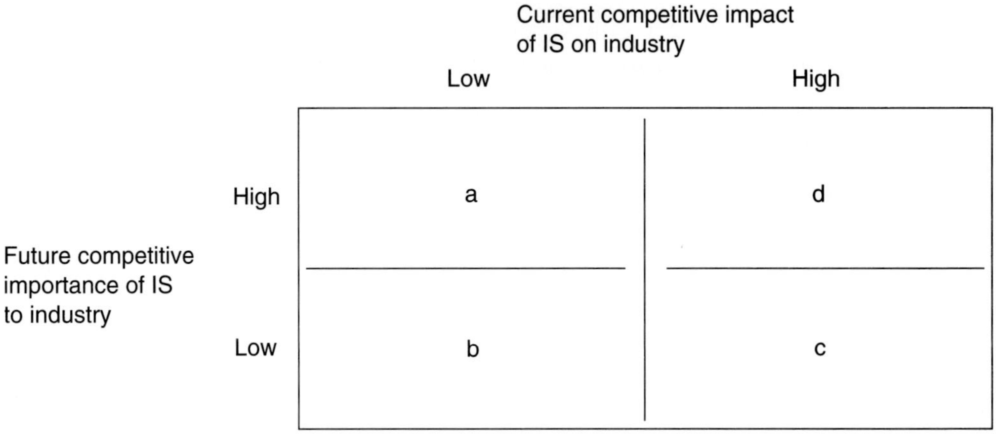

Current competitive impact
of IS on industry

	Low	High
High	a	d
Low	b	c

Future competitive
importance of IS
to industry

FIGURE 3.5   Risk-assessment grid

a firm and the industry from high-current-impact/low-industry-importance position to a high-impact/high-industry-importance position (quadrant c to quadrant d) may bring on governmental action. This is a valuable framework because it is one of the few that makes the risks of SIS explicit. Analysis of SIS risks should be an integral part of an SIS decision, and any framework that aids the decision process by structuring the risk assessment should be included in a manager's framework portfolio (an expanded coverage of SIS risks is the subject of chapter nine).

Information Intensity Grid

The information intensity grid is used to assess the role of information technology and is often used in conjunction with the *Value Chain* framework to evaluate the various information intensities of products and processes.[39] *Information intensity* refers to the amount of information processing required to acquire, process, and then deliver the product to users in its final form. A product's *information content* refers to the amount of useful information within it that is actually received and understood by users.[40] The cement industry's physical product tends to have not much information content in it or in the production process either. The opposite is the case in banking, insurance, and newspapers. These products have an extremely high information content and rely on information technology in the production process. Oil refining uses a high level of information in the production of a very physical commodity. Examples of information-intensive products with a low level of information technology in the production process are becoming increasingly rare. One possible example would be information *hot lines,* which dispense vital information using an old technology, the telephone.

The information intensity grid (Figure 3.6) is useful as a general guide but does not help in specific situations. Trends to increase the information intensity of products and

Information content of the product/service

Low   High

	Low	High
High	Oil refining	Banking
Low	Cement	Hot lines

Information intensity of the process

FIGURE 3.6   Information intensity grid

processes can be followed using this framework. One caveat is that systems that support the high/high information cell may not be as likely to produce competitive advantage because the products and processes are already differentiated. The framework assessment principles do not apply to the information intensity grid.

McFarlan's Five Questions

Warren McFarlan of the Harvard Business School poses five questions that locate SIS opportunities and assess the impact of IT in the competitive arena.[41] The premise is that when managers respond positively to any of these questions, then IT as a resource must be given careful attention. The questions are based on Porter's five forces (ICA) framework. These questions are a rather loose "framework" in deciding where to focus managerial attention. McFarlan provides no specific steps to apply the framework; however, he suggests that the *Strategic Impact Grid* as well as a structure for allocating IT resource priorities be used in conjunction with these questions.

1. Can IS Technology Build Barriers to Entry?   Electronic links to customers that cannot be easily replicated are the typical barrier to entry cited in most literature. However, large capital expenditures on IT can also create exit barriers.

2. Can IS Technology Build in Switching Costs for Customers?   The goal is to create electronic dependencies on a firm's system. Otis Elevator did just that with their OTISLINE maintenance service and callback system. (See more about OTISLINE in chapter five.)

3. Can the Technology Change the Basis of Competition?   The basis of competition in this context refers to how IT can facilitate Porter's generic strategies.

4. Can IS Change the Balance of Power in Supplier Relationships?   Examples are just-in-time inventory/delivery systems or CAD links between organizations. Most interorganizational systems do change the balance of power.

5. Can IS Technology Generate New Products?   A common example is repackaging of an existing database and then marketing it as a new product.

Technology Impact Model

Although this conceptual model is not a true framework, it does provide structure to show the impact of technology on the organization.[42] This model shows two external forces affecting the entire organization: the external technological environment and the external socioeconomic environment. The internal organization is modeled on five elements: (1) structure and corporate culture, (2) corporate strategy, (3) management processes, (4) individuals and roles, and (5) technology. Management processes are the "glue" that holds the organization together. These processes include strategic planning, budgeting, and resource planning—to name a few. The model depicts direct relationships between each of the internal elements.

The two external forces impose changes on the internal organizational elements and shift the delicate balance among the elements. The organization's internal strategy and technological elements are more vulnerable to the external factors than the other internal factors. The model highlights the necessity of aligning the organizational elements. For instance, a particular information technology used by an industry becomes a strategic necessity, forcing the organization to adopt this technology. This is an example of the external technological environment forcing changes in the internal technological elements. This shift would require the organization to realign its strategy, management processes, and essentially all the other organizational elements.

The Technology Impact Model does not facilitate categorization of SIS opportunities. It is also not a classification scheme for SIS impact. In other words, it is not a framework. Yet the model incorporates many fundamental factors like corporate structure, corporate culture, strategy, and technology, which are the requirements for the second framework assessment principle. The model emphasizes individuals and their direct relationships with strategy. Because the model provides for the intentional actions of people who devise and act on a strategy, the first framework assessment principle applies to it as well.

Stakeholder Management Framework

The *Stakeholder Management* framework (Figure 3.7) details a dimension that many other frameworks assume or summarize: the external and internal entities. A stakeholder is "an individual or group who can affect, or is affected by actions taken by the managers of the business." The focus is twofold, the *stakes* that persons have in the organization and the *holders* of the stakes.[43] The goal of stakeholder management is to identify, at various levels, the stakeholder relationships so that a competitive strategy can be successfully executed. That strategy can be supported by an information technology. Each stakeholder can have

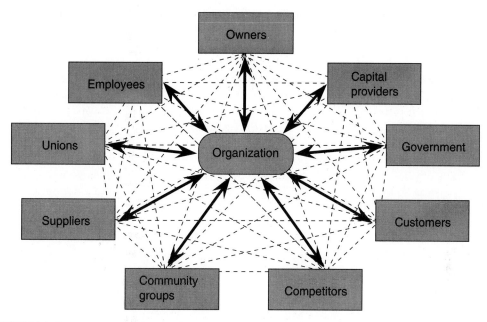

FIGURE 3.7 Stakeholders of an organization

multiple roles; thus, an understanding of individual stakeholder priorities is necessary. For example, United Airlines' pilots are employees and owners, and what may be good for an employee may not be satisfactory for an owner. Furthermore, networks of stakeholders interact with each other. This is indicated in Figure 3.7 by the dashed lines between stakeholders.

The Stakeholder Management framework thus offers a different perspective than many of the other frameworks presented here. It provides a rich, detailed accounting for individuals and groups. Viewed in terms of the three framework assessment principles, the framework scores high on the first two principles (persons and fundamental factors). However, this framework is unsatisfactory in helping managers make timely decisions. The stakeholder interpretation should be used in conjunction with other frameworks mentioned in this chapter.

Strategic Necessity Framework

Clemons and Kimbrough of the Wharton School of the University of Pennsylvania suggest that opportunities for competitive use of information systems are rare and that most applications fall into the category of strategic necessities and thus provide no advantage.[44] They distinguish between systems that are a source of competitive advantage and systems that are a strategic necessity, and hypothesize that most strategic information systems will ultimately become strategic necessities. They base this notion on economic theory and technology transfer experience. As a firm introduces a technology into an industry, it will eventually become a requirement for all remaining competitors. Those wishing to enter the same industry must then have that technology to compete.

A *strategic necessity* is defined as something a firm must have to compete effectively (or at all); it is usually difficult to obtain. The framework divides strategic necessities into two types: beneficial and unfortunate. An unfortunate necessity, the worst-case scenario, cannot be readily abandoned and conveys no advantage. An example is the Cash Management Account (CMA) first introduced by Merrill Lynch and later adopted by other brokerage houses. Customer fees are inadequate to make CMAs profitable but the brokerage houses are unable to discontinue the service. ATMs are the classic example of a beneficial strategic necessity. ATMs are required to compete in the banking industry but they also reduce banks' costs and provide benefits to customers.

This framework is useful for thinking about the impact a particular application or information technology may have on the industry. It may provide some insight into avoiding the unfortunate strategic necessity. Chapter eight gives an expanded treatment of strategic necessity systems.

Business Technology Platform Mapping

Many frameworks presented in this chapter were introduced in the early and mid-1980s. Many neglected the issue of matching the competitive opportunity to an appropriate information technology. Several of the case studies describing SISs even neglected to state which technology was used. Peter Keen introduced this framework to emphasize that technology is immensely important when discussing competitive advantage. The *Business Technology Platform Mapping* framework provides managers with questions and issues concerning IT policy, relations between key business processes and IT, and the IT platform that should be implemented.[45]

Keen's framework has three dimensions: (1) policy drivers, (2) business processes, and (3) platform capabilities. Mapping the relationships among the three dimensions can help managers answer questions about the impact of the firm's IT platform. *Policy drivers* help the firm assess existing IT capabilities and whether there is a business need for an IT platform. There are seven types of policy drivers, which are listed with examples, as follows:

1. Business practicality. The IT base must never impede a practical and important business initiative.
2. Competitive lockout. If the competition uses IT as the base for a successful initiative, we must not be automatically locked out of countering or imitating it.
3. Electronic alliances. We will match the competition in being able to form an alliance, create value-added partnerships, or enter an existing consortium.
4. Reorganization and acquisitions. If we reorganize, make acquisitions or divestments, or relocate operations, our IT systems will adapt quickly and routinely.

5. Third-party intrusions. No firm in our industry, or third parties outside it, will be able to intrude on our areas of strength or into the mainstream of our marketplace.
6. Vendor staying power. We will not be dependent on vendors that will not be able to stay the course.
7. Comparable international capability. The preceding policy requirements will be applicable in an international context.

Business processes are not mutually exclusive. There are seven types of business processes, as follows:

1. Core business transactions are the basis of a firm's operations. Shortcomings in them can have a significant negative impact on a firm's reputation.
2. Current competitive priorities are the stated priorities of critical success factors of the firm.
3. New corporate goals and commitments are the key moves being considered by senior management and are usually included in the organization's strategic plan.
4. Key industry business chains are interorganizational arrangements that involve primary external entities such as customers or suppliers.
5. Cost structure improvements are major plans or targets to improve a firm's cost dynamics.
6. Revenue enhancements are plans to increase revenues via increased volume, new markets, or improved market share.
7. Business invention opportunities are new initiatives that are not part of current plans or strategies.

The IT platform determines a firm's degree of freedom to maneuver in the competitive arena, given one or more policy drivers applied in one or more business processes. IT platforms can be either a major resource or a major hindrance. *Platform capabilities* are listed and explained below:

1. Degree of enablement is the degree of freedom for each policy driver applied in conjunction with each business process.
2. Degree of disablement is the risk of not moving ahead with IT in terms of competitive and organizational opportunities.
3. Impact of reach/range enhancement implies identifying where, when, and how information technology will augment the reach and range, and what impact there will be on business processes and policy drivers. *Reach* is the degree to which information can be directly and automatically shared across systems and services. The goal is widespread compatibility among different platforms of information technology.

Because the framework is complex and difficult to understand without reading Keen's book, managers are unlikely to use it without substantial investment of their time. For this reason, the framework violates the third assessment principle of timely decision making. On the other hand, the complexity allows the framework to score high on the second principle of fundamental factors.

CONTINGENCY FACTORS FRAMEWORKS

Although the previous frameworks are useful, they do not lead directly to understanding the specific factors that organizations or industries must deal with to gain competitive advantage with an SIS. The prior three categories of frameworks classified many dimensions relevant to strategic information systems. Those did not include specific factors that vary among organizations and that may lead to success or failure of an SIS. Knowledge of these contingent conditions can lead to better predictions about the implementation of an SIS. Although these *factors* cannot be easily classified to any preceding category of frameworks, they are called *frameworks* in this chapter and constitute a necessary and informative supplement to the prior three categories of frameworks.

Industry-Specific Factors

Kim and Michelman identified three factors that are important for achieving competitive advantage in the healthcare industry.[46] Many healthcare organizations have various operational and tactical information systems that have led to successful strategic systems. According to Kim and Michelman, three factors have accounted for this success. The first is overcoming political barriers between administrators and physicians. These barriers are a major obstacle because of the historical animosity between the two groups. The second factor involves structural changes that occur as a result of attempting to integrate existing isolated systems. Examples of isolated information systems include those for payroll, pharmacy, medical records, patient classification, and billing. The healthcare industry is noted for its entrenched *islands of applications.* As a result, information between areas is difficult to obtain and communication suffers. The third factor emphasizes the importance of recognizing the strategic use of integrated systems. Kim and Michelman found that healthcare firms that gained competitive advantage did so through their integrated transaction processing systems and information reporting systems. Examples of competitive advantage in the healthcare industry include better bargaining position with suppliers and group patients, increased market share, and higher entry barriers for potential rivals.

This type of analysis is a useful exercise that can be replicated on an industry-specific basis. With Parsons's trilevel framework, a similar analysis of important factors can be done for a particular firm and perhaps for a particular strategy. Because of its focus on the key factors in the healthcare industry, this framework demonstrates a high degree of strength in the second framework assessment principle of fundamental factors. Because this framework deals with persons who can affect the strategy of the firm, it also exhibits strength in the first assessment principle of persons.

Critical Success Factors (CSF)

The CSF technique, suggested by John Rockart of MIT's Sloan School, is widely used.[47] Critical Success Factors are defined as those few key areas in which things must go right for the organization to remain competitive. These areas must be identified, measured, and controlled with constant attention. The CSF analysis has evolved to a role in which it is used by managers as a special-purpose information planning approach to identify opportunities.[48] The analysis can be exercised at various levels within a firm or can be used to establish critical success factors of customers, competitors, and suppliers.

Advantages of this approach are that it is easily understood, it is flexible, it facilitates timely decisions, and it uses a top-down analysis. It is not a true framework because it lacks classification power. Executives define their own classification scheme. One problem with the CSF approach is its reliance on executives' experience and intuition in determining which factors are critical. Thus the usefulness and scope of this framework depend on the subjective ability, style, and perspective of the executives. If the executives do not perceive IT as strategic or potentially strategic, then the CSF analysis will certainly reflect this fact. According to some critics CSF analysis supports only the administrative functions of organizations.

Causal Model of Competitive Advantage

This model attempts to move beyond the realm of frameworks.[49] Its premise is that competitive advantage is caused by possessing bargaining power and/or comparative efficiency. Bargaining power and comparative efficiency are somewhat independent of each other. *Comparative efficiency* is the ability of the firm to produce an undifferentiated product at a lower price. *Bargaining power* is the efficacy of the firm to gain advantage in negotiating with customers or suppliers. Bargaining power is limited by search-related costs, unique product features, and switching costs of customers. The number of available alternatives for competitive advantage is limited by the cost to the customer of the search process. This search process is constrained by the information-processing capacity of the customers (i.e., their ability to efficiently explore alternatives and generate alternatives). A firm will increase its power by increasing its customers' costs in searching for alternative suppliers, by using unique features in its product, and by raising customers' switching costs. Comparative efficiency consists of efficiencies within the organization and between organizations.

To be a predictive model, empirical support showing direction and relevance of the factors causing bargaining power and comparative efficiency is necessary. This has not yet been demonstrated. Because the model is based on the theory of competition, the assumption of using IT to facilitate gaining a competitive advantage is hidden. Although the model may not be suitable for a specific situation, it can serve as a useful general framework.

The Seven-S Framework

This framework is based on the proposition that strategy must be understood in a broad context of factors.[50] The assumption is that effective strategies depend on many contingency factors. The Seven-S framework shows the comprehensive context of an organization and depicts interdependent relationships between seven organizational factors. *Structure* refers to how tasks are divided and coordinated as well as the degree of decentralization. *Strategy* deals with the selection of products and markets. *Systems* are routine organizational procedures to control structure and strategy. *Style* refers to managerial style and corporate culture. *Staff* is concerned with socialization of employees. *Skills* involves the capabilities of employees. *Superordinate goals* are what senior management chooses as unifying factors or guiding concepts. With this framework for SIS, the emphasis is on the *strategy* and *structure* factors.

The Seven-S framework emphasizes the alignment of all the organizational factors in pursuing a particular goal. For example, a shift that occurs in the strategy factor precipitates changes in the underlying *systems* as well as in *staffing, skills,* and perhaps even *structure.* The key concern of the framework then is on the interdependencies among the factors and the impact of changes on the balance, or fit, among the seven factors. This framework is flexible enough to begin at any point and to circumnavigate the remaining portions of the framework. In fact, the initial impact on the seven factors may occur in any order, depending on how the organization interacts with its environment. For instance, if the organization is proactive in introducing new technology into the industry, changes may occur first in the strategy, structure, and systems factors, followed by changes in staffing and skill.

This framework applies to a single organization and does not have an external focus that is so vital when discussing SISs. The framework has been accused of being too broad and lacking guidance about how to align all seven factors. Because it is so general, it also tends toward "analysis paralysis" and thus violates all three framework assessment principles.

DIRECTIONS FOR THE FUTURE

This chapter presented more than 30 frameworks relevant to SISs. The list is by no means exhaustive except in the sense that by the time readers have finished, they will be exhausted. Frameworks will continue to be developed, but clearly we are approaching framework overload.

Current trends in the field will continue while new ones appear. Two trends that seem to impact SIS are (1) globalization and international competition that will open up *windows of opportunity* for first movers, and (2) nonprofit sectors that are increasingly tapping the potential of SIS. We can expect to see case studies depicting these trends.

In most new fields of study, a great deal of descriptive literature emerges. Michael Treacy of MIT suggested in the mid-1980s that we were then at that point in the study of strategic uses of information technology. Treacy recommended that for the future we must (1) address a broader range of topics beyond opportunity identification, (2) incorporate reference disciplines of industrial economics and corporate strategy, (3) devise predictive and explanatory models rather than frameworks, (4) operationalize concepts, and (5) empirically test ideas.[51] A few empirical studies have been attempted. Three recent relevant studies are briefly described below.

Study 1.   Sabherwahl and King pull together many of the important concepts in the SIS field, including those highlighted by the frameworks presented in this chapter, to develop a theory of strategic use of information systems. They call this "pulling together" an inductive approach to theory building. Although they do not attempt to measure such things as competitive advantage or degree of innovativeness, they do demonstrate that patterns can emerge from extensive data collection.[52] They suggest that further study into failed SISs would be valuable.

Study 2.   Triggered by the paucity of information available on the implementation of frameworks, a recent field experiment compared Porter's Value Chain and Wiseman's Strategic Thrusts frameworks as aids to identifying SIS opportunities.[53] Porter's value chain was selected because of its widespread popularity and use. Wiseman's framework was also selected because of it prominence in the field. Each framework was used by ten different medium-sized firms. Criteria for comparison were (1) number of worthy ideas generated; (2) estimated costs of the ideas; (3) estimated length of time required to implement ideas; (4) organizational level of application (i.e., strategic management control or operational control); and (5) cross-classification ability (i.e., could an application found with one framework be classified on the other?). Results indicated that both frameworks were valuable and effective. Some differences between the two favored the Wiseman framework because of its more obvious outward orientation and greater appeal in turbulent environments. Further research in comparing frameworks may shed light on factors that influence firms to use one framework over another.

Study 3.   Jarvenpaa and Ives surveyed CEOs' views on IT using 649 annual reports across various industries.[54] They explored the question of whether IT was more strategic in some industries than others as proposed by the *Strategic Grid* and *Information Intensity* frameworks. Jarvenpaa and Ives found this to be true and suggested that it was important to consider information for competitive advantage in the *specific context* of the technology and the specific industry.

Despite an academic impulse to integrate all these frameworks into a megaframework, there are great advantages in examining SIS from *different* perspectives. There are many dimensions to consider in finding and implementing an SIS, and overlooking an important dimension can have insidious consequences. Thus, familiarity with many frameworks is advantageous. Managers can sift through the frameworks and choose a subset that highlights subjective dimensions relative to their own organizations. The value of the distinctions in these frameworks would be lost in a megaframework.

REFERENCES

1. Wiseman, C., *Strategic Information Systems.* Homewood, Ill.: Irwin, 1988, 98.

2. Cash, J. I., and Konsynski, B. R., "IS Redraws Competitive Boundaries," *Harvard Business Review* 63, no. 2 (Mar.–Apr. 1985): 134–42.

3. Laudon, K. C., and Turner, J. A., eds., *Information Technology and Management Strategy.* Englewood Cliffs, N.J.: Prentice-Hall, 1989.

4. Treacy, M. E., "Toward a Cumulative Tradition of Research on Information Technology as a Strategic Business Factor," Sloan Working Paper 1772–86, *Center for Information Systems Research,* Sloan School of Management, MIT, Mar. 1986, 15.

5. King, W., Hufnagel, E., and Grover, V., "Using Information Technology for Competitive Advantage," in M. J. Earl, ed., *Information Management: The Strategic Dimension.* Oxford University Press, 1988, 75–86.

6. Treacy, "Toward a Cumulative Tradition."

7. Henderson, J., and Venkatraman, N., "Strategic Alignment: A Model for Organizational Transformation Via Information Technology," *Sloan School of Management,* MIT, Aug. 1990, 6.

8. Gilbert, D. R., Jr., Hartman, E., Mauriel, J. J., and Freeman, R. E., *A Logic for Strategy.* Cambridge, Mass.: Balinger, 1988.

9. Porter, M. J., "How Competitive Forces Shape Strategy," *Harvard Business Review* (Mar.–Apr., 1979).

10. Primozic, K. I., Primozic, E. A., and Leben, J., *Strategic Choices.* New York: McGraw-Hill, 1991, 61–63.

11. Cash and Konsynski, "IS Redraws Competitive Boundaries."

12. Porter, M. J., *Competitive Strategy.* New York: Free Press, 1980.

13. Runge, D. A., *Winning with Telecommunication: An Approach for Corporate Strategies.* Washington, D.C.: ICIT Press, 1988.

14. Pedersen, M. K., "Strategic Information Systems in Manufacturing Industries," *Proceedings of the 11th International Conference on Information Systems,* Dec. 1990, Copenhagen.

15. Parsons, G., "Information Technology: A New Competitive Weapon," *Sloan Management Review* (Fall 1983).

16. Porter, *Competitive Strategy.*

17. Porter, M. J., *Competitive Advantage.* New York: Free Press, 1985.

18. Porter, M. E., and Millar, V. E., "How Informations Gives You Competitive Advantage," *Harvard Business Review* (July–Aug. 1985).

19. Laudon and Turner, *Information Technology.*

20. Earl, M. J., *Management Strategies for Information Technology.* New York: Prentice Hall, 1989.

21. Wiseman, *Strategic Information Systems.*

22. Ibid.

23. Bergeron, F., Buteau, C., and Raymond, L., "Identification of Strategic Information Systems Opportunities: Applying and Comparing Two Methods," *MIS Quarterly* 15, no. 1 (Mar. 1991): 89–103.

24. Rackoff, N., Wiseman, C., and Ullrich, W. A., "Information Systems for Competitive Advantage: Implementation of a Planning Process," *MIS Quarterly* 9, no. 4 (Dec. 1985): 285–94.

25. Johnston, H. R., and Vitale, M. R., "Creating Competitive Advantage with Interorganizational Information Systems," *MIS Quarterly* (June 1988): 153–65.

26. Barrett, S., and Konsynski, B., "Inter-organization Information Sharing Systems," *MIS Quarterly/ Special Issue,* 1982, 93–105.

27. Benjamin, R. I., Rockart, J. F., Scott Morton, M. S., and Wyman, J., "Information Technology: A Strategic Opportunity," *Sloan Management Review* 25, no. 3 (Spring 1984): 3–10.

28. Notowidigdo, M. H., "Information Systems: Weapons to Gain the Competitive Edge," *Financial Executive* 52, no. 2 (Feb. 1984): 20–25.

29. Ives, B., and Learmouth, G. P., "The Information Systems as a Competitive Weapon," *Communications of the ACM* 27, no. 12 (Dec. 1984): 1193–1201.

30. Runge, *Winning with Telecommunication.*

31. Rackoff, Wiseman, and Ullrich, "Information Systems."

32. Beath, C. M., and Ives, B., "Competitive Information Systems in Support of Pricing," *MIS Quarterly* (Mar. 1986): 85–96.

33. Ahituv, N., and Neumann, S., *Principles of Information Systems for Management,* 3rd ed. Dubuque, Iowa: Wm. C. Brown, 1990.

34. Feeney, D., "Creating and Sustaining Competitive Advantage with IT," in M. J. Earl, ed., *Information Management: The Strategic Dimension,* Oxford University Press, 1988.

35. Synnott, W. R., *The Information Weapon.* New York: Wiley, 1987.

36. McFarlan, F. W., McKenney, J. L., and Pyburn, P., "The Information Archipelago—Plotting a Course," *Harvard Business Review* (Jan.–Feb. 1983).

37. Hammer, M., and Mangurian, G. E., "The Changing Value of Communications Technology," *Sloan Management Review* 28, no. 2 (Winter 1987): 65–71.

38. Vitale, M. R., "The Growing Risks of Information Systems Success," *MIS Quarterly* 10, no. 4 (Dec. 1986): 327–34.

39. Porter and Millar, "How Information Gives You Competitive Advantage."

40. Lee, M. C. S., and Adams, D. A., "A Manager's Guide to the Strategic Potential of Information Systems," *Information & Management* 19, no. 3 (Oct. 1990): 169–82.

41. McFarlan, F. W., "Information Technology Changes the Ways You Compete," *Harvard Business Review* 62, no. 3 (May–June 1984): 98–103.

42. Rockart, J., and Scott Morton, M. S., "Implications of Changes in Information Technology for Corporate Strategy, *Interfaces* 14, no. 1 (1984): 84–95.

43. Gilbert et al., *A Logic for Strategy,* 106–7.

44. Clemons, E. K., and Kimbrough, S. O., "Information Systems and Business Strategy: A Review of Strategic Necessity," *Department of Decision Sciences,* The Wharton School, University of Pennsylvania, Working Paper 87–01–04, 1987.

45. Keen, P. G. W., *Shaping the Future.* Boston: Harvard Business School Press, 1991.

46. Kim, K. K., and Michelman, J. E., "An Examination of Factors for the Strategic Use of Information Systems in the Healthcare Industry," *MIS Quarterly* 14, no. 2 (June 1990): 201–215.

47. Rockart, J. F., "The Changing Role of the Information Systems Executive: A Critical Success Factors Perspective," *Sloan Management Review* 24, no. 1 (Fall 1982).

48. Wiseman, *Strategic Information Systems.*

49. Bakos, J. Y., and Treacy, M. E., "Information Technology and Corporate Strategy: A Research Perspective," *MIS Quarterly* 10, no. 2 (June 1986).

50. Waterman, R. H., Jr., Peters, T. J., and Phillips, J. R., "Structure Is Not Organization," *Business Horizons* 23, no. 3 (June 1980).

51. Treacy, "Toward a Cumulative Tradition."

52. Sabherwahl, R., and King, W. R., "Towards a Theory of Strategic Use of Information Resources: An Inductive Approach," *Information & Management* 20 (1991): 191–212.

53. Bergeron, Buteau, and Raymond, "Identification of Strategic Information Systems Opportunities."

54. Jarvenpaa, S. L., and Ives, B., "Information Technology and corporate Strategy: A View From the Top," *Information Systems Research* 1, no. 4 (Dec. 1990).

4

The Impact of Strategic Information Systems on Industries, Firms, and Strategies

The meek shall inherit the world, but they'll never increase market share.

—William G. McGowan, Chairman
MCI Communications

INTRODUCTION

Since the early 1960s, computers and information technology have changed the way firms do business and the way they compete strategically. Many executives are concerned about the changing role of information technology (IT), its increasing importance to their firm, and how they expect to manage it. Alex Mandl, CEO of Sea-Land Service, Inc., a $3 billion global shipping company, expressed concern in 1991 that information system (IS) failure could bring his company to a standstill.[1] The cost of IT, future uses of it, and integrating information from different business areas is also of concern to many executives. The airline industry fears that without a redesign of its reservation systems, a system crash is imminent.[2] This has happened in the past and could bring chaos and crisis to airline ticketing. Indeed, although many firms are not sure how to deal with IT, most executives feel IT will play some role in their future. (As John Dillinger said, "You can get more cooperation with a smile and a gun than with a smile only.")

Senior executives differ in their assessment of the impact of IT. Although some firms feel the major advancements offered by IT have already been exploited, others feel IT is becoming significantly more strategic. It is thus clear that the use and impact of IT can vary from firm to firm, and that no prescriptive model exists for executives to examine their IT needs. This chapter attempts to emphasize that IT requirements differ from industry to industry, that each industry is vulnerable to the effects of IT, and that businesses must undergo substantial change to take advantage of the opportunities offered by IT.

Gregory Parsons' three-level framework, described in chapter three, can be used to assess how uncertainties about the use of IT will impact a firm.[3] In brief, Parsons's framework forces a strategic planner or a chief information officer (CIO) to view the possible impacts of IT at three distinct levels: industry, firm, and strategic. It is important to take this more holistic view of IT because different organizations will not use or need IT in the same way. The framework allows a firm to develop a customized view of the potential impact of IT on its own particular industry.

The following section focuses on the impact of information technology at the industry level. All organizations operate in one or more industries. By the nature of their participation in an industry, they are affected by existing or potential uses of information technology. Consider, for example, a bank and its use of ATM technology. Today, an ATM is a necessity of doing business. Consumers of the pre-ATM era would always need to see a teller and bank Monday through Friday only from 10 A.M. to 3 P.M. If a bank were to cater to this market today, it would severely limit its customer base. In this example, the markets as well as the services offered by the banking industry have been changed. In fact, the industry may still be changing as ATMs may offer additional services like ticket sales, airline tickets, or fishing licenses.[4] The section deals with the strategic use of information technology and how it can affect the industry that a firm competes in.

The third section of this chapter reviews the impact of information technology at the level of the individual organization. The competitive posture and performance of an organization is impacted by the scope, intensity, and form of its interrelationships with external forces that are part of the organization's competitive arena. SISs can be used by the organization to give it an edge or defend against an edge gained by one of the forces (e.g., suppliers, customers, competitors). Examining the competitive arena gives insight at the level of the firm as to the potential use of strategic systems.

Strategic information systems are intended to support corporate (organizational) strategies adopted to reach corporate objectives. A *strategy* is a broad course of action that an organization adopts to reach a long-term objective. As firms go through the process of strategic planning, they can use a framework such as Porter's ICA, which was discussed in chapter three. The generic business strategies recognized by Porter include cost, differentiation, and focus. Understanding the competitive forces at work in one's industry helps a firm adopt generic strategies to mediate these forces. Parsons uses these three strategies in his framework on the impact of IT. Charles Wiseman of Columbia University added three more strategies to Parsons's framework: innovation, growth, and alliance. The fourth section of this chapter provides a description of generic corporate strategies and respective SISs that can support them.

INDUSTRY-LEVEL IMPACT OF IT

Consider the publishing of college textbooks. Traditionally, a professor adopted a book by searching through currently available books and choosing the best one. However, in one book, the chapter on integration may be good while the chapter on differentiation is weak. Another book, on the other hand, has an excellent chapter on differentiation. Often, choosing the "best" book is a trade-off of good points and bad points about several texts. Additionally, in fields with rapid change, texts can quickly become outdated. Many teachers in graduate-level courses resort to journal articles and newspaper clippings for lack of an adequate text.

Recently, textbook publishers have made available information systems that allow professors to customize textbooks. By selecting from a publisher's database, teachers can choose specific chapters by different authors, add their own handouts, and receive a finished product in a matter of days. How many students have had to wait weeks for books that the campus bookstore had run out of?

The leader in this technology in 1991 was McGraw-Hill.[5] Forming a partnership with the University of Southern California (USC), McGraw developed a system to offer customized textbooks to USC students. Additionally, they expected to offer an electronic library to students and eventually access to the library via workstations. The college textbook industry, with revenues of $2 billion in 1990, is highly competitive. It is estimated that 10% of college texts can be of this customized nature. The potential for expanding the market to high schools and elementary schools makes it impossible for textbook publishers to ignore this IT development.

In Parsons's model, IT can affect the industry level of a firm in three different ways. First, it can affect a firm's products and services. The new electronic publishing technology is changing the college textbook products from traditional end products to customized texts. It may also offer an electronic product instead of the traditional hard copy. College stores and publishers may become service providers, in that their function will change from providing products to providing a means for consumers to create their own products.

The second industry-level impact of IT may be manifested in changing markets. The emergence of ATMs has expanded the market of bank customers to those who demand electronic products. Similarly, offering customized texts may alter the college textbook market. Customized texts will offer the most current information on given topics and fast delivery of finished products, and can cater to the personal preferences of faculty. Offering this service may cultivate a new market of scholars that would accept textbooks in no other form. It is an intriguing question whether a publishing company that would not offer this service could compete in the new market.

The third industry-level impact is in production economies. In providing customized textbooks to college bookstores, a publisher can gain advantages offered by the distribution cycle. The publisher provides systems that enable professors to select, compile, print, and bind the text of their choice in the bookstore. This eliminates weeks to order texts in the traditional method. Again, how will a college text publishing company compete in the future if they cannot offer this efficiency?

Products/Services

The three ways in which IT can affect products/services at the industry level are by (1) changing the nature of the products/services an industry offers, (2) expediting the distribution process, and (3) creating efficiencies in product life cycles. The primary change that IT has brought to products and services is through the use of electronic over manual media. The advancement of telecommunications technology has made connectivity between remote sites not only possible but cost-effective. During the 1970s, many firms concentrated on automation of well-defined, manual operation–level tasks. The electronic handling of data improved productivity and accuracy, and lowered costs for large firms. It was not long before access to specific services was made available to customers. The nature of products and services has changed as a result of IT. IT has made it possible for firms to electronically link customers to suppliers and thereby offer better services. Aside from the financial industry, other industries that have seen changes in the nature of their products and services include insurance, healthcare, and sales. Providing hand-held terminals to salespeople has allowed them access to inventory and production schedules on a real-time basis. This is much more powerful than telephoning the home office and waiting for someone there to track down the information while a customer waits. Additionally, remote hand-held or laptop computers can perform remote order entry, use E-mail, or provide reports and intelligence information to salespeople.

IT has also changed the distribution process for products. Using electronic data interchange (EDI), information-intensive firms can now electronically transfer invoices, claims, and reports. In the insurance industry, magnetic cards (like credit cards) can be used to file claims instantaneously when a patient receives treatment. This eliminates problems for the patient, physician, and insurer. Some HMOs claimed to have cut their processing costs by 50% with such a system.[6] McKesson, once a wholesaler of nondurable consumer goods, has used IT to transform itself into a value-added distributor. Focusing mostly on pharmaceuticals, McKesson's ECONOMOST system offers economies to customers. A druggist can scan product shelf labels, reorder, and have the orders filled overnight. Once drugstores are tied to such a system, they are more inclined to purchase products from McKesson than other companies. IT offers speed and ease to the product distribution cycle.

The third way that IT changes products is in enhancing the product life cycle. Information systems that offer computer-aided design/computer-aided manufacturing (CAD/CAM) and advanced graphics capability aim to reduce costs of building prototypes and allow designs to be first tested through simulation in an electronic medium before investing in real materials. Recent advances in hardware have made it possible, for example, to graphically model proteins and enzymes.[7] In so doing, the discovery process for new drugs has been shortened. Researchers can model and test compounds cheaply and quickly for viability before entering the expensive and time-consuming laboratory stage. Increasing competition and expiring patents on 80% of the top 50 drugs is causing firms in this industry to seek new ways of shortening the 12 years it takes to introduce new products.[8]

In summary, IT offers electronic products and services, enhanced distribution cycles, and efficiencies in developing new products. The following case illustrates these changes.[9]

Gleason Components Group

Gleason Components Group (GCG) is a manufacturer of components and tools for larger equipment manufacturers. Customers of GCG include Xerox, Digital Equipment Corporation, IBM, Pitney Bowes, Kodak, Black and Decker, Ford, General Motors, Chrysler, and General Electric. Traditionally, component manufacturers competed regionally. Customers existed in the same geographic area, and the component manufacturer with the best products would succeed. However, competition in the late 1980s was increasing for component manufacturers. Customers were becoming increasingly selective on cost, quality, and delivery requirements. Components were increasing in complexity, and customers were requiring electronic links to component manufacturers' facilities. Though many customers had utilized communication technologies to their advantage, component manufacturers had yet to follow suit. Recognizing this shortcoming, GCG made a massive effort to modernize and streamline its processes through the use of IT. Their mission, specifically, was "to provide total customer satisfaction for those customers and markets we serve by being the best components and assembly supplier in the world."

To attack this goal required not only intensified IT investment but organizational changes as well. GCG management worked to change the very culture of their firm to prepare employees for the new technology. By stressing teamwork, consensus, and early participation with customers, GCG employees were moved to a more receptive, open position on new technology. Additionally, GCG invested heavily in training.

Four IT areas that GCG decided to invest in were CAD/CAM, Rapid Response Tool Building (RRTB) Pilot Cell, Materials Requirements Planning (MRP) II, and computer simulation technology. The first CAD/CAM application GCG implemented was in tool development. In the past, customers would send a drawing of a required part to GCG. An engineer would then redraw the part from several perspectives and then design a manufacturing tool to aid in producing the component. This process typically took 120 days. Because the customers' designs were likely to change, this could impact GCG's designs. Many GCG customers already used CAD technology and were beginning to force suppliers to use compatible systems. With intensive training, GCG implemented a CAD-/CAM system that shortened the production time and could asses the impact of design changes in terms of production cost and time. Customers would supply parts information on magnetic tape, and this information could be read into GCG's system rather than manually entered. GCG expects to attain CAD-to-CAD links with customers.

GCG hoped to integrate RRTB Pilot Cell with CAD/CAM technology for prototype tool manufacturing. The RRTB Pilot Cell incorporated CAM-generated data files with CAD capabilities for quickly prototyping required manufacturing tools. RRTB Pilot Cell–ensured prototype tools were built exactly to the manufacturing specifications by linking CAD and CAM capabilities. Their first attempt was in development of a Metal Stamping and Fabrication tool. On a tool that was expected to take 100 calendar days to complete, the production time was reduced to 24 working days. Additionally, efficiencies could be passed on to customers by producing a quality product and shortening the customers' time to market.

GCG's initial implementation of MRP was a failure, largely because the manager responsible was not supportive. An MRP system would have supported GCG in materials planning by managing sales forecasts and supplies, and then generating a materials forecast. Training and having a champion for the technology might have made MRP's implementation more successful. However, GCG still planned to implement MRP II, hoping that more attention to organizational aspects and more help from the MIS support group might help the implementation process. The promise of cost savings and shortened product schedules made MRP technology an attractive investment.

Lastly, GCG expected that simulation technology could offer great gains in manufacturing. Simulation of materials and products on their cycle through different workstations can help streamline and optimize the production cycle. One GCG experience reduced the delivery time of an order to a customer from 11 weeks to 6 days.

IT has changed the products of the manufacturing industry in which GCG competes from paper to electronic. Today, instead of drafting several images of a component and redrafting components when changes are made, a component can be drawn on a computer. The computerized component can be rotated and altered easily and displayed to other departments or other firms. Additionally, components and materials can be managed by a computer to optimize time and cost for production. Shortened product life cycles for components makes a firm like GCG attractive as a supplier in that a customer firm can shorten its own product life cycles. Lastly, GCG can now compete in a global market. Having the ability to link to customers electronically gives GCG the ability to attract and provide quality service to potential customers all over the world.

Markets

IT can also affect demand and segmentation and offer greater geographic distribution possibilities to industry markets. As discussed earlier, the shift in products/services to an electronic base has also created a market of electronic consumers. Many people today cannot recall the last time they saw a bank teller. In the late 1980s more than a third of all bank customers were regular ATM users.[10] Demand from such a large group of customers makes a bank with no ATM a relic.

Similarly, markets for home banking and other electronic financial services are emerging. These markets also have a new and wider range of products to choose from. IT has made possible new financial services product lines such as cash management systems. Merrill Lynch initiated Cash Management Accounts (CMAs) to customers.[11] These accounts offered credit, cash withdrawal, and automatic cash investment to a money market fund. CMAs grew from 180,000 in 1980 to over 1 million in 1983, with an average balance of $70,000. IT thus produced new and automated products and better service, raising demand overall.

IT can also help to support strategies of market segmentation. At a New York hospital, when babies are photographed after birth, the photography company collects data on all the new parents and sells it to a database company.[12] The company sells lists for specific markets to firms like Sears. Sears, in turn, can target new parents with advertising about baby items. Birthday clubs offered by some restaurants are also sources of specialized mailing lists. Blockbuster Entertainment, a video rental franchise, planned in 1990 to sell information on what category of movies its customers rent.[13] Census bureau data are available to everyone. Software packages help marketers map and segment markets graphically and even enhance information with their own databases. However, there is increasing evidence that consumers feel their privacy is being threatened by the sale of such personal information. More people were found by surveys in 1990 and

1991 to be concerned about their rights to privacy. In 1991, the Lotus Development Corporation planned to sell a huge customer database but reversed their plans after receiving 30,000 protests against the sale.

As the GCG case indicates, IT is eliminating geographic barriers to new markets. As such, more industries will face competition on a global scale. The following example illustrates IT-induced changes in markets (whereas the case reflects a failed SIS, it does indicate the potential inherent in IT).

Chemical Bank: The Pronto System

In 1980, the New York City–based Chemical Bank was the sixth-largest bank in the United States.[14] It had a culture of aggressive customer service, providing innovative new products and services to corporate and retail customers. Banking deregulation and the removal of interstate banking restrictions heightened competition among banks for customers. Moreover, banks faced competition from stock brokerage firms as well as large retailers. To compete in the 1980s, banks broadened product lines, improved service, and focused on cost reduction. Many banks implemented online teller access to customer files, automated record keeping, subcontracting data-intensive processing (i.e., check processing), online corporate cash management systems, ATMs, and banking by phone. Chemical, along with other industry leaders, invested heavily in home banking technology, creating a home banking system, Pronto, that would be accessible through videotex terminals in a customer's home. Chemical also hoped to sell Pronto to other banks.

In 1982, a study by Booz, Allen and Hamilton indicated that by 1995, 15% to 27% of American households would use home information services. Optimistic estimates were also given as to how much customers would be willing to pay for a home banking service. A survey recommended that customers using videotex services be allowed to select their own combination of services for a suggested fee of $12 per month. Other advantages that home banking promised were elimination of float inherent in the use of paper checks, lower processing costs, lower mailing and advertising costs, a reduction in the number of necessary bank offices, and increased revenues from customers buying the service.

Videotex would allow customers to access their account through their television screen. Interaction with the screen would be via a hand-held keypad. This system provided color and graphics to customers while other home banking systems were textual and in black and white. In February 1982, a field trial of Pronto was implemented, and 200 homes received Pronto trial systems. The initial use and response was very good. Feedback was collected on user satisfaction and possible improvements. Some users complained of slow response time and poor help screens. When users were polled about willingness to pay for the system, 65% agreed to pay $8 per month, 43% would pay $12, and 33% would pay $16. When polled about purchasing the hardware, 25% quoted $300 as a maximum, 40% quoted $400, and 33% quoted $500. These figures seemed encouraging. However, as the pilot study continued, use of Pronto diminished. A third of the households had dropped out of the study. Of the households that were heavy users, half opted to continue the service for $8 a month or to purchase the hardware for $240. Of those who cancelled the service, slow response time and hardware cost were the greatest reasons for not continuing. Additionally, customers felt that they still had to go to a bank to receive cash and that writing a check was just as simple. Because some institutions would not handle electronic checks at that time, home banking would require managing two checkbooks.

Chemical attempted to increase overall demand by offering new products and services to banking customers. Surveys showed that younger customers were more likely to use the service. Had Chemical continued development, they might have targeted younger banking customers. Allowing customers to link to the bank electronically might have allowed the bank to maintain a greater geographic market, because with home banking, every customer's house can service banking needs through a PC with the exception of cash withdrawal.

Production Economies

IT impacts industries by offering economies of production not possible without computers. IT allows firms to streamline production and make better use of resources. In the trucking industry, fuel usually accounts for between 18% and 35% of operating expenses. IS allows trucking firms to cut costs by monitoring the fuel commodities markets and streamlining purchases.[15] The trucking firm Leaseway provides fuel credit cards to drivers so they can purchase fuel at authorized stations. Though the system cost $1 million to develop, it has cut road fuel costs by 10%. It has also reduced and streamlined accounting in that fuel purchases are electronically recorded into Leaseway's computer system. Monitoring fuel consumption can also reveal inefficient driving styles or faulty vehicles. Northwest Airlines claimed in 1991 that imaging technology helped to cut their ticket processing time in half.[16] Banks exploit imaging technology to reduce costs in paper handling, improve speed and accuracy, and increase productivity.[17] Putnam Investor Services had 2 million investors in 1991 handling $42 billion in assets. The use of imaging in their business showed productivity increases of 30–35% and a reduction in the processing staff of 40%.[18] Another service reported in 1991 that imaging could offer a 30% staff savings and a 50% savings in storage.[19] IT offers new economies of scale not possible ten years ago. These are reflected in the following example.

Automatic Data Processing, Inc.

Founded in 1949 by Henry Taub, a college student working part-time for a local accountant, ADP focused on standardizing manual payroll applications.[20] ADP provided a reliable, confidential payroll service to many businesses. ADP showed continued slow growth through 1957, when they attempted to computerize their operations. As many firms discovered, computerizing operations was not a simple task. What ADP expected to automate in ten days actually took an entire year. During this time, attention to service, traditionally ADP's strong point, suffered immensely. Consequently, their business was failing. By moving their focus from technology and back toward quality customer service, ADP was once again able to build their business. Despite their initial struggle with technology, computers gave ADP significant economies of scale. By the late 1980s ADP was a leader in the data processing services market, earning 9% of total market revenues. This should indicate that the market is highly fragmented, with other computer service firms focusing on different types of services. Historically, ADP offered quality, standardized service in the areas of payroll, financial services, and specialized services (i.e., processing for car dealerships or banks).

ADP's primary business area is employer services, specifically payroll processing. The service includes direct deposits, tax filing, unemployment compensation management, reporting, and on-site manipulation of databases. By providing a standardized product to many consumers, ADP is able to reduce their own costs for processing, as well as the cost of their services to customers. It is described as a case where everyone wins. Customers can save money by outsourcing their payroll functions, and ADP can make money by providing this cost-effective service. In ADP's view, they perform a boring, tedious task for organizations in a cost-effective manner. This frees a firm's IS department to work on tasks that are more strategically significant.

FIRM-LEVEL IMPACT OF IT

In Parsons's three-tier framework of IT impacts, the second tier examines the level of the firm. In examining a firm's competitive arena, Parsons uses Michael Porter's framework of competitive threats.[21] Porter's framework, introduced in chapter three of this book, contains five external forces that affect the way a firm competes. Existing rivals are the most obvious threat to a firm. These are companies that compete against it for the same limited markets and customers. Bargaining power of buyers and suppliers can also represent a significant threat to competition. For example, if only one supplier exists for several competing firms, the firms are in a weak position to demand lower prices or higher quality. Likewise, if buyers are scarce and firms selling to them are numerous, the buyers possess a considerable amount of power. The threat of new entrants into the market is also present. If a firm produces a product or service that is easily or cheaply duplicated, one might expect new competitors to arise. Lastly, there is the threat of substitute products or services. This occurs when competing firms can offer a product similar to those in existence with a better price, service, or feature. When any one of these forces has a powerful position, less profit is attainable by the firm.

The second level of Parsons's framework outlines Porter's five forces as areas where IT can have a strategic impact. In this section, Porter's five forces will be discussed and elaborated with specific examples of the use of IT.

Buyers

Buyers in an industry are strong if they make volume purchases or are made up of large, concentrated consumer groups. If there are only a few buyers for several not well-differentiated suppliers, the buyers can be very powerful relative to the suppliers.

One method for firms to defend against powerful buyers is by building switching costs into their product or service. Switching costs are the costs incurred by buyers when they change from their current supplier to a new one. In changing one's brand of soap, no switching cost is incurred by the consumer. Changing one's personal computer, however, is costly in that the consumer must purchase new hardware and software. By creating significant switching costs, firms can lock their buyers in to buying their products exclusively and thus reducing their bargaining power.

Using telecommunication hookups, Wal-Mart discount stores have made it possible to directly purchase goods from manufacturers instead of salespersons. The power of the traditional buyers, the salespersons, has been significantly reduced. Wal-Mart has also saved money by no longer paying commissions, and they also save time. One industry that may have great control over their buyers is information services. Many more firms are outsourcing their IS activities than in the past, giving outside firms control over all data processing. The firm providing the IS function has a great deal of power over its customers because switching to another information services firm could prove expensive and time-consuming.

Reducing the bargaining power of buyers is one of the most powerful means to compete with IT. Forward integration is a more subtle form of establishing switching costs. With forward integration, a firm adopts some product or service that its buyer would normally perform. The McKesson Drug Company, through its ECONOMOST ordering system, made it possible for pharmacists to order supplies over hand-held terminals that read shelf lists. The products would be sent in the correct shelving order. McKesson added value to their product by facilitating drug purchasing and providing shipments in the correct order. They took over a function that pharmacists traditionally did themselves.

Another method to safeguard against powerful buyers is in determining which market segments produce the most attractive buyers. In determining the requirements of the buyer and the firm's ability to meet them, the growth potential of the buyer, the amount of power the buyer has, and the cost incurred in servicing the buyer, a firm can weed out costly buyers and target those that may produce more profit. Insurance firms typically provide similar coverage to all insured. Instead, insurers could increase profits by offering tailored coverage for different consumer needs. Information on market segments, how much it costs to service them, and special needs they might require is easily attainable. An information system allows firms to analyze data to uncover the most profitable and attractive markets. Consumer databases compiled by some agencies during the purchase of products or services can also provide a rich source of market information. Merging its private marketing data with a purchased customer database can create a powerful marketing tool for a firm. The following case illustrates the use of an SIS to reduce the bargaining power of buyers.[22]

Wickes Lumber

Wickes Lumber, a chain lumber store consisting of 212 lumber franchises, sought to improve profitability by providing computer-assisted planning for building new homes. Wickes customers consisted of general contractors, as well as customers interested in doing their own home projects. This could be anything from installing insulation to building new additions to a home. Wickes stores carried lumber, tools, plumbing and electrical supplies, roofing, siding, insulation, paint, and flooring. Manufactured building components were carried by 13 Wickes stores. In 1982, after the Wickes parent company filed for Chapter 11, Wickes Lumber reorganized and sought ways to increase profits. Changes included improvements in product mix and store layouts, improved purchasing through direct buying, and installation of point-of-sale registers in all stores. Sixty-five of the 212 centers were also closed.

Wickes obtained software through a software house, Integrated Computer Graphics (ICG), that would aid contractors in using customized building components carried by Wickes. They also began selling prefabricated house "shells" that Wickes delivered to building sites. Purchasers of these shells were typically customers building their own homes. Wickes provided ten different home designs, with regional differences in building codes as a modifiable factor. Wickes made money by not only supplying the shell but supplying the products to finish the shell as well. This product area was known as the Affordable Homes Program (AHP).

In the early 1980s, high interest rates caused a slump in the construction market. Sales generated by the AHP greatly decreased too. However, Wickes felt that by providing computerized home customization, they could lock in customers. Most customers were owners that wished to build their own homes. They were believed to be more motivated by economics than by other factors, so Wickes provided a cheaper means of planning a new home. For $200, a customer could buy standard blueprints and customize them. Wickes would assess the markups for feasibility and then offer to return the customers' money or continue planning. Implementing changes to the plans typically took two weeks. Plans were shipped to a processing office in Atlanta and then implemented with an advanced version of ICGs original design software. Computerization made the quick turnaround possible and provided an accurate cost and resources estimate. If the customer made a commitment to purchase $2,000 of building materials from Wickes, the plans and materials list were given to them. Wickes actually lost $300 in producing each customized plan but made it back by selling the materials. Customers also saved money because they did not have to go to expensive independent architects to build a customized home. Wickes provided for the planning step in their building process in a cost-effective manner.

Suppliers

Like that of buyers, the bargaining power of suppliers is great when they are few. If a firm can attain raw materials from only one source, that source has the power to control pricing and delivery with no threat of losing business. Ways to protect a firm against powerful suppliers are, predictably, the reverse of those of defending against buyers. To decrease the bargaining power of suppliers, a firm should avoid suppliers that force significant switching costs. As an example, to safeguard against problems associated with outsourcing the IS function, firms might outsource only processes that are common. For instance, by outsourcing payroll or accounting, fairly standard functions, it may be easy to switch to different IS suppliers. A new supplier of these functions would already understand what was required in providing the service and would likely have experience doing it. In contrast, if a firm wished to switch suppliers of IS for complex engineering designs, they might have more difficulty finding a firm with knowledge and converting their data to a new system.

The use of IT in trucking is a good example of how IT can mitigate supplier power.[23] Trucking companies typically spend 18 to 35% of their operating budget on fuel. By monitoring fuel costs on the commodities market, trucking companies are able to cut costs and somewhat reduce a supplier's power. This type of information system makes all suppliers equal, with no cost in switching whenever the price is advantageous.

A second means of reducing supplier power is through backward integration. Backward integration occurs when a firm takes over as its own provider of a product or service traditionally provided by outsiders. Examples of this tactic are evident in the continued growth of telecommunications. With telecommunication technology, firms can make purchases from suppliers all over the nation without relying on salespeople. By making orders directly, they really adopt the sales function, typically provided by the supplier. Telecommunications thus offers firms a greater source of suppliers as well as reducing commission costs. The following case illustrates how an SIS can reduce supplier power.

Wal-Mart

Sam Walton opened the first Wal-Mart (1962) in Rogers, Arkansas. Warehousing allowed Wal-Mart to control distribution and buy in bulk, allowing them to offer highly competitive prices. This, coupled with tremendous customer service, caused Wal-Mart to grow. In 1970, Wal-Mart stock went public, and the explosion of Wal-Mart into a major retailing giant began. At the onset of 1990, Wal-Mart became the second-largest discount retailer in the United States.

By maintaining several warehouses and clusters of stores in a finite area, Wal-Mart can restock immediately, and cut costs by buying in bulk at a discount. Ultimately this leads to better deals and a reliable selection for the consumer. A fallout area where Wal-Mart is managing to cut cost is dealing directly with manufacturers and, in essence, eliminating the middleperson. This seems to offer retailers close relationships with manufacturers, faster/better communication on sales issues, improved use of buyers' time, and reduced costs. However, sales representatives are claiming that such practices violate the Robinson-Patman Act (the act in essence says it is illegal to receive a discount in lieu of a brokerage fee, much like using a realtor to find you a home, and then cutting your own deal).

Wal-Mart also places great emphasis on courteous customer service and complete customer satisfaction. Employees are treated as business partners and are encouraged to share ideas and actively participate in Wal-Mart's day-to-day business. After a year of service, employees can participate in stock ownership or profit-sharing plans. An atmosphere of teamwork and loyalty is strongly promoted by Wal-Mart management.

Tied into all the avenues explored by Wal-Mart is their innovative uses of technology to improve business. One area that has proved successful is their ability to link different segments of their business (i.e., suppliers with buyers). Though most applications are developed in-house, they also utilize companies such as NCR or IBM for certain applications. For example, IBM provides their electronic mail system.

One major IT area that Wal-Mart has exploited is very small aperture terminals (VSATs) for applications like inventory control, credit card and check verification, loss prevention, and quick response. VSATs are small, portable satellite antennas that offer the advantages of reliability, cheapness, ease of installation, and flexibility. In fact, Wal-Mart found them to be more effective than leased phone lines in terms of cost and performance. For a store that is rapidly expanding, the ability to fully connect remote sites into the company network in one day by simply moving a satellite dish around is a large advantage. Wal-Mart's first VSATs were installed in 1986, and in a year 1,137 terminals were operational. VSATs also provide fully integrated voice, data, and video throughout the Wal-Mart chain.

Supported by their large VSAT network, Wal-Mart was in 1992 the nation's largest user of Electronic Data Interchange (EDI). Some EDI applications include forecasting, planning data, modeling of stock information, replenishment of merchandise, point of sale, and shipping. Wal-Mart has also tempered its use of EDI with intensive employee training programs. The programs seek not only to emphasize smooth operations but also the strategic importance of EDI. Wal-Mart has been accused of strong-arming suppliers to jump on the EDI bandwagon—or lose Wal-Mart business.

Local Area Networks (LANs)-based systems at Wal-Mart stores collect information that aids in the identification of buying trends. Monitoring these trends allows managers to tailor inventory requests to best suit customer preferences.

Substitution

Substitute products can limit profits in an industry or even eliminate industries. The invention of transistor technology has eliminated most uses for vacuum tubes. Two ways in which a firm can compete against substitute products are with relative price performance and product features.

Relative price performance refers to a firm's ability to substitute a product by offering it at a lower cost or improving its perceived value. IT can support offering lower cost by creating efficiencies in bringing the product to market and passing the cost savings along to the consumer. Wal-Mart offers retail products that are also available at other chains but at significant savings to consumers. IT helps Wal-Mart skillfully manage large inventories. Buying in bulk and warehousing lets Wal-Mart demand discounts from suppliers. Savings incurred by use of this strategy are passed on to customers.

If a firm cannot compete on price, it may differentiate its products by offering features that increase perceived performance. Many financial institutions offer credit, cash withdrawal, and money market fund investing. In 1980, with the use of IT, Merrill Lynch marketed Cash Management Accounts (CMAs) that combined all these services.[24] CMAs grew from 180,000 in 1980 to over 1 million in 1983, with an average balance of $70,000. All features of the product had existed previously with several suppliers. The innovation of combining them caused a great strategic advantage. The following case illustrates the use of an SIS to handle the threat of substitute products.[25]

Anaquest

Anaquest (the companies' names are disguised) evolved from the sales division of Ohio Medical Products (OMP). OMP's specialty was strong, cost-effective anesthetic. In 1972, OMP introduced a new inhalation anesthetic, Ethrane. By 1980, Ethrane was used in nearly half of all surgeries requiring general anesthetic in the United States. Anaquest was preparing to introduce Forane, an anesthetic superior to Ethrane, in the near future. Anaquest held patents on both anesthetics. By 1983, half of all surgeries in the United States used Ethrane or Forane, accounting for $75 million in sales. Ethrane and Forane were superior to other products in that they had minimal side effects, worked quickly, and provided a quicker recovery period after surgery. At the time, Anaquest's customer base consisted of approximately 6,000 hospitals across the United States. This was also a time in which healthcare costs began to skyrocket. Government subsidies, based on averages for types of procedures, also caused great incentive for hospitals to cut costs. It was about that time that Anaquest discovered that Forane was falsely perceived as a more expensive form of anesthesia. Narcotics, a substitute for Forane, were sold in single-dose vials and administered directly. To administer Forane required mixing a percentage of a Forane package with oxygen. So unlike the vials, a single bottle of Forane could be used many times. The misconception was so great that some hospitals restricted the use of Forane. Additionally, when used with other drugs, Forane could be administered in smaller doses.

Anaquest, which was just trying to establish its own IS capability separate from OMP, decided to automate its sales force. In 1984, they embarked on a pilot study that would equip sales representative with portable computers. The hardware and software were provided by Grid Corporation and consisted of a laptop computer, an attachable hard drive, graphics, spreadsheet, database, telecommunication, and word processing software. Anaquest began developing its own applications. A comparative pricing program was developed to quantitatively show Forane's price superiority. A clinical references database was developed to give evidence of Forane's clinical superiority. Electronic mail was provided for communication to the main office, and a speakers' file was compiled to allow salespeople to enlist effective speakers for possible promotion.

The pilot study was not without problems. Carrying the external disk drive was cumbersome. Understanding all applications was difficult without documentation. However, the pilot was considered a success. Salespeople felt empowered because they had a tool to bring to the bargaining table. Hospital pharmacists, who were often responsible for ordering, could now see proof that Forane was cost-effective. The salespeople even used E-mail to give each other sales tips. Anaquest decided to continue the pilot for a period of time to ensure that the gains offered by the automated sales force were not just because of novelty. In developing their production system, they used lessons from the pilot study to ease problems like training or human factors–related concerns.

New Entrants

New entrants threaten firms because they can reduce a firm's potential customer base. In an industry that has slow or no growth, new entrants can pose a significant threat (as Khalil Gibran observed, it is only when you are pursued that you become swift). To protect against new entrants, firms can attempt to introduce entry barriers or entry deterrents. Building entry barriers can provide one of the most powerful strategic uses of IT. An entry barrier exists if a firm already in business has a much better position in the industry than a new entrant. Entry deterrents are defensive actions that firms take to discourage new entrants. For example, a large information-intensive firm may own multiple networked computer systems. The capital required to purchase or lease computers, allowing a new business to compete in the market, could discourage new entrants. Supercomputers allow drug researchers to graphically model proteins and enzymes.[26] In so doing, the discovery process for new drugs is enhanced. For a new entrant, investing in IT to be competitive with firms already owning this technology would be quite costly. Cost, however, is not the only way to create an entry barrier. Reputation, service, technology, and experience can also provide a means for building barriers to entry. Imagine the difficulty in trying to penetrate a market where other firms already possess large customer databases and years of experience with specific products. The following case illustrates how IT can reduce the threat of new entrants into an industry.[27]

MBS Textbook Exchange

The resale of used college texts has been an industry in the United States as far back as 1909. MBS was founded at that time as a side business to R. E. Lucas's restaurant business. Lucas would buy books from graduating college students, store them under the counter at the restaurant, and then sell them back to students at a discounted price. Lucas's business proved lucrative and grew to several book-buying branches located near major universities. So called "bookmen" mentally tracked what books were selling and what books were available in Lucas's stores.

The sale of used textbooks is traditionally a market with much more demand than supply. Students who keep their books, and damaged books, further reduce supply. From 1982 to 1986, the annual rate of growth in the sale of used books in the United States was 22%. This growth was expected to continue at approximately 10%. The customer base for used books consisted of 3,500 college bookstores across the nation. A typical bookstore purchased 20% of its books from the used-book market. In 1986, the used-book market yielded sales of $200 million. The main method for buying books was pilgrimage. Buyers would go to used bookstore storerooms and select desired texts. Some companies offered privileges to preferred customers, while others sold books on a first come, first serve basis. In 1985, MBS formed a limited partnership with Barnes & Noble (B&N). B&N was responsible for the management of 150 college bookstores. In return for MBS's purchasing B&N texts at a competitive price, B&N agreed not to compete in the used-book market and to give MBS priority purchasing privileges.

Through 1980, MBS computing capability was strictly for accounting. When Tom Wood, a new programmer, was hired to maintain the accounting system, he saw several possible improvements. Wood observed that knowledge about what books were selling was largely based on rumor and perception. He also observed that when a search was made for specific books in a warehouse, the success rate was a low 15%. Pricing was sheer intuition on the part of the book dealers. Wood, working closely with Robert Pugh, the MBS CEO, developed a plan for the Customer Demand Information System (CDIS). The powerful features offered by CDIS consisted of a database of all books carried by MBS and all customer orders. Requests for books that MBS did not carry were also recorded. The database gave MBS a means of quantifying demand for books in a more rigorous fashion. As a result, MBS had a more accurate estimate of which books were in demand and which books had no more marketable value.

The CDIS system was converted to an online system so that customer orders could be filled directly by phone. MBS encouraged phone orders by offering toll-free calling. Following the installation of CDIS, MBS sales doubled.

MBS also provided an information system called TEXT-AID to managers of college bookstores. TEXT-AID provided computerized management for book orders, sales, and returns. TEXT-AID also had limited sorting and reporting capability. In return for the use of TEXT-AID, stores agreed to supply MBS with $25,000 in used books each year. As the system was used, problems were fixed and familiarity with it brought MBS increased revenue. Training courses were also available to TEXT-AID users. The system evolved to the point where it could handle buybacks from students, as well as place electronic orders. Firmly established in the used-book industry, MBS had the advantages of large capital investment in IT, considerable experience in maintaining the system, and an established distribution network of customers and suppliers. Though these channels of distribution are not difficult to identify, there may be considerable momentum to keep them doing business with MBS. Additionally, by streamlining the entire textbook business, they provide cost savings to students and incentives to campus bookstores.

Rivals

To compete against existing industry rivals, firms can use IT to form a new basis for competition. New product and markets are a means of forming new bases of competition. The introduction of IT continues to change the nature of products on the market as well as markets themselves. It is clear, however, that relationships among firms within an industry must also be cooperative to be healthy for the industry. If firms are too competitive, prices are driven down, and the entire industry loses profitability. Shared IT is an example of how firms cooperate to provide products and services that are beneficial to the industry as a whole. Alliances for ATM networks formed by banks provide nationwide access for banking customers. Pooling resources allowed multiple banks to provide services to customers without the requirement of nationwide branch coverage.

Ultimately, all the techniques for fighting competitive forces aid a firm in being more competitive with other industry rivals.

STRATEGY-LEVEL IMPACT OF IT

After investigating the industry in which a firm competes and the forces against which a firm is acting, the firm can begin to build strategies for managing the competitive environment. These strategies can be supported by strategic information systems. The

SISs can affect firms either directly or indirectly through one or more functions of the firm. What makes IT unique in its strategic impact is that it can touch virtually every function in the firm, and not always in the same way. A supercomputer can assist the research department with quicker development of new drugs. An image billing system can reduce processing time and staff. Electronic mail can eliminate wasted time and money in companywide manual communications. The applications are staggering. Firms should perform careful analysis of their competitive arena, choose appropriate strategies, then examine ways to support those strategies with SISs. (Strategies are not clear or obvious even with the best of hindsight. Sun Tsu, a Chinese general in 500 B.C., said it well: "All men can see the tactics whereby I conquer, but what none can see is the strategy out of which victory is evolved.") The following is a review of the most relevant corporate strategies as they can be supported by IT. These strategies are more illustrative than exhaustive, because both academicians and practitioners have suggested a variety of other corporate strategies.

Differentiation

Differentiation is a firm's ability to distinguish its products from the rest of the market. This concept is inversely tied to substitution. If a product is highly substitutable, it is not differentiated. If all the products in one area are highly alike (highly substitutable), suppliers of these products do not have great freedom to alter pricing. A differentiated product may cause buyers to see it as having no substitute and pay more. A product can be differentiated from competing products either directly or indirectly.

Firms can differentiate products directly by changing product attributes. One way IT can do this is in automation of a firm's sales force. Bridgestone Tire's sales force took advantage of laptop computers to provide information to dealers to increase sales.[28] In a sense, they differentiated on information. The laptop computers enabled salespeople to assess sales demographics for dealers and tailor products to meet the dealers' needs. Product data uncollectible in the past was now current, accurate, and accessible. This points nicely to an indirect way technology differentiates products, by freeing resources so that customer service can be emphasized. The restaurant and hotel industries, which saw a lapse in service during their early stages of automation, later used IT to free managers to service customers better. This leaves number crunching to computers and human interaction to humans. Managers no longer spend their time managing and reporting data but on running the business. Telecommunications is responsible for improving many functions indirectly related to the product. There are several ways by which telecommunications can improve services and products: taking up slack in traditional distribution cycles, providing better coordination, cutting expenses, providing higher visibility, lessening the need for travel, adding links to suppliers and buyers, providing for faster communications, and creating new products.[29] The industries exploiting IT for improved distribution are numerous. Publishing firms,[30] the auto industry, the trucking industry,[31] and even a small pizza chain[32] all find ways to improve their distribution channels, hence paving the way for their product to be sold.

Cost

Being the overall low-cost producer is another area where IT can aid a firm's strategy. This refers to instances where IT offers some benefit that can substantially reduce the cost of doing business. Like differentiation of a product, costs can have a direct or indirect impact. A direct impact is produced by IT when a firm's overall costs are reduced. Firms can do this by exploiting their economies of scale; that is, by virtue of their size, they can perform activities on a massive scale and reduce unit costs. Sunamerica, a large insurance and financial services firm, recently looked at ways of eliminating waste in the processing of paper records.[33] Using imaging technology and electronically processing and distributing most of their transactions, Sunamerica has had a 50% reduction in staff.

A firm that does business on a large scale can use IT to make large gains from small improvements. For example, also using imaging, a bank can cut check-processing costs.[34] If a few cents are saved on each check, a bank that processes millions of checks daily would reap a great cost savings. IT can also enhance a firm's potential for reducing cost by altering some of its already existing functions, enhancing a firm's economies of scope. An indirect way pharmaceutical firms have lowered overall cost is in shortening the time for bringing a drug to market.[35] Advanced graphics terminals aid in designing drugs; computers can graphically display a drug's molecular structure and identify flaws quickly before the drug is further developed.

Focus

A strategy of focus is used if a firm believes it can target a distinct market segment (niche) to gain a competitive edge. In an industry where firms serve large markets, often small firms can enter the industry by finding specific niches and servicing their needs better than bigger firms are able to. Focus is achieved when a firm's ambition is to be either the low-cost producer or offer a highly differentiated product. In this sense focus is a subset of cost and differentiation strategies. IT can help a niche strategy by collecting intelligence to identify segments of the market where this strategy might pay off. Bar-code readers in supermarkets collect data on a consumer's purchases and produce a coupon for the shopper at the checkout. Demographic data from the Bureau of the Census and marketing data are available from many sources. By merging all these data sources, IT will eventually enable most firms to be more focused. This may even become a necessity if firms want to remain competitive in the future.

Growth

A growth strategy can be regarded as the opposite of the niche strategy (i.e., it leads to an expanded customer or product base). A growth strategy is either product or functional. Product growth means expanding existing product lines. Functional growth means expanding a segment of an organization's business. For example, expanding the firm's distribution activities is a functional growth strategy. Wal-Mart, whose growth in the retailing business has been unprecedented, could be regarded as having a growth strategy.

However, their warehousing and bulk buying enables them to cut costs, which is a cost strategy. Their high attention to service makes them appear to follow a differentiation strategy as well. This is a good example of how more than one corporate strategy can be jointly used and be supported by one or more information technology.

Alliance

Alliances can be formed between firms within the same industry (intraindustry), such as banks; they can also be formed between firms belonging to different industries (interindustry). Alliances exist when one or more firms team together to gain some strategic advantage in the industry they compete in. ATM networks provide the best example of an IT-supported alliance between firms in the same industry. By combining ATM networks, banks were able to offer customers nationwide banking at more than just the branches of the customers' banks. Alliances can also be formed in product development, manufacturing, distribution, and other business functions. A later chapter of this book is devoted exclusively to IT-based alliances.

Innovation

Innovation is the strategy used in creating a new product or in altering a process. IT has such varied ways to have an impact, and it affects firms in so many places, that innovations with IT support are widespread (paraphrasing Plato, who said that necessity is the mother of invention, one can argue that innovation is the mother of necessity). To search for the lowest possible air fares, for example, computers exist that run constantly, monitoring fare changes until they obtain a desirable fare.[36] As a result, firms owning computerized reservation systems have begun to charge use fees instead of a flat monthly fee. Mobile data terminals in police cars have shortened response time for 911 calls.[37] They also allow officers to check license plates on a real-time basis. Even the NBA's Indiana Pacers use IT. By analyzing play selection of other teams, they can form basketball strategies to better respond to their opponents' strong points.[38]

Integration

Integration is another instance of corporate strategy with a high potential of exploiting IT. Linking all aspects of one's business or beyond one's business can save costs, improve service, and improve productivity relative to rivals.[39] Integrated systems help strengthen business goals in that different business functions are hooked into communicating with each other and sharing the same information and technology.

Developing an IT-Based Competitive Strategy

Charles Wiseman of Columbia University has suggested a three-step method toward developing a competitive strategy.[40] The first step is to develop a holistic definition of the business area. This includes reviewing the activities to determine how the company provides products to what markets and what technologies support this effort. This information will aid a firm in clearly defining how it differentiates itself in an industry. Supplies are analyzed by their supply risk and profit impact and categorized as strategic, bottleneck, leverage, or noncritical. In this way suppliers' bargaining power can be identified. For example, if a firm makes large-volume purchases, it may be in a position to demand discounts from its suppliers. Analyses of customers and rivals are also performed. Information about how and why customers purchase items and how they perceive products is collected. Rivals are examined on function, organization, culture, human resources, and products. Wiseman suggests firms maintain a strategic intelligence network to continually monitor forces of competition in industry.

Step two involves forecasting trends in the environment. This might include demographic changes in the market or economic changes. The purpose of this step is to find possible SIS areas that may arise in the future. Lastly, step three deals with constructing the actual strategic plan. This includes exploiting strengths and weaknesses of rivals, guarding against environmental factors, counteracting competitive moves by rivals, and the like.

Applying Wiseman's strategic planning approach would require development of a business definition. Like Parsons's framework, all competitive forces need to be examined. Additionally, by predicting environmental shifts, strategy can be aligned with changing needs. Both Parsons and Wiseman present methodologies for developing competitive IT strategies. Wiseman's approach is good in that it is thorough. Parsons's approach is good in that it offers a review of where the industry is and where it expects to go. Using the rigor of Wiseman and the comprehensiveness of Parsons provides a nice tool for building competitive information systems to support corporate strategies.

SUMMARY

This chapter discussed the impacts that SISs can have on industry, the firm, and strategy. Information technology does not only have an impact on products and services, markets and production economies, but on the structure of the industry itself. Firms must examine the industry-level impact of IT to compete. At the same time, firms should be careful that the changes they introduce do not work to their disadvantage. There is certainly a great risk in investing in or developing an SIS that proves unsuccessful. Perhaps the risk is greater in building a successful system that competitors can easily duplicate (in that case, winning isn't everything—it's almost the only thing, with due respects to Vince Lombardi). Developing an SIS is a complex balancing act. On the one hand, firms wish to be technological leaders and innovators. This is highly attractive if great gains in market share or great cost savings are a possibility. However, risks must also be weighed. The Parsons's framework provides managers with a framework for examining industry-level impacts of IT. Understanding the industry in which a firm competes and the external factors associated with that industry is the first step toward building a firm's SIS strategy.

In developing an IT strategy a firm first looks to the industry in which it competes. Examining products and markets in an industry gives a firm ideas about where and how

IT can be applied. The next step in developing an SIS strategy is in examining forces that affect the way a firm competes in an industry. Once the power of threats to competition are understood in their potential magnitude, a firm can begin to use IT to guard or defend against these threats. Electronically linking to buyers and suppliers can help a firm lock into a dependent reliance on the relationship. Significant investment in IT can deter new entrants into the market and give great advantages over existing industry rivals. IT can also distinguish products from substitute products.

REFERENCES

1. Mandl, Alex J., "IS Keeps Sea-Land on the Move," *Computerworld* (April 29, 1991): 67.

2. Dahl, J., and Miller, M. W., "Airlines Concede Ticketing Chaos Could Recur," *Wall Street Journal,* Sept. 7, 1990, 4.

3. Parsons, G. L., "Information Technonolgy: A New Competitive Weapon," *Sloan Management Review,* Sept. 1983.

4. "More Tasks for ATMs," *Los Angeles Times,* Oct. 10, 1990.

5. Lazzareschi, C., "USC Pilot Project Will Customize College Textbooks," *Los Angeles Times,* Sept. 17, 1990, D1.

6. Johnson, M., "Service Delivers Painless Insurance Claims," *Computerworld,* July 15, 1991, 27.

7. Shellenbarger, S., "Lilly's New Supercomputer Spurs a Race for Hardware to Quicken Drug Research," *Wall Street Journal,* Aug. 14, 1990, B1.

8. Green, A. H., "Include IS in the Prescription," *Computerworld,* July 2, 1990.

9. The discussion here is based on Balaguer, N. S., and Stoddard, D., "Gleason Components Group (A)," *Harvard Business School Case,* 9-189-136, 1989 Harvard Business School, 1989.

10. "Crashing the ATM Wall," *ABA Banking Journal,* Sept. 1986.

11. Clemons, F. K., and Row, M. C., "The Merrill Lynch Cash Management Account Financial Service: A Case Study in Strategic Information Systems," *Proceedings of the Twenty-First Annual Hawaii International Conference on System Sciences,* Jan. 1988.

12. Miller, M. W., "Data Mills Delve Deep to Find Information About U.S. Consumers," *Wall Street Journal,* Mar. 3, 1991, A1.

13. Miller, M. W., "Coming Soon to Your Local Video Store: Big Brother," *Wall Street Journal,* Dec. 26, 1990, 9.

14. Quelch, J. A., "Chemical Bank: The Pronto System," *Harvard Busienss School Case,* 9-584-089, Harvard Business School, 1984.

15. Wiseman, C. D., "The Road to Lower Fuel Costs," *Computerworld,* Apr. 4, 1991, 59.

16. Konstadt, P., "The Sharper Image," *CIO,* Apr. 1991.

17. Slater, R. B., "Image Processing: Bank's Big Battle to Beat Back Paper," *Bankers Monthly,* May 1991.

18. Bambrick, R., "Image Management: BIS Award Honors Innovative Use of Imaging Technology," *Today's Office,* May 1991.

19. Constanzo, C., "Image Processing: Imaging's Cost/Benefit Tug of War: Cost Considerations," *Bankers Monthly,* May 1991.

20. Konsynski, B., and Osborn, C., "Automatic Data Processing, Inc.: Computer Services," *Harvard Business School Case,* 9-187-044, Harvard Business School, 1987.

21. Porter, M., *Competitive Strategy: Techniques for Analyzing Industries and Competitors.* Glenwood, Ill: Free Press, 1980.
22. Vitale, M. R., "Wickes Lumber: The Affordable Homes Program," *Harvard Business School Case,* 9-186-057, Harvard Business School, 1986.
23. Wiseman, "The Road to Lower Fuel Costs."
24. Clemons and Row, "The Merrill Lynch Service."
25. Vitale, M. R., and McGee, J. V., "Anaquest: The Professional Services Project," *Harvard Business School Case,* 9-186-275, Harvard Business School, 1987.
26. Shellenbarger, S., "Lilly's New Supercomputer."
27. Ives, B., "MBS Textbook Exchange," *Harvard Business School Case,* 9-188-028, Harvard Business School, 1988.
28. Fitzgerald, M., "Laptops Make Sales Force Shine," *Computerworld,* Aug. 12, 1991, 3.
29. Clemons, E., and McFarlan, F., "Telecom: Hook Up or Lose Out," *Harvard Business Review,* July 1986.
30. Johnson, M., "Publisher Uses Software to Improve Distribution," *Computerworld,* Apr. 15, 1991, 27.
31. Booker, E., "Satellites Help Trucking Firm Keep Tabs on Fleet," *Computerworld,* Mar. 18, 1991.
32. Pastore, R., "Papa Gino's 'To Go' Here to Stay," *Computerworld,* Oct. 1, 1990, 40.
33. Booker, E., "Sunamerica Shredding Costs with Paper Cuts," *Computerworld,* Aug. 5, 1991, 23.
34. Slater, R. B., "Image Processing: Bank's Big Battle to Beat Back Paper."
35. Green, A. H., "Include IS in the Prescription," *Computerworld,* July 2, 1990.
36. Dahl, J., "Agents Rankle Airlines With Fare-Checking Programs," *Wall Street Journal,* May 20, 1991.
37. Wilder, C., "SIM Toots Innovative Horns," *Computerworld,* Aug. 6, 1990, 6.
38. Fitzgerald, M., "Indiana Team Sets Pace for Game Preparation," *Computerworld,* Apr, 29, 1991, 45.
39. Maglitta, J., "New Technology: Taming the Bull," *Computerworld,* Aug. 12, 1991, 53.
40. Wiseman, C., *Strategic Information Systems.* Homewood, Ill.: Irwin, 1988.

CHAPTER

5

The Impact of Strategic Information Systems on the Internal Structure and Processes of Organizations

Change and decay in all around I see;
O Thou, who changest not, abide with me.

"Abide with Me"
—H. F. Lyte.

INTRODUCTION

The Harvard Business School has combined management information systems, organizational behavior, and control systems into one course in its MBA program. The action by the prestigious school reflects the growing belief by practitioners and academicians that there is a new type of management, one that deals with information as an organizational resource. Another lesson derived from Harvard's action is the realization that for an organization to successfully survive in the future, it must make changes. These changes will touch practically every aspect of the organization, from its structure, to its way of doing business, to its personnel.

The last lesson is the subject matter of this chapter. The chapter identifies the organizational changes expected as a result of the introduction of information technology in general, and strategic information systems in particular. These are classified into a number of categories: changes in the organization's external and internal business practices, changes in the decision-making process, and changes in personnel.

The effect of the changes is no more apparent than in the military, which provides an example of changes in organizations due to the introduction of SISs to meet the demands of global competition. The performance of the U.S. military during the 1991 Gulf War was a result of a way of recognizing the changing realities of the environment and adopting a new approach to meet these changing realities. The approach stressed the value of information, its strategic use, and the use of information systems in support of the mission.

In an area characterized by scarce resources, global changes, fierce competition, and added pressures from various stakeholders, the military had to change. The military is an organization similar to any business unit. Its main product is the safety of the country. The customers are the taxpayers. Its suppliers, among others, are the defense contractors. Its competitors are not foreign powers. Rather, the main competition comes from the reduced value of the product, either because of the elimination of external threats, as was the case after the breakdown of the USSR, or because of the rise of a more essential domestic priority, such as social needs.

As a result of the changing environment, the military underwent changes in its internal structure, for example, reductions in personnel and in the number of bases. Changes also occurred in the type of personnel recruited. Changes occurred in its relation with suppliers and customers. More fixed-cost contracts were signed with defense contractors. Efforts were made to streamline procurement. At the same time, the military was able to supply the same product at a lesser cost.

This was achieved by developing alliances, or partnerships, with other countries. The partnerships reduced the cost of doing business and concentrated the effort of the military on what it does best. For example, the Arab countries feared Iraqi leader Saddam Hussein's expansionism but had limited military resources. U.S. forces were needed because of their military capabilities, but without the Arabs, they lacked the required legitimacy, at least in the eyes of the nations in the area. As a result, a partnership developed between the two, the Arab countries paid part of the bill, and the total cost of the operation was thereby reduced.

Changes also occurred in the decision-making process. For example, when the commander of the U.S. forces described the decision-making process in choosing the offensive strategy, he frequently mentioned the *what if* analysis done on computers to determine the feasibility of an alternative. Decisions involved members from the military branches, as well as other specialists such as experts in logistics. This resulted in a better product. Information systems were heavily utilized in operational activities such as determining the logistics needed for troop movements.

Some may mistakenly assume that strategic information systems work for large organizations, such as the military, and not for medium- and small-sized firms. Nothing could be further from the truth. Each firm has a strategy, explicit or implicit, and all firms can benefit from a strategic information system. The remainder of the chapter concentrates on analogies derived from the business world in general and from the Otis Elevator Company strategic information system in particular. We hope readers will notice considerable resemblance among the military example, Otis Elevator, and the other cases in the chapter.

To study the effect of introducing strategic information systems into an organization, this chapter is organized in the following manner. In the next section, a case study of Otis Elevator Company illustrates how strategic information systems can change a company. The case is used to underscore the important issues raised throughout the ensuing sections.

The third section concentrates on organizational decision-making models. It discusses the cost associated with decision making and how these costs vary by organizational level. These models are used in later sections to identify how strategic information systems influence decision making and the organizational level where decisions are made.

The fourth section focuses on the shape of present and future organizations. It is divided into two subsections: the organization relative to its environment and the organization as a closed system where internal changes take place. One classical view presented is Peter Drucker's vision of what the new organization's structure will look like. Although the term *vision* is used here because it was used by Drucker, a better term is *new realities,* because Drucker's vision has already materialized in a number of organizations. The term sheds a guiding light on the shape of the *new organization* and allows us to describe changes, their causes, directions, and destinations.

The fifth and sixth sections, building on previous ones, investigate organizational changes. Section five concentrates on changes in the organization as a whole. It deals with the organization's external linkages, its internal structure, decision making patterns, and work processes. The processes of the new organization blur, if not eliminate, the existing traditional demarcations among functional departments (production, engineering, finance, marketing, and the like). Section six shifts attention from the total organization to the effects of strategic information systems on individuals. Finally, the brief concluding section identifies some of the problems expected in the new organization.

Two issues must be clearly stated here. First, there is no doubt that the developments in information technologies are the driving force behind many of the changes described here. Technology in itself, however, is not sufficient to institute the changes. The reader should not mistakenly assume that the mere use of technology will result in changes. To achieve the full benefits, technology utilization must be within the framework of a strategic information system. For example, the core of the Otis Elevator Company strategic system is a large centralized database and communication equipment. Database technology has been in existence for over two decades. New in the Otis system was the strategic outlook of system developers. That outlook used technological developments and integrated them in the organization, thus changing its way of doing business and presenting Otis with a competitive advantage appreciated by customers and envied by competitors.

The second issue is that strategic information systems are only a vehicle to a much more important concept that must be recognized, believed in, and shared by the whole organization. Information is an important organizational resource that must be treated as such. The success of any SIS and of the concepts behind it depend on recognizing that information is power that must be shared by all.

THE OTIS COMPANY

Otis Elevator North American Operations is a highly dispersed division of Otis Elevator. The company designs, manufactures, sells, and services elevators. It has successfully developed a strategic information system, OTISLINE, that resulted in significant improvements in customer service, sales, and generating new information used by all departments in the company. The success of OTISLINE resulted in its being studied by researchers and practitioners alike.[1]

Industry Background

Elevator sales are cyclical; after-sale service contracts, which are lucrative, stabilize the division's income. However, the service market, unlike the elevator market, is highly competitive, and the cost to service customers of switching from one service company to another is low. As such, excellent customer service is one of the mainstays of any company in the industry. The service market consists of both elevator manufacturers and specialized service organizations. Manufacturers normally receive the service contracts for their newly installed elevators. However, service contract cost is the governing factor for older elevators.

The introduction of microprocessor-based control systems in the elevator cab enhanced Otis's position and allowed the company to significantly increase its sales and market share in the elevator market between 1980 and 1984. Otis was hopeful that technical innovations would accomplish the same effects in its service business.

Division Background

Otis North America had 357 service locations in North America in 1990. The division had four organizational levels. Regional offices reported to the president of the division; zone offices reported to the regional offices and received their reports from district offices. Branch or field offices reported to district offices and dealt direcly with customers.

Prior to introducing OTISLINE, a typical service call during prime time would be answered by one of the branches, and a commercial answering service during nonprime time. The branch or the answering service would dispatch a technician to repair the elevator. Customers used responsiveness to service calls as a criterion to assess service quality. However, this criterion was a function of the branch or the answering service efficiency.

Branches sent to headquarters monthly progress reports that summarized the activities. They did not, however, reflect some of the important information needed by management to control the business. For example, the progress reports did not include all the customer complaints and lacked important information on the history of each elevator and its frequency of breakdown. Additionally, the reports were filtered through four levels of managers, resulting in delays of important information.

Information Systems Background

No strategic information system can be built without the necessary infrastructure, or the appropriate fit with the organization. The first computer was introduced to the division in 1965. All IS applications until 1981 dealt with either accounting activities or factory production control. The first online applications were introduced in 1978; prior to that, all applications were batch-based. In 1981, the company underwent a cost reduction program, which resulted in suspending all new systems development efforts, freezing all new hardware upgrades, and laying off 60% of the programmers. Another objective of the cost-reduction program was to develop a strategic information system, OTISLINE, instead of maintaining applications that replace, but not redesign, manual work processes.

At the time, Otis had the required IS infrastructure. They may not have been an industry leader in terms of computer systems, but they were innovators in terms of elevator design. In addition, the austerity program implemented by the organization and the programmer layoff must have fostered a realization that there was a need for change.

OTISLINE

OTISLINE is a comprehensive strategic information system that was developed in several phases. One early application was the centralization of customers' call-answering activity. The system tracked service calls (the time between the call arrival and the arrival of the technician at the customer location) and service time. As a result, the company was able in 1990 to reduce the customers' wait time. For example, 85% of the calls were answered before the second phone ring, 95% before the third ring. The average arrival time of the serviceperson to the site was 76 minutes, and the service time was 75 minutes. Considering that there were only 357 service locations serving all of North America, the promptness of the response was impressive.

The company also centralized the service data. The database prior to centralization included static customer information (i.e., name and address). The new centralized database added data on sales call management, route management, service performance measurement, cost estimation, and building information. The system produced weekly reports on the status of each branch office. It also produced reports on the frequency of breakdowns by elevator, type of elevator, or other permutation requested by management.

OTISLINE also supplied the company with other valuable information that did not exist under the old system. For example, it became possible to determine whether an elevator broke down because of design problems or improper service. The system also identified weak and strong components in elevators. Hence, the company was able to adjust their spare parts inventory and to predict breakdowns before they occurred. This in turn reduced the number of callbacks.

OTISLINE was a valuable source of information for elevator designers. Parts susceptible to frequent breakdowns could be redesigned. In addition, because OTISLINE identified frequency of breakdowns by elevator type, the engineering group was able to study why certain elevator models were superior to others.

Building on its success, the company expanded the system. For example, it distributed hand-held terminals to its servicepersons, which supplied pertinent information such as history of the elevator and the building, and repair history. OTISLINE also placed higher answering priority on emergency service calls (i.e., calls from passengers trapped in an elevator). Calls were answered by operators trained in dealing with crisis situations. Finally, the company added a microprocessor with communication capability to its elevators. This Remote Elevator Monitoring (REM) system monitored and logged performance statistics. It also communicated elevator problems, thus allowing the dispatch of technicians before an elevator went out of service.

Effects on the Organization

The chapter is concerned with the effects of strategic information systems on organizations, groups, and individuals. OTISLINE affected the division in each of these areas. OTISLINE improved the company's linkage with its customers, and its reputation as a responsive organization improved. Moreover, it gained a reputation as an innovative, reliable company concerned with customer service. As a result of the system, Otis increased its profit and share in the service market while decreasing its cost. In addition to improvements in its service business, the company increased its market share in new elevator sales business as a direct result of its superior service reputation.

Otis management received timely and accurate reports on the performance of field offices. The reports included new and useful information to improve the company's competitive status and increase the organization's efficiency. Furthermore, information generated in the field was shared and used by other departments such as engineering, thus blurring the dividing lines between departments. Sales were reported in less time to production, as well as to service groups. Information was used by engineering to improve elevator quality and develop more effective maintenance procedures.

More important, teams were developing across the organization. For example, OTISLINE was developed by a team whose membership extended over several departments in the organization—IS, dispatchers, service, management. Finally, the capabilities of front-line workers, both dispatchers who answer the service call, and technicians, changed. For example, dispatchers were trained to deal with distressed passengers trapped in elevators, some spoke more than one language, and close to 50% of them had a college degree.

DECISION MAKING IN ORGANIZATIONS

This section investigates three issues in decision making. Two are concerned with decision making at the organization level, and the third stresses decision making at the individual level. At the organization level, the section focuses on how decisions are made and the level of decision making. The section presents two models, each dealing with one of the issues. The models are widely accepted by both academicians and practitioners. They are comprehensive and appropriate for studying how SIS can impact the organization's decision making. At the individual level, the section discusses some decision-making characteristics and cognitive limitations.

Decision-Making Models

The Cuban Missile Crisis is one of the most researched crises in political science and in decision-making theory. It was the basis for a seminal work by Graham Allison on organizational decision making.[2] Prior to his work, it was assumed that organizations, as well as governments, follow the rational actor model, which suggests that entities (e.g., organizations or groups) behave as a single, rational individual who searches for an optimal solution, or, following Herbert Simon's alternative model, looks for a satisfying solution. Allison presented two new models, the Standard Operating Procedures and the Negotiator.

The *standard operating procedure model* suggests that decision making in organizations uses the available standard operating procedures (SOPs). Thus, management follows SOPs when making a decision. If a new problem arises, solutions are normally developed according to how previous problems were tackled. Regardless of what management decides, the implementation of any decision is influenced by the standard procedures.

For example, it was suggested that the downing of the Korean Airline flight 007 by the Soviet Union was due to the strict Soviet adherence to the SOP, irrespective of any mediating circumstance, such as being a civilian-scheduled flight with passengers. Another example occurred during the Cuban Missile Crisis. At the time, military airplanes were parked in a wing tip–to–wing tip formation. President Kennedy, taking no chances, gave an order to disperse the planes to minimize losses in case of an unexpected attack. A short time after the order, he requested an intelligence report and photographs, which indicated that his orders were not implemented. One explanation was that what President Kennedy ordered was not part of the SOP, and as such, it was not carried out.

The SOP model underscores the deeply rooted problems associated with organizational bureaucracy and inflexibility. The inflexibility is not only in decision making but also in decision implementation.

The *negotiator model* assumes that an organization consists of groups. Each group competes with the other groups for scarce resources and power. During a decision-making process, the individual groups choose the course of action best suited for them, and not for the organization as a whole. If a problem does not directly affect the group, then its representatives are open for negotiation and align themselves with whoever offers the best deal. The deal may take various forms such as a favor or future alliance in another problem of some importance to the group. This decision-making process, exemplified by the political establishment, serves as the basis for agency theory.

Level of Decision Making

Agency theory states that an organization is a nexus of contracts among self-interested individuals.[3] The principal (entrepreneur) employs agents (employees) to perform some service on his or her behalf. The service performed by the employees is facilitated by the delegation of decision-making authority from the principal. The theory assumes that all the parties involved are utility maximizers, that is, they attempt to maximize their own utilities. Hence, it is possible that some of the decisions taken by the agents (employees) will not maximize the utility of the employers (i.e., stockholders of a firm). The principal can limit the deviation by using a number of approaches. The principal can monitor the performance of individuals, which will result in the owner's incurring *monitoring costs*. The principal can request progress reports, resulting in *bonding cost* (i.e., the cost of developing the report). In addition, the principal may incur an *opportunity cost* owing to the deviation that may still exist in spite of monitoring and bonding. This is a *residual loss*. The sum of the three components is the *agency cost*. Agency cost increases as the decision-making level moves down and away from the top.

Furthermore, in any organization, the employees away from the top have better access to local information. This information is a necessary ingredient in making the correct decision. However, there is a cost associated with collecting the information and transmitting it up the ladder toward the top. This cost, the *decision information cost,* consists of information-processing costs such as communication, documentation, and opportunity costs due to poor information transmission, as well as delay in information required by top management for decision making. The decision information cost increases as decisions move away from the information source (i.e., when they move upward and closer to the top).

Agency and decision information costs compete with each other. The optimal decision-making level is where the sum of the two costs is at a minimum. The level determines whether the organization should be centralized or decentralized. Centralized decision making is closer to the top, whereas decentralized decision making moves the decision-making authority downward.

Quality of Decision Making

Both Allison's models and agency theory advance the notion that the quality of the decision-making process in organizations can be improved. Artificial intelligence and psychological research have identified other constraints on decision making. The normative approach to problem solving recommends analyzing a problem, identifying criteria used to rank the alternatives, identifying the alternatives, and ranking them based on the criteria identified, and choosing the alternative with the highest ranking. For example, when deciding which car to buy, criteria may be price, horsepower, repair record, number of passengers, and gas consumption. The alternatives may be a Corvette, a Ford Lincoln Continental, a Mercedes Benz, and a Toyota Lexus. The decision maker should investigate how each alternative ranks along the various criteria and assign a score for each alternative-criterion combination. The car with the highest total score is the best alternative.

However, in a complex problem, instead of following this normative methodology, decision makers frequently retrieve from memory (either their own or from their computer's) a similar problem and adopt a modified version of the previous solution. Cognitive constraints bias the retrieval process to those problems that are recent, or those that strongly influenced the decision maker in the past. Also, the constraints frequently cause decision makers to neglect important facts that do not conform with their mental model.

SISs remove some of the impediments of decision making identified above. Prior to discussing how SISs achieve this, the next section reviews additional organizational characteristics that may be impacted by SISs.

The Organization's Structure

Historically, organizations were depicted as pyramids with senior management constituting the narrow top and blue-collar workers representing the large base. Middle management existed in between. The primary concern of top management was the organization's survival. Strategic decisions dealt with the internal linkage between various departments, distribution of scarce resources, or new products. Middle management's primary function was to connect the top with the base; that is, to convert decisions into actions to be carried out by the base, and to collect and consolidate information from the bottom to the top. Organizations were internally structured, or segmented, into autonomous functional divisions, each responsible for a specific set of activities (e.g., engineering, production, marketing).

EXTERNAL RELATIONS

The historical view has undergone, and is still going through, major changes. Change in the view of how organizations relate to the environment occurred when competition, both national and global, started to affect profits. In addition, the environment surrounding the organization became more actively involved. Organizations realized that they were not closed systems. Extensive ties and dependencies either developed or were suddenly recognized between the organization and its customers, suppliers, and other stakeholders in the environment. The outside began to influence the organization. In the 1990s, an organization may still be depicted as a pyramid; however, its base, instead of resting on solid ground, rests on pillars. These pillars represent the linkage between the organization and the environment. Without careful maintenance of these pillars, the organization's stability is threatened. That is why decisions must account for the stability of these pillars (i.e., the linkage between the organization and its suppliers, customers, rivals, and the other stakeholders).

Organizational Shape

In addition to the changes occurring in the organization and its ties with the outside environment, other changes affected the organizational structure itself (i.e., the shape of the pyramid). The first occurred with the introduction of computers. As will be discussed later in this chapter, traditional computer applications reduced the size of the base of the pyramid. The change resulted in a new shape: the pyramid remained about the same at the top two layers of senior and middle management, but the width of the base was reduced.

As economic conditions fluctuated, a second change took place. The most logical way to cut costs became the reduction in the number of middle-level managers. This meant reduction in size instead of level; the number of layers remained the same but the width of each layer changed. This took place in the late eighties and early nineties, when large layoffs of white-collar workers occurred. These cost-reduction measures did not affect the work processes in the organization.

The Organization of the Future

To fully understand the possible changes in the internal structure of an organization, a picture of how the future organization will look is needed. Such a picture was proposed by Peter Drucker in 1988.[4] In a classic paper, Drucker offered his vision of the shape of the new organization. "The typical large business 20 years hence will have fewer than half the levels of management of its counterpart today, and no more than a third of the managers," says Drucker. "The typical business will be knowledge-based, an organization composed largely of specialists who direct and discipline their own performance through organized feedback from colleagues, customers, and headquarters. . . . It will be what I call an information-based organization." Paraphrasing the elegant words of Drucker, the new organization will reduce the number of middle-management levels, and business activities will be performed by teams.

The new, flatter organization is depicted by Drucker as an orchestra, with one leader responsible for all the groups. Each group is highly specialized and responsible for one type of instrument. The new organization consists of several teams, each technically qualified and specialized in a set of functions. Business activities are conducted by teams. For example, in a hospital, surgery is performed by a team of specialists. Team members represent the various organizational functions needed to conduct an activity. The description of the new organization is brief, but one characteristic must be emphasized: the organization is an *information organization.* Managers as well as workers depend on information. Information is shared by all concerned. Data is input once at the local level, processed by the system, and distributed to all concerned. The organization is flat because strategic information systems are responsible for the aggregation of data and the generation of information needed by the different groups. Additionally, the systems act as communication media and replace some decision-making processes.

ORGANIZATIONAL CHANGES

This section identifies some of the driving forces for the organizational changes and investigates some of the changes expected, owing to the introduction of SISs. These include changes in the decision-making process; changes in the organizational structure, both vertically (number of levels) and horizontally (departmental division); and changes in flexibility. The section draws from the models reviewed in previous sections and from case studies or organizations which have introduced SISs.

The section starts with a discussion of the relation between technology and SIS. It identifies the differences between the two and how they work in tandem to change organizations. It then concentrates on the concept of information as an organizational resource. Following these, the section identifies the organizational changes due to the introduction of SISs.

Technology and Strategic Information Systems

Technology now allows organizations to collect large amounts of data that were impossible, or too costly, to collect in the past. Strategic information systems convert these data into information and allow organizations to increase the *information content* of their products. For example, the new California driver's license contains digitized image and fingerprints of the driver, and other information that makes it practically impossible to forge. The digitized image and other stored data, such as driving record of the holder, changed the way the California Department of Motor Vehicles (DMV) is conducting business. An information system determines whether and when a driver's license is scheduled for renewal. If the driving record is above a minimum level, a notice is sent to the driver, who can renew the license by mail. If, on the other hand, further intervention is required, a different notice is sent to the driver.

One question should not be left unanswered. SIS enables an organization to increase its competitiveness. However, the DMV is a monopoly. No other organization competes with it or produces the same product. The system can still be considered an SIS, because it increased customers' satisfaction (a goal of any service organization), reduced costs in a time of severe budget cuts, and increased revenues by linking several systems into one, such as traffic ticket management.

This example underscores how strategic information systems and technology interact. Previously, a driver's license had a photographic picture of the owner. Technology permitted the use of digitized image and removed one of the constraints that required the physical presence of the owner during the renewal process. Strategic information systems eliminated all the constraints by utilizing the technology, adding other pertinent information such as the driver's record and the rules that define an acceptable driving record, and linking the parts together. It is the strategic information system that increased the information content of the product.

Information as an Organizational Resource

Peter Drucker argued that the new organization would be information-based. The issue deserves further discussion, because it is the driving force behind the expected organizational changes. To compete in the environment of the 1990s, internal and external information must be perceived, accepted, and used as an organizational resource. Historically, on the average, only 20% of the data collected by any functional department in an organization was shared by the organization. Eighty percent of it was reserved for internal departmental use. One reason for this unevenness is the cost associated with sharing the data and converting it into information. Another is cognitive limitations. Information improves decision making, but more information means added complexity. All human decision makers have limited cognitive capability, and the added complexity leads to confusion, instead of better decision making.

Strategic information systems invalidate both these reasons. In an SIS, data collected by one department are readily available to all. More significantly, the cost of converting data into information has been reduced, because it is performed by the SIS. Although an SIS does not relax the cognitive limitation, it presents an excellent means of complementing cognitive abilities. For example, the information is available in the computer, is displayed on a terminal, and does not exhaust humans' short-term memory.

Changes in Linkages with the Environment

A strategic information system changes the linkage between the organization and its environment. It affects the organization's relations with its customers, suppliers, competitors, and other external entities.

For example, American Hospital Supply Corporation's ASAP system (described in chapter one) tied the customer to the organization. By installing a computer terminal in the customer's location, it facilitated fast customer orders and reduced the cost of order processing. The system was originally envisioned to serve customers who were too small to justify a sales representative. The installation of a terminal connected only to the organization's computer limited the customer's alternatives and locked the customer in.

Strategic information systems provided Otis Elevator with a competitive advantage. Otis differentiated its product by improving the quality of its after-sale service and as a result increased its market share. For the sales side, the information collected by the servicepersons was shared with engineering and resulted in improved elevator design. For the service side, the engineering group developed better maintenance procedures and easier-to-maintain elevators.

OTISLINE presented Otis Elevator with an opportunity to differentiate their products by adding a new service. For example, by redirecting emergency calls, the well-trained operators provided the customer with additional service—reduction of the tension in a stalled elevator.

Linkage with customers is one type of external relation; another is with suppliers. SISs present organizations with an opportunity to develop different types of relations with suppliers. For example, *just-in-time* systems change the relations between an organization and its suppliers. They reduce both inventory costs and time to place and receive an order.

Relations with competitors are also changed by SISs. Besides product differentiation that results in additional pressures on the competition, an SIS changes the rules. For example, American Airlines' SABRE system provided the company with information unavailable to its competitors. The rules were so much changed in favor of American Airlines that some airline companies went to court to change the rules.

Improvements in Decision Making

An SIS improves the quality of the decision-making process and increases the number of optimal or more satisfactory decisions. Compared with the previously described decision-making approaches, strategic information systems reduce the need for SOPs because the systems contain these procedures. As mentioned earlier, standard operating procedures are required by organizations to streamline their activities, but there is a rigidity built into the procedures. An SIS facilitates changing the procedures, because it distributes new information, thus eliminating the need for training or generating additional documentation. This also results in added flexibility.

An SIS reduces cognitive biases and increases the number of optimal decisions by structuring the decision-making process. For example, one module in Mrs. Fields Cookies system schedules the production of cookies for each specific store. The limits on the number of variables affecting scheduling is set by constraints preprogrammed into the system instead of the short-term memory limitations of a store manager. This approach reduces human cognitive biases, because the production schedule is the same as long as the input is the same. The scheduling rules are built into the system.

Another example is the American Express Advisor system. It sets the credit limits and approves card holders' purchases according to a set of rules. The system makes all standard decisions and refers exceptions to human experts. It reduces the workload of experts by filtering out routine decisions and decreases the decision time, thus allowing the organization to serve more customers. This example reflects an additional benefit of SISs: they add a great deal of flexibility to the organization, thus allowing it to change as the market and economic conditions change.

An SIS also provides new information that is impractical to generate without such a system. For example, Otis Elevator engineers have access to a wide array of information regarding elevator performance—which elevator design is superior to others, which parts break down the most, and the like. This information is genrated by OTISLINE and supplied to engineers to improve the design process. Additionally, the service persons have access to a large maintenance database. The database includes information on the elevator in question such as its history, previous breakdown record, and next scheduled maintenance. Information is also organized in terms of the elevator type, cause of similar problems for a given type of elevator, and maintenance and repair information. The availability of this information has improved the quality of repair and reduced the number of callbacks. In addition, multiple and complex variables need not be remembered by employees, because they are stored by the system and displayed on the screen.

Strategic information systems present more timely and accurate information on which decisions are based. For example, OTISLINE generates management reports that are better in terms of quality, content, and timeliness than the pre-OTISLINE reports. The accuracy, timeliness, and completeness of the information, as well as the support of human cognitive abilities and the increase in problem structuring, interact to improve a normative decision-making methodology. This statement does not suggest that SISs will improve decision making in general. However, it does suggest that SISs will give normative methodology a better chance for success.

Changes in Organizational Structure

Two types of structures are of concern—vertical and horizontal. Horizontal structure has to do with the horizontal compartmentalization of the organization, that is, its various departments. The vertical structure relates to the number of levels between the management and the local data collection points.

Horizontal Structure

Strategic information systems affect the horizontal structure of the organization. The need to change and the driving force behind it is the importance of the information as an organizational resource. SISs facilitate this change. An organization performs a successive conversion of inputs to outputs, which adds value to the final product. The conversion process has been historically segmented into a number of activities. This segmentation, and its sequential characteristics, became ingrained in management thinking: engineering develops, production manufacturers, marketing sells, and so on. In addition, management theories considered the segmentation as a fact.

Porter's *value chain* framework, described in chapter three,[5] in addition to adopting the same segmentation, enforced another misconception. It stengthened the sequential attribute of the activities. The term *chain,* at least implicitly, portrays a sequence of events (i.e., one activity after the other). A major drawback of these segmentation and sequencing ideas is that both notions developed before computers existed. Given information technologies, the question is whether the same product can be developed without such segmentation, or whether an additional benefit can be added to the three identified in the value chain framework. Can strategic information systems redesign the work processes, and thus the horizontal structure of organizations?

Most organizations traditionally used computers as calculators for number crunching or as a replacement of mundane manual processes. However, this is not the objective of a strategic information system. To demonstrate the differences between a traditional computer system and an SIS, it is helpful to review the effects of information systems on the work processes in one of the well-established departments in any organization, finance and accounting.

Historically, finance and accounting performed a number of well-defined, structured processes, as well as some unstructured tasks. For example, bookkeeping and payroll are well-structured accounting functions that lent themselves to computerization. The automation of both functions was one of the early computerized applications and represents a traditional computing function. It saved personnel in the lower pay scales owing to the computer's ability to perform calculations faster and more accurately, but it did little to change the actual work process.

The advancement in the technology allowed for the introduction of newer, more powerful applications that added structure to previously unstructured problems. For example, capital-investment problems, which used to take person-months to complete, take minutes with a spreadsheet package and personal computer. More important, these new tools offer "what if" analyses and no longer require a financial expert to handle them. The function could thus move from the expert's to the manager's domain.

As a result, financial functions are being absorbed and combined into activities carried out by other departments. Finance departments are shrinking with the help of information technologies. This trend is leading some researchers to predict that future finance departments will be limited to consolidators of data and to providers of financial data and infrastructure needed by others for management accounting.[6] Other predictions suggest that information systems may become "the keeper of the technical standards and infrastructure, but ownership and management of applications and even of hardware may shift to the user department."[7] This finding is supported by the introduction of expert systems, which contain expert knowledge and can be used by laypersons.

This brief history supports the contention that information technologies will force certain activities to be absorbed and work processes to change. Some may argue that finance and accounting are support and not line functions. The next two examples show how strategic information systems will change the work processes in line functions.

Two common approaches to software design are product life cycle and prototyping. Product life cycle approaches program development in a sequential manner. A need is identified when a user requests a new application. An analyst discusses requirements with the user and develops specifications for the application. Using the specifications, a programmer writes the program. The program is tested by the programmer, then sent for testing to a quality assurance group. Finally the program is approved by the user, and the final software product is released. This approach has several disadvantages. For example, the cost of changing the program because of an error or a user request increases by orders of magnitude with each succeeding phase of the development. The probability of a change is high, because the user does not inspect the product until it is completely developed.

As a result, a different approach developed, called *prototyping*. Prototyping involves all the groups in practically all design phases. After the user defines the requirements, the program is divided into modules and dummy modules are created. These first modules show the input and output screens, using dummy values. Users comment on what they see to provide feedback to developers. The comments are incorporated in a new version, again shown to the user. This process continues until the users approve the modules. As each module is developed, it is tested by the quality assurance group. In addition, the quality assurance group is involved in the design because they set criteria for good programming practices.

This example, although it does not pertain to a strategic information system, shows how changes in work processes can improve a software product. It also underscores the importance of information as an organizational resource. Information is shared by all groups when it is most needed. The user approves a module when it is still a dummy module, the test group tests each module, and so on. It also underscores the superiority of teamwork over the sequential approach.

The second and similar example comes from the automobile industry, where manufacturers have adopted the same approach in new car introduction. The team responsible for the design includes engineers, market specialists, production experts, product specialists, and quality control specialists. The actual car development process is carried out in parallel, thus reducing the chances of a design flaw causing problems during production, or increasing production costs because of retooling requirements, or performing poorly because design did not consider some market requirements. Using this team approach, the Ford Motor Company succeeded in reducing new car development time by 50% and in reducing the labor time requirements by a similar percentage.

Vertical Structure

Middle management's primary responsibility is translation of top-level decisions into actions, communication of decisions and required actions to the lower levels, and collecting and directing data to the top. SISs can and do perform most of these functions. Strategic information systems are a better distributor, conduit, and communicator of information. Research suggests that over 50% of messages transmitted by people is lost. The Otis Elevator Company encountered delays and inaccuracies in field reports. The reports went through four levels of management and took a month to reach the top. OTISLINE produces accurate reports on a weekly basis. It aggregates data and generates exception reports. In some cases, the CEO is informed of problematic elevators with an extremely high repair frequency.

In addition to the improvement in the quality and reduction of time in the decision-making process, the decision-making level is a function of a number of cost factors. An SIS changes these cost factors by reducing the communications costs, the data manipulation costs, and the opportunity loss. SISs collect and transform data into information. The data gathering can take place at the local level. The information is available to management in a very short time and can be used immediately for decision making.

OTISLINE has changed reporting costs because servicepersons do not have to write a report. They call in reports based on a predefined format in their manual. Information is available to management at various levels shortly after the call. Servicepersons' reports do not have to be manipulated by supervisors, nor delayed in the mail. As a result, the decision-making level is changing and the number of organizational levels is decreasing.

An Interim Summary

The flat organization, as envisioned by Peter Drucker, is a direct result of recognizing information as an organizational resource. A strategic information system is a vehicle to implement this concept and change the organizational structure and its way of doing business. The system performs the collection of the data and their conversion to information. The system is a better information conduit in all directions, and a better distributor of information. The system reduces impediments on the decision-making process and, in some cases, performs the actual decision making.

These attributes of an SIS affect the organizational structure. SISs will reduce the number of middle-level managers whose primary functions are communication and information channeling between local information gatherers and top management. This will result in cost saving and in flattening the organizational structure. Furthermore, teams will be formed to carry out the various work processes. Teams are faster, more flexible, and less bureaucratic than conventional functional departments. The teams consist of specialists in various fields, including linkage with the outside, product design, production, marketing, and other important areas of the organization.

The redesign of work processes, more popularly termed *business reengineering*, has another benefit, which materialized in the 1980s in a number of firms. The new processes along with strategic information systems add flexibility to a firm, thus increasing its ability to change and compete in a turbulent environment. For example, the product development time is 50% less than what it was in 1985 for Black and Decker, with similar claims from Xerox and Ford.[8]

Corporate managers need to rethink how they are doing business and how to utilize SIS ideas creatively. Case study after case study prove that if the work processes are not redesigned, not only will company costs increase, but they also will lose the potential benefits expected from an SIS. For example, shortly before Christmas of 1991, GM announced major cost-cutting decisions, including laying off 9,000 white-collar workers and 15,000 blue-collar workers, and the closing of 21 facilities. The number of layoffs was scheduled to reach 74,000 during the following few years. The move was widely analyzed by experts and media pundits. One prevalent and agreed-upon conclusion that surfaced was that the cuts were not enough, and that GM has to first and foremost change its way of doing business. Cutting work force did not affect GM's disadvantage of requiring 44 hours of labor per car in 1991, while Ford was able, in 1985, to reduce labor hours per car to 18.

Additional Flexibility

Flexibility is a measure of the organization's ability to change and adapt to its new environment. It has a temporal and a quality dimension. These two dimensions distinguish and underscore important organizational characteristics. The temporal dimension includes both the time an organization takes to decide and the time it takes to implement a decision. The quality dimension reflects the ability to adopt the correct change. Time, cost, and problem-structuredness differ among types of decisions. For example, strategic decisions require a long time to implement and a high cost to change. The problem itself is unstructured and includes many difficult-to-predict variables. For a farmer, a strategic decision deals with the type of crop to plant. The decision must consider factors such as market demand for the crop at the time of harvest. It must account for weather variations for extended periods of time. The cost of changing the crop is extremely high and may require the farmer to wait until after the harvest. The farmer as an example illustrates an important characteristic of strategic decisions. The length of time is a function of the business, and not an absolute measure of time. In other words, in agriculture, a strategic decision may vary from less than a year to many years, depending on the crop.

Strategic information systems play an important role in adding flexibility to an organization. In addition to improving the quality of the decision-making process discussed above, these systems reduce the time needed to make strategic decisions and the time to implement them. SISs reduce the time needed to collect data and information. For instance, field reports can be generated on a weekly or daily rather than monthly basis.

SISs also reduce the time for decision implementation. For example, price changes in supermarkets are entered once in the computer. The sales clerks do not have to memorize individual prices, nor is the price identified on each unit sold. Newer systems display the price on a liquid crystal device on the shelves. Additionally, the systems adjust the inventory, determine what items are sold and their average stay on the shelves, and make numerous other decisions that were time-consuming in the past. They are now available at the store manager's desk practically instantaneously. They also support other departments, such as purchasing, where the SIS reduces the time required to place a reorder.

In addition to reducing time, strategic information systems greatly improve the organization's ability to find and adopt a correct decision. SISs present decision makers with new information that reduces the complexity of the decisions. For example, new information generated by OTISLINE is used by various departments to improve their decision making. Another benefit from SIS is the change in the degree of problem-structuredness. The degree of structuredness is a function of the accuracy of information. For example, weather forecasts have improved because of the availability of more accurate data.

Strategic information effects are not limited to strategic decisions. For example, Mrs. Fields Cookies production scheduling system changes as new rules are programmed into the system. The system requires a minimal amount of learning by the store manager when adding a rule or deleting one. The new decision-making process is changed instantly. No training programs for store managers or new companywide procedures or documentation are required prior to implementing the change. The system thus reduces the negative impediments described by Allison in the standard operating procedure decision-making model. It also adds a greater deal of flexibility and shortens implementation time.

Support of the Team Approach

Contemporary information technologies such as telecommunications facilitate another important function of an SIS: to support work done in parallel rather than serially. Groups, or teams, will develop. Hence, product design, for example, need not be carried out serially. With information technologies, it is possible to compose work groups, even in the extreme of geographical dispersion, that work in parallel. For example, Japanese automobile manufacturers use design teams with members from all pertinent departments. The automobile television commercial that suggests that "the quality is built in" embodies this concept, because one of the new team members is a quality control engineer.

There are a number of benefits from this team approach. It reduces the development time because work is carried out in parallel. Production does not have to return a design to engineering because of problems like increased production costs owing to unclear specifications. It also improves product quality, because production methods and quality control procedures are considered while designing the product.

More and more, information technologies are facilitating group work. Numerous activities may be carried out in parallel instead of sequentially. For instance, a design report may be developed in parallel, with relevant members adding to the same document and commenting on other members' input. Ideally this process would reduce project development time.

INDIVIDUAL CHANGES

SISs will affect personnel skills and activities. This section discusses how two types of individuals, managers and workers, will be affected.

Managers

The flatter organization and the redesign of work processes will eliminate or reduce the need for middle-level personnel. In addition, information systems will reduce the work load and allow managers time to gain knowledge in diverse areas. Managers, who will be responsible for coordinating the work of teams, will have to acquire diverse knowledge in a number of areas. The previous brief review of the changes in finance and accounting provided an example of activities previously reserved for certain departments that will be transferred to other managers in the future.

Management skills will change, as numerous decisions will be made by the system. As one IS manager remarked after installing a scheduling and production control expert system:

> Our training program changed radically after we put the expert systems in. We weren't investing training dollars into managers on how to create a schedule and how to do a production plan, because they really didn't need to know. All they needed to know was push the button, and it's going to recommend something.[9]

Managers will become the environmental scanners for new trends. The definition of management as *getting things done through people* will soon become obsolete. A better definition of managers may become *technical environmental scanners, and controllers of resources.*

Workers

The military is moving activities more and more toward built-in machine intelligence and reducing the knowledge and training levels required by its personnel. For example, late 1980s contracts awarded by the military specify a lower educational level and shorter training period required for computer maintenance. This trend is similar to the trend concerning managers in that it reflects a shift to superficial knowledge in numerous areas from in-depth knowledge in one area. The same is true with regard to the new software systems developed for personal computers that are highly user-friendly. These systems allow laypersons to use what in the past was reserved for specialists. For example, the same worker may use a word processor, retrieve data from a database, and compare numerical options by manipulating a spreadsheet.

One should not assume, however, that workers will become the new untouchables. New duties and new functions may be assigned to them. For example, in some banks and credit card companies, the telephone operator can provide services reserved in the past for supervisors (e.g., approve an increase of credit limits).

In the service industry, workers are also the first line between the organization and its customers. As such they can be the environment scanners. For example, information systems in a retail store report actual sales, but the sales clerks may report lost sales because an item is temporarily unavailable or is not carried by the store.

These examples suggest that combining new functions will require better training. For instance, some airlines have acquired hotel chains and car rental agencies. Reservation clerks, using a computerized reservation system (an SIS), then became responsible for reserving a flight, a hotel, a car, and for providing any additional services a customer might need. The clerks had to be trained in several functions, as opposed to having in-depth knowledge in only one area. Likewise, OTISLINE increased the requirements of the dispatchers and improved the efficiency of its servicepersons. The new dispatcher, as mentioned earlier, is college-educated, speaks more than one language, is experienced in dealing with people under emotional stress, and is familiar with Otis history, products, and computer systems.

The new worker will also have to be sufficiently aware of the environment to sense and report changes, as agency theory suggests: the new worker is the source for all data entering the system. The ability to identify important data may become an important measure of performance. In other words, new workers will also be environmental scanner, in addition to their main functions.

CONCLUSION

The chapter has developed a plausible scenario on how SIS will impact orgnizations and how organizations will change to meet the new challenges of the 1990s. It also warns against confusing some of the present traditional changes with what it recommends as SIS-induced changes. The two may be similar in terms of short-term cost savings, but there is a great deal of difference in terms of the change processes. As one commentator remarked:

> Inefficient business processes have been automated for the past three decades, making it harder than ever to change them. But the imperative to change is clear. In the current economic doldrums, companies cannot afford the luxury of unproductive people and pro-cesses. In many corporations, however, the easy solution—massive layoffs and/or asset sell-offs—may turn [out] to be worse than the problem. Shrinking the size of payroll or asset base does not fundamentally change the way the business is run. Merely "hunkering down" in a trough of the business cycle and waiting for the upturn is no longer sound business strategy. By the time the economy rebounds, a more innovative, flexible competition—perhaps based outside the U.S.—may have beaten you to the punch.[10]

Jean-Jacques Rousseau said, "We want to penetrate everything, to know everything. The only thing we do not know is how to be ignorant of what we cannot know." What was lacking in the discussion in this chapter were the new problems that will confront future managers. Peter Drucker's vision of the new organization identified four such problems: (1) developing rewards, recognitions, and career opportunities; (2) creating a unified vision in an organization of specialists; (3) devising a management structure for teams; and (4) ensuring supply, preparation, and testing of top management people.

Besides these problems, another set exists that is as mysterious as it is dynamic and varied. What problems will the organization face during its transformation process? We already know our current problems; with the help of Drucker's vision, we know some of our future problems. What we do not know are the problems that will occur during the organization's reengineering, or transformation. Regrettably, experience in organizational evolution is limited. Only two major evolutions in the concept and structure of organizations have occurred since the development of the concept of the modern organization. The first took place when the distinction between ownership and management materialized. The second took place when DuPont and Alfred Sloan pioneered the present segmentation in organizations to functional departments such as production, engineering, marketing, and accounting.

Unfortunately, the chapter ends without attending to these problems. It does, however, end on a different note. The change is coming, and it is not about a little boy crying wolf. Too many organizations did not perceive the change and most such firms are not around to lament it. The chapter at least highlights several important change characteristics, and more important, the notion that strategic information systems can assist us in dealing with changes. That is not to say that SISs are prerequisites to the organizational changes reviewed in this chapter. However, SISs introduced to help organizations maintain and improve their position in the competitive arena will also facilitate these organizational changes.

REFERENCES

1. McFarlan, F. W., and Stoddard., D., *OTISLINE, Harvard Business School Case Services,* 9-186-304, Harvard Business School, 1986.
2. Allison, G. T., *Essence of Decisions: Explaining the Cuban Missile Crisis.* Boston: Little, Brown, 1971.
3. Gurbaxani, V., and Whang, S., "The Impact of Information Systems on Organizations and Markets," *Communications of the ACM* 34, no. 1 (Jan. 1991).
4. Drucker, P., "The Coming of the New Organization," *Harvard Business Review,* Jan.–Feb. 1988.
5. Porter, M., and Millar, V., "How Information Gives You Competitive Advantage," *Harvard Business Review,* July-Aug. 1985.
6. Gibson, C. F., and Jackson, B. B., *The Information Imperative.* Boston: Lexington Books, 1987.
7. Ibid.
8. Rockart, J., and Short, J., "IT in the 1990s: Managing Organizational Interdependence," *Sloan Management Review,* Winter 1989.
9. Fitzgerald, M., "Cooking with Expert Systems," *Computerworld,* Oct. 15, 1990.
10. Wilder, C., "Time to Make Hard Changes," *Computerworld,* Dec. 16, 1991.

CHAPTER

6

The Impact of Information Technology on Strategic Alliances

*If you look at the world in a certain way
everything is connected to everything else.*

—Umberto Eco, Foucault's Pendulum, 1990

INTRODUCTION

Business alliances are not a new idea. There have been business alliances as long as there have been businesses. Many centuries ago, Phoenician merchants set up joint ventures to limit their risks in overseas trading. In recent years, however, there has been a tremendous surge in the number of alliances. "The day of the stand-alone corporation has passed," states James Senn of Georgia State University, an expert on global information technology issues. "Leading firms in industries as diverse as retailing, textiles, pharmaceuticals, and automobiles are changing the way they do business. . . . The most successful enterprises are looking beyond their corporate boundaries. They recognize the advantage, and the necessity, of creating special business relationships with external enterprises."[1]

Information and information technology are the driving forces behind many of these alliances, as the two sections of this chapter demonstrate. The first section examines the impact of *information* on alliances. *Alliances* are defined as the joining of efforts and resources by two or more partners. More and more firms are pressured into such joining of efforts because of the increasing role of information and organizational knowledge in the design, manufacturing, and marketing of products and services. The section discusses the increasing information intensity of products and services due to information technology infusion, bundling of products, and exchange of product information with other participants in the marketplace, and increasing product customization.

The second section addresses the need for firms to form alliances owing to the pressures from *information technology*. Firms that have installed only intraorganizational systems in the past, that is, systems that automated tasks within the firm, suddenly find

104

themselves linking their computers to those of their suppliers and customers for electronic order entry and payment processing. Other firms see the opportunities of further developing interorganizational systems to implement just-in-time inventory management systems, fully coordinated with their suppliers. Other firms move on to electronic markets in bold strategy or simply out of the necessity to remain in business. Whatever the current state of a firm, the consideration of a wide variety of alliances is becoming a strategic necessity for most.

Understanding the threats and opportunities of information technology-based alliances may become indispensable for the survival of firms in the competitive arena of years to come.

THE IMPACT OF INFORMATION ALLIANCES

The Phenomenon of Business Alliances

The number of business alliances formed in the 1980s has increased dramatically. More domestic joint ventures were announced in a single year of the early 1980s than in the previous 15 or 20 years. In Europe, cooperative agreements increased roughly tenfold between 1980 and 1985, and international joint ventures involving U.S. firms and overseas partners nearly doubled in the years after 1978.[2] The greatest changes occurred in service industries such as advertising, financial services, communication systems and services, and database development and management. Cooperation also blossomed among manufacturers of electrical equipment, consumer electronics, computer peripherals, software, electrical components, and aerospace products.

While the 1980s saw a record number of takeovers and buyouts, the 1990s have already seen alliances that would have seemed unthinkable just a few years earlier, such as the alliance between the former arch rivals IBM and Apple Computer, Inc. For many firms such alliances are a dramatic departure from the traditional management philosophy of owning and controlling all principal assets and selling their products through their own sales force. Such is the case for IBM Japan. Between 1980 and 1988, IBM Japan created 17 joint ventures, set up relationships with 9 leasing firms, sold products through 136 dealers, allowed 107 other companies to remarket its products, and formed relationships with nearly 800 software organizations.[3]

What Is an Alliance?

An alliance, in this chapter, is defined as the joining of efforts and resources of two or more partners with the intent of serving to the advantage of all joining partners. This definition does not require allying partners to preserve their separate identities, thus including mergers and acquisitions as forms of alliances, nor does it require the partners to pursue a common objective.

Most alliances, however, do serve a common purpose. In the classical form of a business alliance, the cartel, the associating partners seek to reduce competition to raise or maintain profits. For example, consider the wave of consolidations in the banking industry in the early 1990s, which created a system of fewer but larger banks. Driven by mounting loan losses, especially on real estate, many institutions sought cost savings and market dominance through mergers. The most prominent of half a dozen such mergers announced in the summer and fall of 1991 were the mergers of Chemical Banking Corp. and Manufacturers Hanover Corp., and NCNB Corp. of Charlotte, N.C., and C&S/Sovran Corp. of Atlanta and Norfolk, Va. Emerging from these consolidations were the nation's third- and fourth-largest banks with $135 billion and $116 billion in assets, respectively. Chemical planned to reduce its annual expenses within three years by $650 million through the elimination of 6,200 jobs and the closure of 70 branch offices in the New York area, including its old Park Avenue headquarters.

Alliances may also serve the purpose of sharing risks, of bringing together complementary resources in developing products and bringing them to markets, or of fostering organizational learning and the transfer of knowledge between firms. Alliances can be formed aggressively to harness opportunities and build profit and market share, or defensively to fend off threats from competitors or new market entrants, or otherwise strengthen a company's strategic positioning through changes in the competitive area. Increasingly, information technology plays a role in the resulting strategic decisions.

In the case of automated teller machine (ATM) networks, information technology has changed the marketplace of consumer banking by creating a new electronic delivery channel for banking transactions previously assisted by tellers. The systems required to implement and maintain this technology are growing too large and too costly for any single bank or even small groups of banks to develop and run. As a result, banks are now forced to enter into strategic alliances to gain access to efficient ATM network services. Regional networks of automated teller machines were the fastest-growing segment of electronic banking business in the 1980s. These networks may face a struggle for survival in the 1990s as the business climate is reshaped by mergers and growing competitive pressures among banks, networks, and technology companies. The changes are forcing banking companies that own regional ATM networks to consider whether their franchises have reached maximum value and, if so, to contemplate mergers or sales of their stakes. Some bankers believe that regional ATM sharing arrangements will be replaced in the 1990s by national networks such as those run by Plus Systems, Inc., and MasterCard's Cirrus System, Inc. The prediction is that as few as 20 from the most aggressive and innovative of the 75 to 80 shared networks will remain in the mid-1990s.

Types of Alliances

Alliances can be categorized in many different ways, depending on the point of view taken. Table 6.1 gives an overview of several different ways of categorizing alliances.

The first two categories, which are based on *organizational form* and *choice of the alliance partner,* apply to alliances in general and do not necessarily imply a major role of information or information technology. The latter three categories, however, imply an increasing emphasis on information and information technology. *Product alliances,* as discussed later in this chapter, involve increasing amounts of information embedded in the product, bundled with it, or required in its manufacture and distribution.

TABLE 6.1   Types of alliances

Organizational Forms of Alliances

* Acquisition

* Merger

* Joint venture

* Agreement

Choice of Alliance Partner

* Intra- or interfirm alliance

* Intra- or interindustry alliance

* Supplier–customer (vertical) alliance or competitor (horizontal) alliance

Desired Product

* Product development alliance: creation of new products

* Product extension alliance: creation of new uses, markets, or applications for existing products

* Product integration alliance: creation of new offering by combining products or parts of products

* Product distribution alliance: utilization of new channels of distribution for a product

Formality of Arrangement

* Informal arrangement, temporary, open-ended, infrequent

* Formal contract, clearly defined scope, frequency and duration

Resources Shared

* Traditional resources: land, labor, or capital

* Knowledge

The *formality of alliance arrangements* is impacted by shortening product life cycles and the shortening time to market in many industries, which lead to less formal contracts of more limited scope and shorter duration. These often involve increased communication between firms and lower organizational levels.

The final category is based on whether the exchange or creation of knowledge is a primary consideration in the alliance. This distinction is based on the argument that the role of information accumulated by firms and transformed into knowledge is a key enabler of *knowledge-based alliances.*

Knowledge-Based Alliances

Joseph Badaracco of the Harvard Business School proposed the distinction of alliances based on the role of knowledge and organizational learning.[4] As an illustration of this distinction, consider the example of the IBM/Apple Computer, Inc. alliance. This alliance is similar to the above examples in its objective to share resources and save costs, but although organizational learning played no part in the banking industry, it is of prime importance here. IBM and its competitor Apple Computer, Inc signed a contract in September 1991. The two firms agreed to form two joint ventures to create new computer operating systems based on object-oriented technology and desktop multimedia software. Apple Chairman John Scully foresaw a "renaissance in technological innovation." Both companies, declared IBM President Kuehler, would "continue to vigorously compete" while forming joint ventures to develop technologies too expensive for any one company to undertake.[5]

Traditional forms of alliances focused on the sources of wealth of classical economics: land, labor, and capital. Now knowledge emerges as another source of equal importance, with a tremendous impact on the interrelations of firms. It is easy to observe that there is a vast pool of potentially commercializable knowledge that is expanding rapidly. This vast amount of knowledge is now becoming available for commercialization in products and services and growing to be a major global economic force. To apply this exploding body of knowledge, firms need to reevaluate the way knowledge flows within and between organizations. Business alliances and information technology are two primary vehicles in this new interorganizational learning and commercialization of knowledge.

Knowledge-based alliances are a new idea. Italian city-states forbade, under pain of death, the export of knowledge about silk making.[6] What has changed is the speed and capacity for the migration of knowledge. Consequently, corporations must actively manage the forces of knowledge creation and knowledge migration with the same attention they devote to other market forces. Windows of opportunity become more fragmented and of shorter duration. Collaboration helps firms learn from each other and thus accelerates the movement of knowledge. New competitors emerge who often create additional alliances to enter new markets and quickly expand the scale of their operations. Established competitors must respond, and increasingly in recent years they have done so by forming alliances—to lower costs and risks, to expand markets, and to learn or create new knowledge. In turn, less enduring, more open-ended cooperative arrangements result in knowledge-driven forces that are reshaping competition, creating new threats and opportunities for firms, and leading managers to build yet more alliances.

Knowledge Links

Badaracco uses the term *knowledge link* to denote cooperative arrangements in which there is an explicit intent to create new knowledge or to foster interorganizational learning. This intent distinguishes a knowledge link from a different cooperative arrangement widely used in past decades, the *product link*. In a product link a company relies on an outside ally to manufacture part of its product line or components. Examples of this are GM's, Ford's, and Chrysler's minority equity investments in three Japanese carmakers in the early 1970s. In these arrangements there was no attempt to learn from the partner. Knowledge links, by contrast, enable personnel from both firms to work together closely. Often partners in knowledge links are not companies but organizational units or other bodies such as labor organizations, universities, and government bodies that can together build specialized capabilities.

The Migration of Knowledge

With the evolution of data processing systems in businesses, many firms have come to distinguish between the systems they use to run the business and the information stored in these systems, and to recognize this information as a corporate asset. This creates opportunities for strategic leveraging of this information and the knowledge embedded in the organization for competitive advantage in the marketplace. In doing so, however, a firm must be aware of the threats of migrating knowledge.

When knowledge crucial to an industry migrates to firms with lower costs, greater flexibility, or the capacity to improve the knowledge, other companies face challenges that affect activities such as finance, marketing, and manufacturing, as well as their corporate culture and strategy. The migration of knowledge tends to raise costs and lower revenues. It makes a firm's profits more variable and hence riskier. When knowledge migrates to firms that can produce a product more cheaply, other firms lose revenues because they then sell fewer units and often do so at lower prices. Even clones of very low quality, as IBM has learned, can do damage.

As an aid to the corporate strategist threatened by leaks of migrating knowledge, Badaracco offers a distinction between two categories of knowledge, migratory and embedded. *Migratory knowledge* can move very quickly and easily because it is encapsulated in formulas, designs, manuals, or books, or in pieces of machinery. If individuals or organizations with the appropriate capabilities get the formula, the book, the manual, or the machines, they can get the knowledge (as Yogi Berra said, "You can observe a lot just by watching"). Thus, reverse engineering is the extraction of knowledge from a product. *Embedded knowledge,* by contrast, moves slowly because it resides in social relationships. A team, a department, or a company has knowledge embedded in its organization and procedures and "knows" things that none of its individual members knows, and this knowledge typically is not fully articulated.

This distinction places technological issues, which are addressed in the remainder of this chapter, in the proper organizational perspective. Other information technology observers agree with Badaracco on this point: "Technical aspects are not the major issue in inter-organizational [relationships and] systems. The technical issues are often minor when compared to the relationship issues. The major challenge is building the new 'electronic relationships'. This often requires reevaluating current practices and educating many levels of employees."[7] Knowledge-based alliances are fundamentally based on the capabilities of the cooperating firms and require leadership, trust, and commitment. This, much more than plants, cash, or technology, seems to be a fundamental asset for a growing number of industries in the 1990s.

The Increasing Information Intensity of Products

The increasing role of information and information technology directly affects the products and services of many, if not most, firms. These products and services continually require more information to produce, more information to be embedded in or bundled with the product or service, and more technology to distribute and market. This typically forces firms into cooperative relationships with other firms to install the supporting systems and to bring together the added information and technology required to deliver the added value to the customer.

The added information is in some cases attached directly to the product. For example, garden bulbs that formerly sold in bulk now sell in packages with planting instructions, a pamphlet, and perhaps a coupon offering a discount on future purchases. The receipt on which the customer's purchases are totaled at the cash register no longer is blank on the reverse side but also has imprinted coupons and promotional messages. In addition, these messages may be generated and customized at the point of sale, based on the customer's purchase just being made. Even shopping carts were available in the early 1990s with on-board calculators or computers, directing the customer to desired products and keeping tabs on the running total of purchases.

Information-Technology Infused Products

An example of a large firm differentiating its services by means of information technology infusion is Blue Cross/Blue Shield.[8] This Massachusetts health insurance company is fighting back with information technology after six years of dwindling market share and increasingly ferocious competition in the late 1980s. It shifted its business from traditional indemnity insurance to cost-controlled managed healthcare. The key to the new product offerings was the use of information technology in response to market demands as in a point-of-service plan that Blue Cross sold to AT&T in 1991. The plan offers AT&T employees the core benefit of an HMO network of providers but also the option of using physicians or hospitals outside that network (for an additional fee). The plan requires integrated claims systems for hospitals, physicians, pharmacies, and subscribers that can recognize in-network from out-of-network claims, tell the provider what the eligibility is, and tie together the components of healthcare before paying a claim. This means that there are now complex intertwined systems and healthcare components where previously there was relatively little overlap among the different claim groups.

Bundling of Products and Services

Every product and every delivery channel is a candidate for bundling with other products and services. Where in the past a bank mailed its customers monthly statements, today bundled with that statement come brochures, advertising, and direct marketing materials, all packaged to maximize the impact of a single mailing. Such a change invites or even requires the sponsor of the delivery channel, in this example the local bank, to form alliances with other enterprises, such as insurance underwriters and mail order retailers, to create a bundle of products and services suitable to the recipient of the mailing. Meanwhile, information technology of various kinds is the prerequisite for bringing all the resources together.

Citicorp bank has bundled many different services with its Visa credit card. One of these services is offered in a joint program with American Airlines. For every dollar of purchases the customer charges on the Visa card, a mile is credited on American Airlines' frequent flyer program.

Sears Roebuck and IBM have jointly created Prodigy. At an expense of more than $500 million, these companies have assembled a package of over 400 electronic data services including home banking, grocery shopping, and restaurant reservations to be delivered across a standard telephone network to millions of American homes. Individually, these services would be used so infrequently and cost too much for customers to find any of them worthwhile. But IBM and Sears have perceived that these services have considerable appeal when bundled together.[9]

Product Data Exchange Specification

Even manufactured goods and components that may appear to have minimal information embedded in the product itself come with extensive documentation. Complete machine-readable specifications revolutionize product design, manufacture, and distribution. Product Data Exchange Specification (PDES) is a standardized method of digitally defining a given product throughout its critical design and manufacturing stages in terms that computers of various types can fully interpret.[10] Such a standard will help cut development time and result in a product closer to the original designer's intentions. And it will also give manufacturers greater flexibility in designing and producing a wider variety of products on short notice and in short runs.

The United States Navy uses such a standard. Rather than keeping rarely used parts for seafaring vessels in stock, a complete part description is stored on a computer. When the part is needed, an order is placed remotely to an automated manufacturing facility on land where the part is manufactured automatically from the stored specification within hours of the order, then flown by aircraft to the vessel where it is needed. Again, much closer cooperation between the participating organizations is a prerequisite to make such systems work than was the case in the past.

Customized Products

The use of information technology reduces switch-over costs in manufacturing processes, lowering the break-even quantity in production series, and brings products and services from related markets closer together.

McGraw-Hill's Custom Publishing System customizes textbooks to order for a particular college course.[11] In an agreement with the University of California at San Diego, McGraw-Hill will make available on a database an extensive inventory of its texts and journals. Professors will use a terminal to mix and match chapters, articles, and even unpublished manuscripts into a cohesive textbook. The order will then be transmitted to a high-speed printer where as many as 90 pages of book-quality type can be printed every minute. Within hours, the selections will be printed, bound, and ready for sale at the campus bookstore. However, for the project to fully succeed, other publishers must become part of the McGraw-Hill system through a cooperative venture or set up their own databases. Once again, interorganizational cooperation is a key to the success of the strategy.

The advertising industry is undergoing a new wave of applying technology to finer marketing targets. Newspapers offer more zones and delivery options than ever before, including combinations of full-run advertising with inserts and supplemental postal mailing for selective market coverage. *PC Magazine* has teamed up with Zeos International to create a new first in the industry—full-run magazine advertising customized to the individual subscriber. If John Doe was a subscriber to *PC Magazine* for the November 28, 1991, issue and opened to page 49, he would find a notice printed in the middle of the page reading: "To: MR JOHN DOE. Be sure to call ZEOS before you buy the next system. Read this ad . . . then call ZEOS at 1-800 . . ."

One can easily imagine an extension of this communication channel between the service provider and the advertiser. In the above example, the advertiser takes advantage only of the magazine's information about the subscriber's name. However, more information may be available to further customize the advertising, to the point where the innovation threatens to invade privacy. This has been suggested in the case of the electric utility employees who, when they enter the customer's house to read the meter also record that the house could use a paint job.[12] This information then becomes an item of significant value to a target marketer to whom the information can be sold and who might, in theory, even include an advertisement with the next mailing of the electric bill.

THE IMPACT OF INFORMATION TECHNOLOGY ON ALLIANCES

There are many new information technologies that have a major impact on the way firms do business. Advances in database technologies, communications technologies, imaging technologies, and others are penetrating into a wide range of business processes as technology costs decrease and the range of their profitable applications increases. While technology costs continue to decrease, costs for energy, materials, and labor have risen, making a stream of new information technologies profitable for application to business problems. As more applications are computerized and more information is stored in machine-readable form, it becomes more attractive for firms to transmit these data wherever needed. This avoids redundant conversion and regeneration of data.

The Evolution of Interorganizational Computing

As products, services, and production processes become more information-intensive, there is also an increase in the need to transfer this information between the firms engaged in the design, manufacture, marketing, and distribution. This gap is filled by a growing number of interorganizational computing facilities.

Interorganizational computing consists of the sharing of computerized information and/or computerized systems between two or more separate companies.

Interorganizational computing can be viewed as an extension of the past evolution of data processing systems from single applications to integrated groups of applications to enterprisewide computing, and, now, to interorganizational computing. Table 6.2 summarizes these four waves of computerized systems.

Computers were first applied to business problems in single, stand-alone applications (Wave 1). Transactions such as university enrollments were captured on punch cards processed in batches to produce printed reports. Later magnetic disks and multiuser operating systems brought about the advent of online systems (Wave 2). Applications could then be accessed from terminals by a few keystrokes. Customer records and billing information could be reviewed on a screen while the consumer was still on the telephone with a request or complaint. Inventories were converted to point-of-sale perpetual record-keeping systems, and management began to access online data through management information systems. As these online systems grew, however, it became apparent that the same information was frequently needed in many different departments of the same company but was inaccessible from one computer system to the next. To this day, most companies have difficulty bringing together all the different records kept on a customer in separate production, marketing, and billing systems.

In the 1980s many firms were building enterprisewide computing networks (Wave 3) because they recognized information as a fundamental asset. Computer systems are increasingly evaluated by their effectiveness in facilitating the flow of information in addition to their effectiveness in storing and manipulating it. The improved flow of information is accomplished by the installation of systems with open interfaces and intelligent networks, which allow many different types of workstations to connect with a variety of networks and hosts through routers and protocol converters.

Interorganizational computing (Wave 4), from a systems point of view, is a logical extension of the first three waves. The same technology formerly applied to information flows within a firm in *intraorganizational systems* is now applied to the operational problems between firms in *interorganizational systems.* From a management and control point of view, however, interorganizational computing raises a completely new set of issues and concerns. How does one manage and control systems that are not under the control of a single firm? How does one manage and control the flow of information in such systems? Where

TABLE 6.2 Waves of computerized systems

---

1. Single, stand-alone applications (1960s; focus on computerization of a single business; use of batch processes, magnetic tape–based).

2. Online and integrated application systems supporting several applications (1970s; focus on computerization of all processes in a single business area; use of disk-based, online systems).

3. Enterprisewide computing, executive information systems (1980s; view of data as a corporate resource across dissimilar computer systems).

4. Interorganizational computing (late 1980s; recognition of the need to leverage data and information technology across separate companies).

---

are the boundaries of ownership, liability, and responsibility? What are the legal and regulatory implications? However, as James Senn asserts, "if partnership beetween firms is a matter of commitment and communication, inter-organizational computing is an essential vehicle to operationalize the commitment and communication."[13]

Not unlike the beginning of intraorganizational computing, interorganizational computing tends to begin at the operational level. Often it is the purchasing department wishing to exchange computerized records on orders placed with suppliers. Or it is engineering that can benefit from receiving product and part information in machine-readable form. Such systems, generally called *Electronic Data Interchange* (EDI), can grow at the bottom tier of an organization without much awareness in the executive suite, but they can also grow into systems of strategic importance. Full-fledged *interorganizational systems* (IOS) and *Electronic Channel Support Systems* (ECSS) mark the technological growth of such interfirm links. These systems, described immediately below, become strategic tools for companies with a profound impact on their position in the marketplace.

One well-known firm cut the number of its suppliers to improve quality, to manage parts on a full-cost basis, and to shorten the business process. In a four-year period it reduced the number of its suppliers from over 9,000 to fewer than 2,500, but electronically shared manufacturing information with the suppliers it retained. As a result, the materials-receiving cycle was reduced from several weeks to just four hours. Shop floor problems traceable to defective materials and components were reduced by over 95%. Inventories were dramatically lowered at all manufacturing stages.[14]

Electronic Data Interchange

Electronic data interchange is accomplished by transmitting information from one organizational unit to another in an agreed-upon proprietary or standardized electronic format.

The first benefit of EDI is the avoidance of repeated data entry at the receiving unit. It is estimated that 70% of all business data manually entered into a computer are manually reentered into another.[15] As a way to streamline everyday business transactions, EDI is emerging as one of the most useful computer applications.

Many EDI projects originate in purchasing, with the computer-to-computer exchange of order entry, shipment notification, and electronic invoicing. Typical EDI linkages are depicted in Figure 6.1.

The purchasing clerk of the customer firm establishes a computerized connection with the order entry department of the supplier. This connection can be as simple as two personal computers connected by telephone and modems. Then, instead of tracking purchase orders and receipts with paper documents that are delayed in the postal service and must go through many hands at both the supplier and the customer sites, transaction records are transmitted electronically, eliminating the paper trail along with the need to enter the information from the paper document into the computer systems at both companies.

The process repeats itself for the ordered item between the manufacturer's plant and the customer's receiving department. Rather than tracking the flow of documents between the two companies, the updated electronic records are passed as shipment notification.

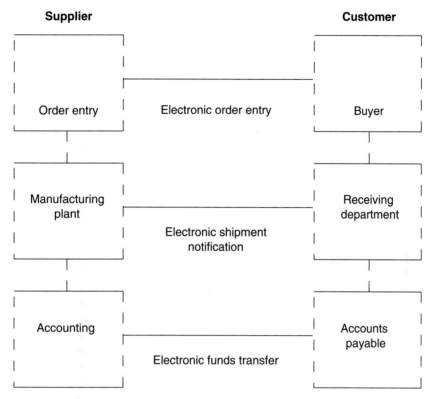

FIGURE 6.1   EDI linkages

Finally, the customer's accounts payable department sends an electronic fund transfer to the supplier, either directly or through a bank or other intermediary.

Systems based on EDI can cause major changes in the business operations of both participating organizations, because they may eliminate the need for many traditional business functions such as order entry, accounts receivable, accounts payable, billing, and invoicing. A grocery wholesaler can use EDI with its trading partners. The electronic documents can be exchanged via a third-party *value-added network* (VAN). The wholesaler can thus save on each purchase order it processes. An automobile manufacturer can make electronic payments to its hundreds of EDI trading partners through arrangements with banks offering EDI payment systems services. The EDI linkage could save the automobile buyer hundreds of dollars on the price of an automobile.

Interorganizational Systems

The interorganizational communication channel can grow from the mere exchange of formatted electronic records to support the sharing of databases and applications. Such shared systems are commonly called *Interorganizational Systems* (IOS). They provide additional benefits to both customers and suppliers. Customers benefit from increased quality of products and services. They are also enabled to do joint development of products and to benefit from shared pricing and inventories. For example, an IOS extends a manufacturer's control into the operations of its suppliers and enables major structural changes in the manufacturer/supplier relationship. IOSs allow a just-in-time environment to be created for both the customer and the supplier. The customer might receive quality control information along with the goods being shipped, allowing it to reduce personnel formerly involved in checking quality. Organizations can also transmit engineering drawings electronically to streamline the research and development function.[16]

Levi Strauss and Company, the California apparel manufacturer, created a new electronic data interchange services department in 1989 charged with improved customer service, more efficient merchandise turnover, increased sales, lower inventory costs, reduced order lead times, and more rapid and accurate merchandise replenishment. One of the users of the new EDI services was Designs, Inc., a chain of over 60 retail stores in the eastern United States that sells Levi Strauss clothing exclusively. Designs has spent over $1 million developing software for its computer systems to take advantage of LeviLink. Using vendor marketing, Designs has reduced the time to replenish shelf stock by 3 to 14 days.[17]

IOSs are different from intraorganizational systems in many ways. James Cash of the Harvard Business School identified four key characteristics that distinguish IOSs:

1. IOSs introduce new and different challenges to a company's internal control, planning, and resource allocation systems. Such systems are not under the control of a single firm and therefore require different management control procedures and coordination across organizational boundaries.

2. Legal questions arise as a result of the information exchange across the organizational boundaries and between separate legal entities. When does an electronic message become an order? What constitutes an unfair business practice? What government regulations apply in interstate transactions? How can consumer interests be protected?

3. There is a new role for IOS facilitators who act as intermediaries, such as the CIRRUS nationwide network of automated teller machines.

4. IOSs generally have a broader and more significant potential competitive impact than the traditional internal uses of information systems technology. Interorganizational information links that started out with EDI to improve operating efficiencies may lead to electronic markets if pricing information becomes available online. A manufacturer could then scan the offerings of its suppliers and place an order based on the price or availability of offered products.[18]

Electronic Channel Support Systems (ECSS)

ECSSs complete the expansion of the pipeline that stretches from EDI to IOS: "An ECSS seeks to exploit the full capabilities of the rapidly evolving communications and information technologies for the purposes of acquiring, creating, distributing, and presenting knowledge rather than just data or information between organizations. . . . Where EDI and IOSs have changed organizational structures within an organization's extended enterprise, ECSSs have the potential of modifying the structures of entire industries."[19]

Firms can become involved in interorganizational computing as IOS participants or sponsors. One or more *IOS sponsors* develop and implement the system, bearing the risk and the advantages of the early entrant. Other firms can join the IOS as *IOS participants*, typically after the system has been implemented. Each participant or sponsor of an IOS or ECSS must choose a level of participation in that system. Chapter three has already mentioned Barrett and Konsynski, who identified five levels of participation, ranging from a remote access of a system that is owned and operated entirely by another firm to sponsoring a network of systems that operates at many sites. At each level of participation there is an increase in the degree of participant responsibility, cost commitment, and complexity.

At *Level 1* a firm simply accesses a system that is run and operated by other companies. Participant responsibility is limited to interacting with the system according to the set procedures and protocols. The cost is determined by the compatibility requirements and changes in manual procedures. *Level 2* participants design, develop, maintain, and share a single application such as a customer order processing system. The firm has complete authority over the application, modifications, and enhancements. Costs usually depend on the scope of the application, the complexity of the environment, and the degree of integration. Higher costs are offset by the ability to optimize the internal functions. Level 2 participation may also change the dependencies between participating and nonparticipating firms in the marketplace.

Level 3 participants take responsibility for a network in which lower-level participants may share. An example would be a manufacturer building a network of linkages with authorized dealers. This level of participation can entail a substantial complexity as network functions are added to the set of applications. Costs rise as the network's design has to be negotiated with many different lower-level participants. The resulting benefits include improved communication as well as potential growth in sales volume.

Level 4 participants develop and share a network with diverse applications that may be used by many different types of lower-level participants with whom the level 4 participant may not have a direct product/market relationship. Examples are automated clearinghouses such as for financial transactions or insurance claims.

At the highest level of participation, *level 5,* any number of lower-level participants may be integrated in real time over complex operating environments. Examples of level 5 participants are data utilities of similar scope such as current voice or broadcast utilities. The Consumer Credit Authorization Clearing House (CCACH) has evolved into a level 5 participant. Each location in this point-of-sale network has many different providers of credit available to most consumers. The consumer chooses the desired credit line for an individual purchase. Neither CCACH nor the seller can determine in advance which credit line will be used. In this way CCACH must establish and maintain simultaneous transaction linkages between the seller and many credit service firms.

Nellie Blye Manufacturing (NBM) sponsors an automated manufacturing facility. The manufacturing process is a joint venture between NBM and three other highly specialized firms. A prototype assembly plant is operated with direct communication links to NBM's mainframe from 20 microprocessors, which access databases located in the R&D departments of the other participants. NBM's mainframe directs the necessary manufacturing, accounting, and quality control processes automatically, transfers data continuously, and controls the assembly process.[20]

In general, the definition of a participation level is independent of the system's technology and focuses on the purpose of the system and the targeted organizational objectives. Some potential strategic objectives are to attain a competitive edge, maintain market leadership or share, or to enter a new product or market area.

With each level of participation and increasing investment in IOSs and ECSSs, the strategic focus tends to shift. Often IOSs are viewed at the outset as opportunities to cut operating costs but later are recognized as vehicles for improvements in products and services. At that highest stage of development, IOSs tend to lead toward electronic markets where the consumer is in direct contact with the supplier through the intermediary electronic systems.

Electronic Markets

An *electronic market* allows buyers and seller to exchange information about market prices and product offerings through a computerized system. Such a system replaces traditional intermediaries and forces sellers to form cooperative arrangements with new information technology–based intermediaries or with other sellers or service providers to sponsor a new electronic market. In a fully developed electronic market, the role of the new intermediary can become relegated to the provider of the communications medium through which the buyer and seller communicate directly with each other. Other intermediaries use the communication channel as a vehicle for adding value.

Such is the case in one of the first large electronic markets that is also one of the most successful, Reuters Holdings PLC. Monitor Dealing Service. This service, launched in 1981, enables money dealers to complete foreign currency exchange transactions through one of over 170,000 Reuter video terminals in 78 countries. Dealers are able to contact their international trading counterparts through the Reuters network in no more than four seconds, regardless of location. Reuters not only provides the communications medium for the online trades but also enters each closing deal into an up-to-the-second record of current exchange rates, which it displays on the terminal. As a result of the Monitor Dealing Service, foreign exchange services now account for more than half of Reuters's revenue and have given the company a dominant position in the worldwide market for many years.[21]

In an attempt to create electronic markets in the futures and futures options market, Reuters formed a landmark alliance with the Chicago Mercantile Exchange in 1988 and brought a new global Post Market Trade system online the following year. This system offered an unprecedented 24-hour-a-day access to a global market, including money managers who previously were constrained to Eurodollars and other currencies in other time zones.[22]

Electronic markets reduce the cost and time required to acquire price and product information and allow the buyer to consider a very large number of offerings from many different suppliers. Buyers benefit from electronic markets in two ways. First, they are likely to enjoy lower prices because of increased competition among sellers; second, they are better informed about the available products and thus may choose sellers who better suit their needs and do so more quickly.[23]

Comp-U-Card, marketed by Citibank and a number of other banks, offers private buyers price information about brand name products. If the buyer decides to purchase an item, the system automatically selects the lowest-price supplier for that item and the product is directly shipped and charged to the buyer. This ensures that the buyer gets the item at the best price in a way that would not be possible without access to an electronic market. Even if consumers were to visit several stores to compare prices, they would have no way of knowing if the item were available at a lower price in another city or state. Insurance Value-Added Network Services (IVANS) is an electronic market created by a group of independent insurance agents concerned about their loss of market share to direct sales forces from State Farm Allstate.

Even saloons are threatened by electronic markets, as the following story demonstrates:

> When Los Angeles screenwriter David Freeman wants to relax at the end of his workday, he doesn't leave the house or even get up from his computer terminal. He hits a few keys and is instantly among friends. He can discuss the cocaine trial of Washington's Mayor Marion Barry or the crime wave by New York's Zodiac killer, indulge in shoptalk about $3-million screenplays, tell a joke, give advice, gossip or simply sound off. In another place, at another time, Freeman might have strolled down to the local tavern, bumping into friends and acquaintances along the way. Instead his fingers do the walking—and talking. He has become a denizen of a 1990s-style electronic watering hole—a bulletin board system that links more than 800 screen writers throughout Southern California.[24]

Like other systems, electronic markets tend to follow stages of development. They tend to evolve from nonelectronic markets through an intermediate stage of a *biased electronic market.* When a firm sponsors a new electronic market system, it is often tempted to bias the system in favor of its own product offerings. For example, American Airlines' SABRE system initially listed American's flights before those of any other airline. This bias in the system made it easier for travel agents to book flights on American. Likewise, American Hospital Supply Corporation's system initially allowed electronic orders only of its own products.

After the intermediate stage of a biased system, electronic markets tend to evolve to unbiased systems and from there may progress further to personalized systems. In the examples of American Airlines and American Hospital Supply Corporation, the electronic market systems were forced by market and regulatory pressures to move to unbiased systems. SABRE reservation services later became available directly to consumers through Prodigy, CompuServe, and other services without the need for an intervening travel agent.

THE ORGANIZATIONAL IMPACT OF INTERORGANIZATIONAL COMPUTING

Interorganizational computing has a dramatic effect on the way firms conduct their business. Entire organizational units may be disbanded while new ones are created. Management faces new and complex issues in the management and control of cooperative ventures, the flow of information and knowledge in these ventures, legal issues, new electronic intermediaries, strategic choices of participation and sponsorship of cooperative systems, and more.

Organizations participating in an IOS may experience changes in several areas. Specific business processes such as order entry or quality control may require a change in procedures that precipitates changes in the skills needed by the employees and, in some cases, the emergence of a new staff category. Higher-order effects include the development of new or changed organizational style, structure, and strategy. In a reverse order of organizational impact, top management may decide on a new or changed strategy that in turn precipitates structure, style, and operational units. The order of change among the elements appears to vary depending on whether the organization is reacting, in a participant role, to an IOS implemented by another organization, or whether it is the proactive sponsor of the IOS.[25]

Among key managerial issues is the information technology planning process, which must deal with the firm's organizational culture, stage of information technology development, and the criticalness of information systems activities in relation to the company's achievement of corporate goals. Repeated studies have suggested that a clear correlation exists between effectively perceived information systems activities in an organization and a focused, articulated, and appropriate planning process.[26] The rapid change in technology requires continued meetings of information systems staff and management groups to stimulate the identification of appropriate profitable new applications. As the technology changes, planning becomes increasingly important to prevent the proliferation of incompatible systems. The trend to database design and integrated systems requires a long-term view in information systems projects, while the scarce qualified personnel imposes limitations on new projects.

A Shift from Organizational Hierarchies to Markets

There is another effect of interorganizational computing that is subtle in specific instances but has a wide-ranging impact. That effect is the shift away from organizational hierarchies toward market systems.[27]

Organizational hierarchies and *markets* are two basic mechanisms for the coordination of the flow of materials or services through adjacent steps in the value-added chain. *Markets* coordinate the flow through supply-and-demand forces and external transactions *between* different individuals and firms. Market forces determine the design, price, quantity, and target delivery schedule for a given product that will serve as an input into another process. The buyer of the good or service compares as many sources as possible and makes a choice based on the best combination of those attributes. *Hierarchies,* on the other hand, coordinate the flow of materials through adjacent steps by controlling and directing it at a higher level in the managerial hierarchy *within* an organization. Managerial decisions, not the interaction of market forces, determine the design, price (if relevant), quantity, and delivery schedules at which products from one step on the value-added chain are procured for the next step. In this case buyers do not select a supplier from a group of potential suppliers; they simply work with a single predetermined one. Hierarchies typically have lower coordination costs than markets, owing to the absence of the extensive bidding and procurement necessary in markets, but they tend to have higher production costs because they are not free to buy from the cheapest source.

A number of factors affects the relative advantages and disadvantages of the two mechanisms. Two factors in particular are *asset specificity* and *complexity of product description.* The more specialized a product or service—whether it is due to its specialized purpose, high cost, specific location or short shelf life—the greater the need for close coordination and greater control between both supplier and recipient. If either goes out of business or changes its need for the product, the other may suffer sizable losses. The same is true for products that are too complex to describe. Items with simple standardized descriptions such as securities and commodities are much more easily traded on an open market than complex items such as business insurance policies or large computer systems.

Information technology is creating a shift in favor of markets over hierarchies. Databases and high-bandwidth electronic communication channels can handle and communicate complex, multidimensional product descriptions much more readily than can traditional modes of communication. Similarly, products and product components formerly regarded as highly specific can now be produced and delivered more quickly and at lower costs owing to reduced switch-over costs, automated design and manufacturing, and computerized inventory control systems. As a result, products such as personal computers that were once considered specific are now traded in open markets as commodity items. For example, IBM, Xerox, and General Electric have in recent years substantially increased the proportion of components from other vendors contained in their products. This kind of *vertical disintegration* of production activities into different firms has become more advantageous as inventory control systems and other forms of electronic integration allow some of the advantages of the internal hierarchical relationship to be retained in market relationships with external suppliers.

Value-Adding Partnerships

As information technology eases and speeds the flow of information, alliances of small companies find themselves in a position to realize some of the advantages of vertically integrated companies through the formation of *value-adding partnerships* (VAPs). Usually companies in a supplier-customer relationship hold each other at arm's length for fear of losing bargaining power and thereby losing control over profits. In fact, organizations often try to weaken their suppliers or customers. By contrast, the participants in a value-adding partnership understand that each player in the chain has a stake in the other's success. Their partnership orientation means they view the entire value-added chain as a competitive unit and they work toward the common goal of making the whole VAP competitive. VAPs can also secure the benefits of economies of scale by sharing such things as purchasing services, warehouses, research and development centers, and, of course, information.[28]

The hub of one of the most successful VAPs is McKesson Corporation, the distributor of drugs, healthcare products, and other consumer goods. Under fierce competition from large drugstore chains, McKesson realized that if the independent stores they serviced died, it would soon follow suit. To protect their business, McKesson's managers began to look for ways to help customers. McKesson developed ECONOMOST and a series of follow-up computerized systems. The initial order entry and inventory management system of 1969 was expanded nationwide in 1975. This system offered participating stores access to better technology than was available to others while allowing them to retain their autonomy and adaptability. The independent stores were free to respond to the needs of the local areas and form closer ties with their communities. This gave them an advantage over the chain stores, whose managers had to answer to headquarters and could be transferred from one location to another. McKesson benefited handsomely from the success of the stores. Its sales to pharmacies soared from $900 million in 1976 to over $5 billion by 1987.[29]

It is easy, however, to make the mistake of thinking that McKesson's network is nothing more than a computer system with terminals in someone else's building. Although the McKesson VAP grew out of the company's computer system, it was the managers who understood the relationships along the entire value-added chain and the need for each link in the chain to be as strong as possible.

VAPs, at their best, combine the coordination and scale of large companies with the flexibility, creativity, and low overhead usually found in small companies. VAPs share knowledge and insight but aren't burdened with guidelines from a distant headquarters. Unlike companies connected only by free-market business transactions and guided by competitiveness, they do not perceive their trading partners as adversaries and therefore are not motivated to ship shoddy materials, squeeze margins, delay payments, pirate employees, steal ideas, start price wars, or corner a critical resource—all practices that reveal a lack of concern for the supplier's or customer's well-being. At the same time, they are not bound by the directives of an integrated hierarchy. Too many large companies focus on few competitive dimensions, which makes it difficult for smaller organizational units to perform tasks that require distinctly different orientations and values. A business that emphasizes cost leadership, for instance, may run its factories well, but its R&D, design, or marketing functions may have trouble innovating. Participants in VAPs don't have long forms to fill out and weekly reports to render. They can act promptly, without having to consult a thick manual of standard operating procedures. In an increasing number of industries, they are proving to be fiercely competitive against both large companies and small independents.

IMPLICATIONS OF INTERORGANIZATIONAL COMPUTING

The following suggestions are offered as a tool to reflect on the issues presented in this chapter and the implications for corporate management.

Recognizing the Realities of the Marketplace

- Firms must recognize the information and knowledge embedded in the structure of the firm, in its products, and in the delivery channels as a source of value. They must also recognize their technology infrastructure as a fundamental source of value.

- Competitive leveraging of both information and information technology will be a strategic necessity in coming years.
- Leveraging of information and information technology requires cooperative agreements with suppliers, customers, competitors, and intermediaries.
- Interorganizational systems are becoming a strategic necessity and part of the infrastructure of many industries.
- Firms should consider the potential advantages of participating in an electronic market or of sponsoring one. Such a market may increase the sales of their current products or services and provide a potential source of new revenues.

Recognizing the Realities of the Firm

- Firms considering an alliance must have a clear, strategic understanding of their companies' current capabilities and the capabilities they will need in the future.
- Before committing to an alliance, firms should assess the values, commitment, and capabilities of prospective partners.

Tenets for Managing Alliances

- Firms must structure and manage their alliances like separate companies.
- Firms must change their core operations and traditional organization to enable themselves to learn from alliances.

Tenets for Managing Information Technology

- A firm's information infrastructure, including data processing, storage, communications, and input-output capabilities, is a central asset in any electronic integration initiative.
- As traditional technology with low entry costs is replaced by systems based on information technology with very large development costs, firms must seek to hedge risks and costs in alliances with competitors, with firms in other industries, and with new providers of intermediary services.
- Firms' information systems groups should begin to plan the network infrastructure that will be necessary to support internal and external interconnections with other firms.
- Firms should consider whether more of the activities they currently perform internally could be performed less expensively or more flexibly by outside suppliers whose selection and performance would be coordinated by computer-based systems.
- To plan for EDI, firms should develop a list of business transactions currently performed, analyze the current *gateway* application that will potentially be linked to and receive data from an EDI application, develop a list of potential EDI trading partners, and create a revised data flow that reflects how EDI will replace manual operations.

REFERENCES

1. Senn, A., "Inter-Enterprise Links Will Impact Corporate Performance," *Executive Brief,* Society for Information Management, Premier Issue (Third Quarter 1990): 1.

2. Badaracco, L., Jr., *The Knowledge Link.* Boston: Harvard Business School Press, 1991; also, Harrigan, K.R, *Strategies for Joint Ventures.* Lexington, Mass.: D.C. Heath, 1985.

3. Badaracco, *The Knowledge Link,* 6.

4. Ibid.

5. Daly, J., "IBM, Apple Seal Promise-Laden Pact," *Computerworld* 25, no. 40 (Oct. 7, 1991): 1.

6. Badaracco, *The Knowledge Link,* 10.

7. McNurlin, B. C., and Sprague, R. H., "Cooperative System," in *Information Systems Management in Practice,* 2nd ed. Englewood Cliffs, N.J.: Prentice-Hall, 1989, 73.

8. Johnson, M., "An IS Approach to Managed Care," *Computerworld,* 25, no. 20 (May 20, 1991): 89–93.

9. Konstadt, P., "Marriages Made in Armonk," *CIO,* Sept. 1990, 60–64. See also Malone, W., Yates, J., and Benjamin, R. I., "Electronic Markets and Electronic Hierarchies," *Communications of the ACM* 30, no. 6 (June 1987): 484–97.

10. Francis, B., "Competitiveness: A New Standard," *Datamation* 35, no. 14 (July 15, 1989): 53–55.

11. Cusack, S., "Innovator Wins Award" *Computerworld,* 24, no. 46 (Nov. 12, 1990): 92. See also Smollar, D., "Customized Books From Computer in Works at UCSD," *Los Angeles Times,* Oct. 17, 1991, A3.

12. Wilder, C., "Innovation or Invasion?," *Computerworld,* 24, no. 21 (May 21, 1990): 76.

13. Senn, "Inter-Enterprise Links," 1.

14. Ibid.

15. Rochester, J. B., ed., "The Strategic Value of EDI" in *I/S Analyzer* 27, no. 8 (Aug. 1989): 1–16.

16. Primozic, K., Primozic, E., and Leben, J., *Strategic Choices.* New York: McGraw-Hill, 1991.

17. Rochester, "The Strategic Value of EDI."

18. Cash, J. I., Jr., "Interorganizational Systems: An Information Society Opportunity or Threat," *The Information Society* 3, no. 3 (1985), 199–228.

19. Primozic, K., Primozic, E., and Leben, J., *Strategic Choices,* 137f.

20. Barrett, S., and Konsynski, B., "Inter-Organization Information Sharing Systems," *MIS Quarterly,* Special Issue, 1982, 93–105.

21. *Reuters Holdings PLC Products & Technology,* Reuters Holdings PLC, Mar. 1989.

22. Katz, R., "Merc's Deal With Reuters Brightens Future Trading," *Wall Street Computer Review* 5, no. 6 (Mar. 1988): 8.

23. Bakos, J. Y., "International Information Systems in Vertical Markets," Graduate School of Management, University of California, Irvine, 1991.

24. Pristin, T., "Replacing Corner Saloon With a Computer," *Los Angeles Times,* July 22, 1990, B1.

25. Cash, "Interorganizational Systems," 213f.

26. Cash, J. I., Jr., McFarlan, F. W., and McKenney, J. L., *Corporate Information Systems Management,* 2nd ed. Homewood, Ill.: Irwin, 1988, 210.

27. Malone, T. W., Yates, J., and Benjamin, R. I., "The Logic of Electronic Markets," *Harvard Business Review,* 67, no. 3 (May-June 1989): 166–170.

28. Johnston, R., and Lawrence, P. R., "Beyond Vertical Integration—The Rise of the Value-Adding Partnership," *Harvard Business Review* 66, no. 4 (July-Aug. 1988): 94–101.

29. Ibid.

Global Strategic Information Systems

*America is the land of opportunity if you are
a businessman overseas.*

—*A new Far Eastern proverb*

INTRODUCTION

As we enter the 1990s, there is little doubt that information technology will diffuse throughout the world and will become the backbone of an increasingly independent global economy. This chapter explores how competitive advantage may be obtained in a global marketplace by using SISs. It illustrates how information technology, with its ability to compress time and space, and to share and distribute resources over geographical boundaries, can offer opportunities for organizations to leverage advantages of market size, geographical scope, or market niche.

In a global economy, a firm is no longer limited to domestic suppliers. If the cheapest subassembly for your product is from Taiwan and you use just-in-time manufacturing, no problem. Taiwan is only a day away. In a global economy, a firm is no longer limited to domestic customers. If customers for your product live in Brooklyn, Iceland, Terra del Fuego, and Fiji, don't despair—it can still be sold profitably. If you are clever, you may even dominae the market. Even after-sales service and support are not the problem they once were. In a global economy, a firm is no longer limited to the domestic labor force, domestic engineering talent, even domestic managerial wisdom. You can pair up German and Japanese engineers with Italian specialists to design a product to be made in Malaysia. And none of your design staff ever have to leave home. Information technology has shrunk space and time to let you mix and match all these elements, just as if they *were* domestic.

Doing business on a global scale was common before the widespread use of computer information systems. However, it has largely been recent advances in telecommunications and computer technology that have turned businesses of every size and type into global competitors. Multinational corporations (MNCs) now account for most of the world's economic activity. Global competition was until a short time ago suitable only for large companies. Now, even small, domestic firms can suddenly find themselves pitted against a nondomestic competitor. For example, a U.S. auto body parts supplier could find that its competitor is Japanese, rather than a firm down the road in Detroit.[1]

Often, a nondomestic competitor will be larger and have greater financial resources, lower production costs, or greater product sophistication. Increasingly, it also could be a modest-size firm with a carefully crafted SIS. The rapid infusion of information technology into the world economy has had profound impacts. Existing businesses are being reshaped, while new types of businesses are being created. For example, a new class of freight mega-carriers is projected to develop, largely because of information technology.[2] Fewer businesses than ever are immune to global competition. Fewer still can avoid the strategic use of information technology. Currently, most firms do not have an international IT strategy coupled with a worldwide network, but the number that do is increasing. The advantages are too great and the downside is too painful. Reuters was losing money in 1964, then in 1973 it methodically began to build its international networks. Now, it has become *the* global market for currencies, carrying both financial and bank quotes. Reuters' Dealing 2000 system allows traders around the world to enter orders into the system, which will then automatically match them.[3] Its SISs have played a key role in moving it ahead of rival Dow-Jones as a supplier of financial information.

In this chapter, no attempt is made to distinguish between SISs that provide sustainable competitive advantages and those that provide only fleeting advantages or are strategic necessities—systems required for a firm to stay in business. Such distinctions can be tricky and usually are not all that helpful when planning global systems. (More about these distinctions is discussed in the next chapter.) Some theorists argue that no competitive advantage is sustainable. Obviously, without constant renewal, any system can be copied or, worse, improved upon by a hungry competitor. Thus, the most compelling argument for pursuing global SIS is survival. The day may soon come when a global SIS will be essential to any healthy, growing company. Most researchers studying global business agree that even now, some centralized IS is critical for global multinationals.[4] As more companies compete globally, the need for centralized ISs will grow as well.

The remainder of this chapter presents the pitfalls of global SIS, a look at what the history of global business can teach us about the use of global IT, an examination of the business drivers of global SIS and how they link to corporate strategy, and details about internally and externally oriented SISs. The chapter closes with a look at the challenges and opportunities of global ISs.

GLOBAL PITFALLS

Before describing global systems and strategies, we note that along with their considerable benefits, global systems pose difficult and unique problems. The issue is not just scale; large global systems are more difficult to create and manage than equivalent domestic systems. Some problems are inherent in doing business abroad: different languages, cultures, and customs. Some of these problems are merely annoyances. Others can stymie an integrated global network. Different regulations and regulatory agencies worldwide can make creating a single network an infuriating puzzle. Independent post, telephone and telegraph (PTT) operations in some countries can block network hookups or inflate their costs excessively. Lack of local computer supplies and service technicians coupled with restrictive import regulations can transform simple hardware breakdowns into logistical nightmares. Regulation of transborder data flows can hinder—or even block—the movement of both basic transaction data and critical management information. Even internal barriers can hinder global SIS deployment. Independent-minded subsidiaries may resist new systems for fear of losing autonomy or control. Home office staff, on the other hand, may resent how IS resources are drained away to support remote sites.

Adapting American-designed computer systems for other languages, particularly those using pictographic alphabets, can pose serious technical challenges. Proposals for new character-coding schemes have been discussed since the early 1990s but are probably years away from adoption. Until then, language can remain a problem. On the other hand, computer systems can be a powerful tool to overcome language differences. Research at the University of Texas has focused on applying artificial intelligence to problems of multilingual negotiation and communication, as well as to coping with the red tape of international trading.[5]

Although burdened with such implementation problems, global SISs are still the wave of the future. One payback of the rapid growth of global systems is that as more systems are established, implementation barriers will begin to fall. Early pioneers may have faced daunting problems, but those that follow inevitably find that the trail has been cleared for them, and their job made much easier. Of course, pioneers usually derive the greatest competitive advantage from their SISs precisely because they took the risks of being early adopters.

As for cultural barriers, global trade builds bridges between cultures and homogenizes customs. As far back as 1983, Levitt claimed that consumers had become alike throughout the world.[6] Some argue that considerable differences still exist, but the signs of convergence are everywhere. When McDonald's serves Big Macs on Red Square in Moscow, one can be sure that some customers are alike the world over. Although society may bemoan the loss of cultural diversity, the job of technologists becomes easier as cultures blend worldwide. Furthermore, as countries, states, and cities realize that they, too, are competing in the international marketplace for the manufacturing plants and offices that will support their future economic health, they will doubtless move to lessen the existing barriers to international systems and improve the communications infrastructure. Heathrow, Florida, has tried to become the "city of the future" by installing $2 billion worth of telecommunications systems over ten years, including a full fiber-optic network and the first residential installation of Integrated Service Digital Network (ISDN) in the United States.[7] The Far Eastern trade centers of Hong Kong and Singapore both have established EDI networks to simplify trade by reducing paperwork and the time spent to move goods in and out of their ports.

A SHORT HISTORY OF GLOBAL BUSINESS

How did global business markets and industries arise? The answer to this question can help guide those who are trying to build SISs in support of global strategy.[8] Although international trade has flourished for centuries, global business as we now know it has existed only a relatively short time. Before the turn of the century, single-unit, single-function organizations were the rule. Market forces shaped production and coordination costs. International trade was confined to merchants and traders. In the latter part of the nineteenth century, technological innovation enabled many firms to transform themselves into multiunit, multifunction organizations. The enabling innovations included improvements in transportation, communication, and production technology. The resulting transformation first took the form of forward integration, where companies took over their own marketing and distribution. Later, backward integration incorporated purchasing and control of raw and semifinished materials, where companies took over their own suppliers. The companies that expanded across national borders to achieve such integration became the first multinationals.

Not all large firms immediately became multinationals. The first firms to "go international" were mainly those with large capital investments, such as Standard Oil, or those that mass-produced commodity products. For these firms, the unit cost dropped rapidly with increased scale. When domestic markets were exhausted, these companies turned to other countries to absorb excess capacity created to exploit economies of scale. Labor-intensive firms did not show similar cost reduction, and thus were slower to seek the advantages of wider international markets. Only when new production technologies supported mass production did these industries expand globally. Thus, technological innovation harnessed by managerial coordination stimulated the move to global business. For example, the invention of automatic canning machines enabled some food processing organizations to become global giants.

But just as technology can provide bounty, it also can take it away. In the post–World War II era, technology transfer out of North America—largely to Asia and Western Europe—seriously eroded U.S. dominance in many industries. The Japanese, in particular, transferred vast amounts of technology from the West to build themselves into a power in international trade. In addition, both Japanese and Europeans have taken over many U.S.-based firms.

Today, high-speed transportation and communications are required to move raw and finished materials quickly enough to achieve economies of scale in fast-changing markets. Advanced computers and telecommunication networks, combined with more efficient and faster transport in jet airplanes have opened the doors to firms previously excluded from global competition. Now more than before, competition is based on function and strategy.

The important thing to remember is that technology was the key enabling factor in creating multinational businesses. It continues to be so today. Now, the technology most likely to influence the expansion of global business is information technology. As communication and coordination costs drop at a breathtaking rate, the new challenge is to create strategies that optimize the concentration or dispersion of critical resources. It is no longer necessary to choose exclusively between concentration and dispersion when designing an organization. Those who exploit information technologies will earn competitive advantage by finding the best balance between these two modes. Building products in a variety of locations based on the most favorable conditions is known as "rationalizing" operations. Although costs are a primary driver of rationalized operations, availability of labor and materials or favorable regulations also can influence task distribution.

BUSINESS DRIVERS

The best global strategy for any firm depends on its resources, market, competition, and configuration. In other words, strategy should be driven by business realities. In a 1991 study of 25 firms competing globally, the following list of business drivers was derived:

1. *Global consumer-customer.* Firms that serve travelers—airlines, hotels, rental car and credit card companies—need worldwide databases. Corporate customers with global operations are demanding more integrated worldwide services.

2. *Global product.* The product is either the same worldwide (e.g., Coca Cola) or is assembled by subsidiaries throughout the world (e.g., security, currency exchange, real estate). Information systems can manage worldwide marketing.

3. *Rationalized operations.* Different subsidiaries build different parts of the same product based on availability of skills, raw materials, or favorable business climate. A computer manufacturer might build software in the United Kingdom, monitors in South Korea, and circuit boards in Taiwan. IT coordinates operations.

4. *Flexible operations.* Operations are moved from one plant to another in response to labor problems or shortages of raw materials. Common systems simplify these moves.

5. *Joint resource.* National subsidiaries may share facilities or workers. For example, the European subsidiaries of a petroleum company jointly own tankers. A material resource system tracks the location of each resource.

6. *Duplicate facilities.* A chemical company uses nearly identical plants to produce gases in different countries. Production systems are easily shared.

7. *Scarce resources.* A chemical company requires that high-cost compressors be available in each of its worldwide plants. High cost prevents storing them at every facility, so a parts logistics system coordinates compressor use.

8. *Risk reduction.* Risks associated with currency conversions, multiple global markets, and multiple traders are alleviated. A multinational bank develops a global risk-management system for currency trading.

9. *Legal requirements.* Information requirements mandated by laws in one or more countries are consolidated. Financial regulations imposed on a subsidiary necessitate corporatewide information requirements if the subsidiary intends to sell or use products made elsewhere.

10. *Economies of scale for systems.* One corporatewide system is used to reduce data center requirements, duplicateed development, and maintenance efforts.[9]

Management also needs to match the style of the industry in which it seeks to compete. This is one reason certain industries thrive in certain countries, though there are no structural reasons why that should be so. For example, Italians do well in markets characterized by focus, niche marketing, and breathtaking change: lighting, furniture, footwear, and woolen fabrics.[10] Other countries show similar style-industry matchups.

The earliest form of multinational corporation is the multidomestic firm, which consists of a home base or host firm that directs the operations of a loose amalgamation of overseas subsidiaries. Before the arrival of modern telecommunications and the easing of barriers to trade and transborder data flows, the multidomestic approach made sense. A company could be active in many markets, often selling the same or similar products, but with very decentralized management. To attempt to centralize control would raise coordination costs to the point where they might wipe out any economies of scale in production. Many firms today continue to use a multidomestic configuration.

A transnational firm, on the other hand, can retain much of the local flexibility of the multidomestic, while exercising greater corporate control over the entire enterprise. Probably the most beneficial aspect of transnationals is that the degree of concentration or dispersion can be tailored to the needs of the particular situation. And given the appropriate internal resources, it can be retailored in the future, if circumstances warrant it. For example, glass is best made locally, because it is composed of commodity available materials and is costly to ship. However, glass manufacturers can gain considerable advantage by pooling global research and development in a single location. Conversely, manufacturers of videocassette recorders achieve better economies of scale if they manufacture their product in a single location but allow sales and marketing to be handled independently in each country to which they export.[11]

Transnational firms have become possible only because of the stunning advances in telecommunications and transportation. Without these technologies, the coordination costs and problems of centralized control would be nearly insurmountable. Becoming transnational can increase a firm's competitiveness but it also requires more tightly linked information systems.

In some industries, such as financial services, transportation, and communications, global strategies linked to global SISs are essential. As early as 1983, 51% of Manufacturers Hanover's profits came from overseas. Without an international network, it would soon have become noncompetitive. Some highly successful firms like Reuters have built their entire business around a global information network and its related information systems. Most airlines now derive some if not most of their profits from reservation systems. If those carriers serve international routes, their systems must be global, too. As noted above, producers of bulk and commodity items have long competed globally without integrated SIS. Now, however, rapid changes in markets, currency, and prices make the use of IT to support global sales and production essential.

The most important factor in the strategic use of IT is ensuring the alignment of global SIS with corporate strategies. A computer system that supports strategy A, when the company using it is pursuing strategy B, can do more harm than good. Economies of scale in worldwide production can be squandered by fragmented communication networks and missing or delayed information.

If the strategy of a multidomestic firm is cost leadership, then the best centralized SIS will provide strong support for all subsidiaries. Each subsidiary should get rapid access to resource, market, and financial information. If the goal is product differentiation, then the multidomestic should have a system that "gets out of the way" of the local subsidiary to encourage local responsiveness to market needs. The SIS needs of a multidomestic are usually less demanding than those of a transnational, because global integration is not needed. The host company mainly needs to monitor the subsidiaries to make sure they don't get into trouble, provide information as needed, but otherwise stay clear.

If the transnational's goal is cost leadership, an SIS provides opportunities for global economies of scale. If differentiation is the corporate strategy, then a global SIS could provide the leverage to penetrate new markets.

INTERNAL SISs

Strategic systems can either be entirely internal to a firm or they can link to external entities. Each type of system has its own special role. Internal SISs can take various forms to support a mix of strategies. Internal SISs are used only by individuals and groups within the organization. They support an organization's management and staff as they design, produce, sell, and service products. They provide the information needed by central management to administer widely dispersed operations. Internal SISs can support niche, differentiation, innovation, and cost strategies in any combination. A networked computer-aided design system allows product engineering to take place on more than one continent simultaneously, reducing development time, increasing the number of independent perspectives on a problem, and ensuring *round-the-clock* development without relying on multiple shifts or overtime in one location. These intensive efforts can yield the competitive benefits of reduced time and cost, and increased potential market share. In slower-paced days, the 3M Corporation could test a new product in the United States, fine-tune it, then later roll it out in Europe. Soon, firms like Canon exploited these long introductions to learn from the U.S. introduction, and introduce products in Europe first.[12]

Talent from around the world can use networks to help solve intractable design or technical problems. At Digital Equipment, an engineer can put a problem on the network of 50,000 terminals and VAX mainframes around the world, go to bed, and the next morning find a half dozen solutions.[13] A pharmaceutical house links research centers in four countries to obtain simultaneous multiple governmental approvals, vastly decreasing time to market for new drugs.[14] Networked systems can coordinate the work of specialists on three continents as if they were located in one facility.

Internal systems are particularly helpful in rationalizing operations, usually in support of cost-leadership strategy. Production tasks can be shifted to sites around the world where specialized talent is available to handle it. Offshore software development can ease critical shortages of expensive U.S. software development talent.[15] Work can be assigned where the labor costs are the lowest. This is a particularly vexing problem, because constantly shifting labor costs have forced companies to establish overseas manufacturing locations. Britain's labor costs are 20% less than those of the United States, while labor costs in Japan, which used to be 30% less, are now the same as those of the United States.[16] Dow Chemical allocates production across borders to optimize internal production and external purchases of supplies. A sophisticated system considers everything from currency and taxes to transportation and production costs to select the cheapest plant.[17]

A tightly integrated global information system can reduce management costs by allowing a centralized group to control operations in plants with a wide geographic distribution. Internal SISs can enable rapid communication between far-flung operating and management sites. Basic systems process orders promptly so that the right products manufactured overseas are assembled and shipped on time to the right customer. When production is dispersed and fragmented, this can be a special challenge. It is now simple, using telecommunications, to create effective international teams that were impossible to form before. Electronic mail and FAX are the only sensible ways to send messages conveniently and quickly from London to New York to Tokyo. Networked internal systems mean that overseas personnel can often get more access and better service from headquarters than from local facilities. This difference often provides critical cost, time, and product differentiation advantages. Conversely, the input from diverse cultures—with different intellectual and practical perspectives on business—can help stimulate innovation and create new ways of competing.[18]

Where markets are volatile, an internal SIS can provide central management with instantaneous reports on sales. This information can be used to make important product design and distribution decisions. The Italian firm Benetton mass-produces "half-garments" that are finished (dyed) according to local requirements for the week. Four thousand retail stores are linked to provide daily sales and inventory. Using the network, a CAD system, and an automated warehouse, Benetton makes clothes to match local tastes and rapidly changing fashion trends.[19] Firms like DuPont feel that in the new competitive environment, corporate managers should have immediate access to any data they need from around the world for decision support. In the case of DuPont, this means an information system that links over one hundred businesses and over twelve hundred different products.[20]

Internal SIS can, if needed, feed information both ways, enabling an approach the Japanese call *glocalization,* where a global strategy is carried out with distinctly local flavors. Corporate headquarters can constantly review and monitor local activities, exercising either rigid or lax control as circumstances dictate. Conversely, local managers can easily draw on corporate staff for information and guidance.

EXTERNAL SISs

The most exciting and profitable SISs often exist outside the firm, in the boundary between the firm and its environment. These also are the most challenging to create. External SISs connect the firm with suppliers, customers, and other organizations both inside and outside a particular industry. These information alliances (reviewed in chapter six) are becoming more common, as fewer and fewer companies have the resources to go it alone in the global marketplace. In the world market, the largest U.S. firms are dwarfed by the Global 1000.[21] And even these giants often resort to alliances to build on complementary strengths, increase geographic reach, or reduce risk. To some extent, the IT revolution of the last decade also has fostered the appearance of companies that look more like the single-unit, single-function firms of the nineteenth century than the industrial behemoths of the midtwentieth century. With access barriers to international trade growing lower every day, even small start-ups can move quickly into active global competition.

The first applications of external systems are usually up- and down-stream from company operations, in alliances with suppliers, freight carriers, and buyers. All three have powerful incentives to build and sustain alliances. Sometimes these are simple order processing systems that use EDI linkage to handle purchase orders and invoicing. Between sophisticated firms, the connection can be much more intimate. Boeing uses computer-aided design jointly to design components online with foreign suppliers.[22] Costs are reduced, while the ability to innovate improves. Often, interorganizational alliances are composed of more than a single system or firm. These SIS chains connect multiple systems and entities, each of which leverages the unique strengths of the partners' systems. As global trade grows, these chains are likely to proliferate. Currently, they tend to include supplier, freight carrier, and manufacturer. A single case shows how these systems connect. Gateway 2000 purchases Asian-made personal computer parts for assembly at its PC manufacturing plant in South Dakota. It then ships finished machines directly to users throughout the United States. Using Federal Express's International Expressfreight Service, it can order parts when it needs them and count on delivery within two days. Its just-in-time manufacturing requires not only jet airfreight and automated ordering systems but also Federal Express's computerized customs clearing system, which initiates custom checks *before* the goods reach the States to ensure quick clearance.[23] In this case, at least three distinct interorganizational systems are operating: the link between Gateway 2000 and its Asian suppliers, the link between Gateway 2000 and Federal Express, and the link between Federal Express and local customs. Presumably, Gateway 2000 also has an internal system to handle its direct marketing and manufacturing activities. As more firms develop global SISs, such multiple-system chains will become common.

From the upstream perspective, external SISs usually support marketing, sales, and service. The Federal Express freight system mentioned above is a good example, where Federal Express is putting thousands of terminals in customer locations throughout the world to speed up shipping orders and tracking inquiries. Other freight carriers have or are planning similar systems. These systems primarily foster product differentiation or cost reductions.

SISs can become selling points themselves. Particularly in the information services and freight industries, SISs are a key part of the service being sold. In a 1991 survey, shippers ranked good information systems third, behind cost and reliability, among carrier selection criteria.[24] Singapore has used EDI to stimulate its growth as an international trade center. Its TradeNet system was created to speed the review and approval of trade documents. More than 500 companies have subscribed to TradeNet, and more than 95% of government permits are processed in 15 minutes rather than one to four days. Permits are automatically routed to port and aviation authorities to speed up the physical clearance of goods. TradeNet processes excise duties, customs fees, and funds transfers.[25] Hong Kong has similar trade- and customs-oriented systems.

The effects of such SISs are multilayered and mutually reinforcing. Value is added by each system. The use of various technologies by cities to entice businesses to their locality has a secondary effect on the firms that elect to go. The telecommunications infrastructure, composed of fiber-optic cabling and advanced digital switches, and the related information systems, such as electronically based permit/approval systems, enhances not only the competitive position of a city but also of those firms that choose to do business there. The more aggressively these services are used, the more advantages accrue for both parties. Learning of these prime locations can be a key piece of strategic information itself.

SISs can foster, or result from, strategic alliances between competing firms. Airline reservation systems are a good example of how SISs build alliances, even between competitors. Most reservation systems now involve alliances of at least two or three airlines. Some, particularly the two European systems, Amadeus and Galileo, represent alliances among 14 airlines altogether.[26] These alliances are needed in part because the resulting system is too large for any single firm to develop and sell to travel agents. And the value of each system is enhanced by the cooperation of the partners.

Some alliances are built on shared risk, whereas others are built on shared expertise. Germany's MBB joined General Electric to build jet engines, while Matsushita worked with Phillips of the Netherlands on consumer electronics. These alliances of large multinational corporations create entities with truly global scope.[27] The best alliances leverage the links between strategic systems. In the two alliances just noted, the SIS should encompass at least computer-aided design and engineering (CAD/CAE), and electronic mail.

Strategic alliances form to leverage complementary services between noncompetitors. Or the alliance may extend the geographic scope of comparable firms in two parts of the world.

Although the most common alliances are between large organizations, globalization also can result in alliances between smaller firms. Because the firms are small, the relative advantages can be much larger. Often, these firms are composed of professionals who support other global-oriented organizations. Lex Mundi, a nonprofit worldwide membership organization founded in 1989, provides a network of contacts that can enhance the resources of a law firm internationally, without the expense of a foreign office.[28]

Some external SISs function in a *receive-only* mode. These systems are a special case of environmental scanning for decision support. Early detection of trends in support of an early-mover strategy can often be enhanced by systems specifically designed to monitor key factors. These *early warning systems* can be as simple as a connection to global E-mail, bulletin boards, and routine news reports, or they can be as sophisticated as fuzzy-logic, expert screening systems. Either way, the rapid link to the world's information networks can play a pivotal role for those seeking early advantage.

GLOBAL SIS CHALLENGES

One special challenge of globalization is the result of feedback on systems and processes. Sometimes these systems change the environment so much that they themselves must adapt. Many successful firms—especially the Japanese—now rely on a strategy of *glocalization*—emphasizing the local attributes and conventions related to a product and market. However, improvements in global communications inevitably bring market homogenization. So while firms must plan for a diversity of approaches in the near term, they must be alert to possible convergence and remain flexible enough to respond with product and marketing changes that can take advantage of more homogeneity. In this fashion, greater economies of scale can be realized. For a company supplying manufacturing firms, increased globalization will usually result in more worldwide consistency in orders from customers, as they, too, globalize their products. "We want to get the product as close to the customer's place of operation as possible, but we also need to remember the needs of our customers, and many of our customers are *global* customers," states Hans Huppertz, director of Corporate IS, Dow Chemical Corporation. The challenge is to customize for the local customer, yet retain a single common access for global customers. Dow's global customers include the global Ford Motor Corporation, which orders products in Latin America, Canada, the United States, and Europe.[29]

Another challenge of global systems is that as more companies go global, the already rapid rate of change will increase still more. Even without burgeoning technology, increasing rates of change are a guaranteed feature of the international markets of the future. One need look no further than the changes in Europe planned after 1992, when a single European Market was to be created by the cooperation of the members of the European Community. Traditional patterns of business will be upset, as transborder trade becomes far simpler. Competition will heat up, and companies will have to realign their operations and their SIS to deal with this new environment. Despite all the prognostications regarding Europe, companies will have to maintain vigilance to events unfolding there. Ironically, the dropping of trade barriers in Europe may benefit U.S. firms as much as anyone. Because Europeans have had to work across many borders for years, they tend to adapt easier to transborder problems. Brad Power, of the Index Group, observes that IS units in the United States tend to think more homogeneously.[30] With European trade much more homogenized, U.S. companies should feel right at home. Regardless of who comes out on top, post-1992 Europe both poses a special challenge and also serves as an exemplar of things to come in global business.

The other revolution that will change international business irrevocably is the dismantling of the Soviet Union. Although the final shape of Eastern Europe and the Soviet republics is difficult to foresee in 1993, there will clearly be many new opportunities for global business resulting from the fall of communism. Information technology will probably play an even more important role than ever before, as the Eastern European countries struggle to develop their own currencies and markets.

The stunning ability of IT to shrink the globe is perhaps best exemplified by events that occurred during the abortive Soviet coup in August 1991. Glasnost had resulted in the creation of an electronic mail link between a Russian computer group called Demos and a computer in Helsinki, Finland. Computer users throughout the world found themselves to be long-distance participants in the events in the Soviet Union because of this telecommunications link. Computer users outside the Soviet Union transmitted news broadcasts and information to Demos, which in turn distributed it electronically on its own network to major organizations inside the country. In turn, the Soviets transmitted what information they had to the outside world. Some of these transmissions were formal, others were personal. Information was often more available to the Soviets from sources thousands of miles away than from just outside their windows.[31]

Global systems have the power to reshape our world. We need only apply the imagination, intelligence, and fortitude to forge these new international links.

REFERENCES

1. Mannheim, M., "Global Information Technology: Globalization, Competitive Strategy and Information Technologies," *Proceedings of the Twenty-Fourth Annual Hawaii International Conference on System Sciences* 4, 1991, 172–81.

2. Browne, M. J., "Prospective Freight Mega-Carriers: The Role of Information Technology in Their Global Ambitions." *Proceedings of the Twenty-Fourth Annual Hawaii International Conference on System Sciences* 4, 1991, 192–201.

3. Keen, P. G. W., *Shaping the Future.* Boston: Harvard Business School Press, 1991.

4. Ives, B., and Jarvenpaa, S. L., "Applications of Global Information Technology: Key Issues for Management," *Management Information Systems Quarterly* (Mar. 1991): 33–49.

5. Lee, R. M., Dewitz, S. D., and Chen, K. T., "AI and Global EDI," *Proceedings of the Twenty-Fourth Annual Hawaii International Conference on System Sciences* 4, 1991, 182–91.

6. Levitt, T., "The Globalization of Markets," *Harvard Business Review* (May 1983): 92–102.

7. Keen, *Shaping the Future.*

8. The discussion here is based on Chandler, A. D., "The Evolution of Modern Global Competition," in M. E. Porter, ed., *Competition in Global Industries.* Boston: Harvard Business School Press, 1986.

9. Ives and Jarvenpaa, "Applications of Global Information Technology."

10. Porter, M. E., "The Competitive Advantage of Nations," *Harvard Business Review* (Mar.-Apr. 1990): 73–93.

11. Porter, M. E., "Competition in Global Industries: A Conceptual Framework," in M. E. Porter, ed., *Competition in Global Industries.* Boston: Harvard Business School Press, 1986.

12. Keen, *Shaping the Future.*

13. Horwitt, E., "Globalization: Key to Corporate Competition," *Computerworld,* (Aug. 20, 1990): 46–48.

14. Roche, E. M., Power, B. L., Ferreira, J. F., and Crescenzi, A., "The Multinational CIO," unpublished paper, School of Business, Seton Hall University, New Jersey, 1991.

15. Keen, *Shaping the Future.*

16. Ibid.

17. Roche et al., "The Multinational CIO."

18. Porter, M. E., "The Competitive Advantage of Nations."

19. Roche et al., "The Multinational CIO."

20. Ambrosio, J., "Opening Systems to Span the Globe," *Computerworld,* (June 24, 1991): 75–77.

21. Ives and Jarvenpaa, "Applications of Global Information Technology."

22. Porter, M. E., "Competition in Global Industries: A Conceptual Framework."

23. Lubove, S., "Vindicated," *Forbes* (Dec. 9, 1991): 198–202.

24. Browne, "Prospective Freight Mega-Carriers."

25. Keen, *Shaping the Future.*

26. Carey, S., "Airline Systems For Reservations Near an Alliance," *Wall Street Journal,* Nov. 15, 1990.

27. Roche et al., "The Multinational CIO."

28. Wierzbicki, B., "Stretching the Law," *Computerworld,* (Oct. 1, 1990): 93.

29. Fiderio, J., "Information Must Conform in a World Without Borders," *Computerworld,* (Oct. 1, 1990): 91–95.

30. Kramer, S., "National Flavors in the Global Stew," *Computerworld,* (Oct. 1, 1990): 93.

31. Millican, A., "Soviet PC Users Stage Own Coup," *Los Angeles Times,* Sept. 6, 1991, B3–B4.

CHAPTER

8

Sustainability of Information Technology–Based Competitive Advantage

I would rather be first in a small village in
Gaul than second in command in Rome.

—*Julius Caesar*

INTRODUCTION

The percentage of top executives of U.S. companies who feel information systems (ISs) hold the key to competitive advantage for their companies during the 1990s has dropped in recent years. According to *Computerworld/Anderson Consulting* surveys conducted in 1989 and 1991, the percentage decreased from 86 to 75%.[1] Many companies have found that heavy investment in information technology (IT) does not always result in increased market share. Information technology includes computer hardware and software, communications, and office technology. Although IT is a critical and growing part of many companies, few systems can provide a sustainable competitive edge. Most systems can be imitated or improved by competitors, and any initial strategic advantage may be competed away. It seems that pioneering don't pay, as Andrew Carnegie once observed.

If competitive advantage with IT is so elusive, why should a firm devote resources to evaluating and implementing strategic information systems? First, interest in SIS remains strong. Of the companies interviewed for *Computerworld's* 1991 *Premium 100* survey, 74% indicated they were very likely to install information systems to provide a competitive advantage during the following year.[2] Being able to more clearly identify systems that provide or support competitive advantage is of value to management. Second, even if a potential IT application does not provide long-term, or sustainable, competitive advantage, a company may be forced to implement it to remain competitive (as Machiavelli said, "In a world of lone wolves, it is much safer to be feared than to be loved"). Such applications are known as *strategic necessities*. Being able to forecast that a potential application is likely to be a strategic necessity will help managers avoid possible costs and risks associated with being the first to introduce the application.

This chapter examines the nature of competitive advantage with IT. It will be shown that IT can support a sustainable competitive advantage under certain circumstances and neutralize a competitive disadvantage in other situations. The elusive problem of measuring competitive advantage will be discussed, as will the various methods of maintaining a competitive edge. Strategic necessities will be described in more detail, and current thinking on the general subject of sustainable competitive advantage with information technology will be summarized.

HOW TO RECOGNIZE COMPETITIVE ADVANTAGE

A number of questions arise about the issue of sustainability of competitive advantage. Some of them relate to definitions of terms. Defining and measuring competitive advantage and sustainability have proven difficult in practice.

From the economist's point of view, *competitive advantage* is a straightforward concept. Michael Porter of the Harvard Business School has defined a competitive advantage as an activity that yields a sustained, better than normal return on investment.[3] Evaluating an activity with this criterion can be difficult. Is a normal return associated with the company's industry? Or is it to be compared with the average return of the company's other competitive activities? How long must the advantage be sustained to qualify as competitive? From the economic perspective, the advantage must be sustained until the investment required to support the activity has been recovered and enough additional profits are captured to provide a better than normal return. But how are profits measured for this purpose? Are profits using the company's and its industry's accounting principles and procedures reasonably representative of the return on investment for the activity? Do the company's accounts reflect the appropriate value for the investment?

Academics have suggested a number of alternative measures of competitive advantage in an effort to address these problems. Improvement in competitive position has been measured by increase in market share, although an increase in market share has not always been accompanied by an increase in profits.[4] Decrease in costs has also been used. This is not always an appropriate measure because an activity that decreases a company's costs may not improve its competitive position relative to other firms in its industry, unless the company is pursuing an overall cost leadership strategy. Increase in sales has been used to measure competitive advantage, but with the same limitations as increase in market share. Increase in the number of customers also has been suggested. The obvious limitation related to this method is possible concurrent changes in profit per customer. Return on assets and return on sales can have the same accounting limitations as return on investment. Finally, increase in a firm's common stock price can be used as a measure of competitive advantage. Because stock prices usually reflect a number of factors in addition to the issuer's competitive situation, this approach does not yield a consistent indicator.

Considering the variety of imperfect measures described above, it becomes apparent that a contingency approach to the measurement of competitive advantage is necessary. This approach measures the extent to which a strategic information system impacts areas critical to the survival and growth of a company. These critical areas vary with companies and industries, and they can be determined with a variety of techniques, including, for example, critical success factors and IBM's Business Systems Planning.[5] Both of these techniques were originally developed to determine the information needs for an organization and its management.

Critical success factors (CSFs) are the few things that must be done right for a company to achieve successful competitive performance. They are determined by interviews with key executives in an organization. The executives are asked to explain the company's strategic goals in terms of the critical factors required to attain them. This is followed by additional interviews designed to better define both the goals and factors and to develop measures of success in achieving the goals.

Business systems planning (BSP) is a top-down analysis of an organization that starts with interviews of top management to determine, among other things, the company's objectives and environment. Critical success factors are included as part of this analysis. Additional information on the company's business processes is gathered. Business processes are the activities through which a firm designs, produces, markets, delivers, and supports its products or services. This information is used to further define the relationship among the company's objectives, environment, and critical success factors.

Even if the issue of how to measure competitive advantage can be resolved, additional questions arise concerning the sources of competitive advantage, particularly in the area of custom-oriented SISs. If improved customer service is considered to be a competitive advantage and the improvement is due to the implementation of a strategic information system, how much of the increased, better than normal return on investment should be attributed to the SIS? How much should be attributed to other company resources and capabilities used to create the competitive advantage? Information systems researchers have not been able to separate the respective contributions of strategic information systems and other strategic factors in most observed instances of competitive advantage. Current thinking on this issue focuses on the nonquantitative impact of a proposed strategic information system on competitive position when allocating resources to information technology (IT) programs.[6] Clear guidelines for assessing the contribution of strategic information systems to competitive advantage have not been developed, and the results of blind investment in such systems are beginning to surface. As mentioned in the introduction, the percentage of top executives of U.S. companies who feel information systems hold the key to competitive advantage for their companies during the 1990s has dropped in recent years. Many companies have found that heavy investment in information technology does not always result in increased market share or other indications of competitive advantage.[7]

SOME EXAMPLES OF IT-BASED COMPETITIVE ADVANTAGE

Consider some of the better-documented (perhaps over-documented) strategic information system examples. American Hospital Supply Corporation's ASAP system for order entry and inventory control, described in chapter one, was considered to be a major contributing factor for a dramatic increase in market share, sales, and earnings in the late 1970s and early 1980s.[8] Although there is no published information on the return on investment directly attributed to ASAP, a review of available reports indicates that both the company and outsiders felt the system provided a clear competitive advantage.

Similarly, American Airlines' SABRE reservation system is regarded as a competitive advantage because it has always led the computer reservation system industry in market share. The impressive magnitude of the return on investment for SABRE can be indirectly estimated by the system's $1.5 billion valuation in 1988 versus a cumulative investment of $350 million reported in 1991.[9] SABRE also has provided profit margins in excess of those associated with American Airlines' asset-laden airline business.[10]

When measured by increase in market share, Merrill Lynch's Cash Management Account (CMA) is an example of a strategy supported by information technology that is a competitive advantage. The CMA account created the central asset account market, and Merrill Lynch dominated the money fund management business from the CMA account's introduction through at least 1987.[11] However, the company's return on equity consistently remained below the industry average in the same period, except for 1982. Perhaps the ROI for the CMA account exceeded the industry average for similar services; this information is not available. Clearly, the CMA account was not a competitive advantage for the entire company using the ROI criterion.

McKesson Drug Company's ECONOMOST order entry and customer support system is an example of a strategic information system that improved a company's financial results but did not qualify as a competitive advantage using traditional criteria. While sales increased and costs decreased at McKesson as a result of the introduction of ECONO-MOST, the company did not achieve sustainable, higher profitability. In fact, none of the companies in the wholesale drug distribution industry realized higher-than-average profits. What did happen was that the industry consolidated, becoming more efficient in the process. Direct distribution by drug manufacturers also decreased. Many of the benefits realized from the restructuring were passed on to customers through lower prices, although the larger companies in the industry improved their financial situation by modernizing their facilities and boosting productivity. Eric Clemons and Michael Row, of the Wharton School, University of Pennsylvania, believe that a large portion of the improvement in productivity and profitability was due to information technology.[12]

They also feel that systems like ECONOMOST are strategic necessities in the wholesale drug distribution industry. Such systems are necessary to compete in the industry, but they are not competitive for any firm. What should have happened if McKesson had not introduced ECONOMOST? It's possible that another distributor could have implemented a similar system, putting McKesson at a competitive disadvantage. Additional discussion on strategic necessities follows later in this chapter.

Eric Clemons and Bruce Weber of the Wharton School have documented another possible competitive advantage using information technology. Barclays de Zoete Wedd (BZW) is a British securities dealer that implemented an automatic order execution system known as TRADE in June 1988. Customers, who include small brokers and money managers, use software and network connections provided by BZW to evaluate market prices and execute orders with BZW. TRADE was implemented to increase BZW's share of the small-order market and to lower the company's dealing costs. The jury was still out in 1991 on whether TRADE will result in a sustainable competitive advantage, and economic analysis by BZW of the proposed investment in the system indicated that TRADE should accomplish its objectives and enhance BZW's total business relationship with its customers as well. Results through May 1989 supported this forecast.[13]

SUSTAINING A COMPETITIVE ADVANTAGE

Charles Wiseman of Columbia University makes an argument for pursuing a *contestable advantage* when circumstances dictate.[14] He cautions against subscribing solely to the economist's view of competitive advantage, which requires sustainability. A competitive advantage is regarded as sustainable when it can be maintained, regardless of competitors' behavior or industry evolution. Anything less is considered to be a contestable advantage; even though it may be vulnerable to later imitation or improvement by competitors, it is worth investing in.

One proposal to measure sustainability places contestable and sustainable competitive advantages as points on the same scale.[15] Sustainability is then described as a function of the durability of a gap in capabilities that separates a company from its competitors. The capabilities are reflected in some product or delivery attribute that is a key buying criterion in the market. A key buying criterion compels the customer to purchase from a specific company instead of other providers. Sustainability can be defined as the ratio of the cost (to a competitor) of closing the gap to the value of the advantage (to the company) created by the gap. Higher ratios indicate more sustainability and less contestability:

$$\text{Sustainability} = \frac{\text{cost to close gap}}{\text{value of gap}}$$

The smaller the ratio, the higher the temptation for rivals to imitate. The higher the ratio, the more sustainable and incontestable the competitive advantage. This mathematical model can help managers compare the sustainability of possible competitive advantages.

It may be that most competitive systems are contestable. A recent survey indicates that many strategic information systems provide competitive advantage for only 12 to 18 months.[16] However, a review of the strategic management literature reveals that the majority of scholars of business policy subscribe to the view of sustainable competitive advantages rather than to the contestable variety.

Because sustainability is desirable even if it is not always attainable, how is it achieved?

Barriers to Imitation

For certain classes of innovations, barriers to imitation can provide a sustainable competitive advantage. Copyrights, patents, and trade secrets provide differing levels of protection from imitation, and in some cases, government regulations can provide comparable protection. For innovations based on information technology, these traditional means of blocking imitation generally have not proven effective. The technology is readily available, and its applications can not only be duplicated but improved on by competitors. Legal protection usually is not available or effective. As an example, Merrill Lynch patented its CMA account, but this has not proven to be an effective barrier to imitation by other financial institutions.[17] Even so, companies are trying to enforce what they feel are their rights to intellectual property; witness the ongoing legal maneuvers in 1991 related to spreadsheet and database management systems for personal computers. As another example, Innovis Interactive Technologies, a unit of Weyerhauser Co., filed a suit in 1990 charging that Osmose Wood Preserving Co. violated its copyright on backyard deck design software.[18]

Preemptive Strikes

When descriptions of strategic information systems first began to appear in both the business press and academic journals, much was said about the use of information technology to keep customers happy captives,[19] the competitive power of information,[20] and the use of IT as a competitive weapon against competitors.[21] Although some of the claims were overblown and many of the prescriptions misdirected, the competitive advantage of the *preemptive strike,* or being the first to implement a strategic information system, has been demonstrated by at least four of the classical examples of successful SISs. American Airlines' and United Airlines' computer reservation systems, American Hospital Supply's ASAP system, and Otis Elevator's OTISLINE maintenance system were the first applications introduced in their markets, and they continue to dominate their industries into the early 1990s. The preemptive strike offers benefits often known as *first-mover effects.* These are the competitive advantages and disadvantages available to innovators in a market.

Both economists and business strategists have studied the benefits and drawbacks of being a pioneer, the first company to introduce an innovation in a market. Table 8.1 details some of the advantages and disadvantages of being a pioneering application adopter. Note that many of the entries are directly applicable to an IT application. Other entries are appropriate when considering competitive advantages supported in some way by a strategic information system. As will be discussed later, IT can be used to leverage other strategic resources and capabilities at a company's disposal (it is tempting to state here the Technology Rule: He who has the technology rules).

Consider the following examples of disadvantages encountered by companies that followed competitive systems innovators. Of course, these disadvantages also can be regarded as advantages for the innovators.

Citibank was the leading U.S. bank in the field of international corporate banking in the early 1990s. The institution made pioneering investments in a global electronic delivery base in the 1970s while other banks continued to implement separate systems for different lines of business. Followers have been saddled with lesser market positions and the additional burden of catch-up expense.

The Publix supermarket chain in Florida was able to capture a growing segment of the financial market by preempting the state's major banks in electronic funds transfer at

TABLE 8.1 Pioneering application adopter advantages and disadvantages

Advantages

More or most market share

Highest product prices

Key customer retention by staying current with product market, technology, and the like

Customer loyalty associated with first product on market

Retention of customers owing to buyer switching costs

Preemption of product input factors (labor, suppliers, distributors, etc.)

Preemption of location (including shelf space)

Preemption of investment in plant and equipment

Control of strategic information (preventing imitation)

Competitor response lags (leaving a clear field)

Learning or experience curve benefits

Enhanced reputation (being known as a leader)

Network externalities (product value increases as more customers adopt it)

Buyer evaluation costs (new buyers of product avoid evaluation of competing products and purchase the market leader)

Advertising and marketing channel crowding for followers' products

Disadvantages

High development risk (unknown product demand)

Higher development costs than competitors'

Free-rider effects by followers (taking advantage of the pioneer's investments in R&D, buyer education, infrastructure development, employee training, etc.)

Resolution of technological or market uncertainty for followers (emergence of the dominant design)

Vulnerability to later shifts in technology (which may occur while the current market leader's older technology is still growing, causing difficulty in perceiving and addressing the threat)

Incumbent inertia (the pioneer's susceptibility to being locked in to specific fixed assets, reluctance to cannibalize existing product lines, and organizational inflexibility)

the point of sale. The chain's cash registers act as point-of-sale banking machines, eliminating any need for the banks' ATMs in the supermarkets.

Thompson Holidays, a United Kingdom firm, was the first to introduce a videotex-based system to link customers and travel agencies. The system has become the de facto standard in Europe, although other system operators were actively pursuing Thompson.[22]

Banc One of Ohio was able to preempt a major market niche by offering information processing services to other financial institutions. Merrill Lynch used Banc One's Visa processing capabilities to support Cash Management Account for a number of years before establishing a bank in New Jersey in 1984. In 1985 Banc One's services to Merrill Lynch were reduced to check processing, a commodity in the financial industry.[23]

Rosenbluth Travel in Philadelphia experienced phenomenal growth in sales and earnings in the 1980s. Sales increased from $40 million to over $1 billion, and earnings were the sole source of funding for the company's expansion.[24] Rosenbluth pursued a strategy of differentiation through value-added service by the innovative use of information systems to provide lowest-cost travel costs and expense reporting for its corporate travel customers. Larger competitors, including computer reservation system operators, were beginning to catch up, but Rosenbluth still maintained its competitive edge up to 1993.

Continual Improvement

As strategic information systems have become more common and documentation of their performance over time has become available, empirical evidence has confirmed the need to continually improve them to sustain competitive advantage. As part of an effort to maintain the company's lead over imitators, American Airlines has added new travel-related services to SABRE's database to broaden the system's product line and software to support travel agents' business operations.[25] American Hospital Supply Corporation continued to customize the ASAP system to the specifications and requirements of different hospitals to effectively outdistance imitators.[26] McKesson's ECONOMOST system has not been improved at a sufficient rate to preempt imitators, and it has not resulted in a competitive advantage.[27] As for Merrill Lynch, the information systems associated with the CMA account were never the major source of competitive advantage. Instead, the competitive advantage of the CMA account is based on Merrill Lynch's quality of service, the broad variety of products and services the company offers, and customer switching costs that would be necessary to move an account to another institution.[28] IT has played an important but supporting role in the realization of this competitive advantage. Product improvements for this application have consisted of offering new products through the CMA account and offering specialized versions to various segments of the market.

Otis Elevator's OTISLINE maintenance system, another classical strategic information system that has provided competitive advantage, continues to be improved. Otis is implementing hand-held radio data terminals for use by field technicians, while Schindler Elevator, an archrival, is introducing a new remote elevator monitoring system based on the Integrated Service Digital Network (ISDN) standard.[29]

Continuing research on the relationship between IT and competitive advantage appears to support the theory that strategic information systems are rarely capable of being a competitive advantage in themselves for a company. They are much more likely to contribute to competitive advantage by leveraging other resources and capabilities of a firm.

LEVERAGING RESOURCES AND CAPABILITIES

A new model for strategic analysis appears to be emerging. It has its roots in past economic theories of profit and competition, including those of David Ricardo, Joseph Schumpeter, and Edith Penrose.[30] There has been a resurgence of interest in the role of a company's resources and skills in strategy formulation. According to the so-called *resource-based view of the firm theory,* the objective of strategy formulation is allocation of a firm's resources and capabilities to activities. Resources are considered to be long-lived productive capabilities, including intangible assets and people-based skills. A capability is the capacity for a set of resources to accomplish an activity, and capabilities are what a company can do as a result of teams of resources working together. Resources can be considered the source of a company's capabilities, and its capabilities are the main source of its competitive advantage.[31] As an example, a company's IS employees, hardware, and software can be considered some of the resources used in implementing and developing a strategic information system. Effective delivery, support, and improvement of the strategic information system in coordination with other functions or departments in the firm can be considered a capability of the company.

With this theoretical approach as a basis for analysis, a strategic information system can be evaluated for its ability to support and strengthen the use of a company's resources and capabilities to gain and maintain a competitive advantage. A couple of other concepts are necessary to fully explore this approach.

First, *complementary assets* are assets necessary for an innovator to exploit an innovation.[32] They are necessary for efficient commercialization of an innovation and have higher economic value when used with the innovation than for other purposes. As an example, programmers and analysts who specialize in industry-specific systems like computer reservation systems can be considered as complementary assets to these systems.

The degree of competitive advantage provided by an innovation depends on the accessibility or cost of complementary assets for the innovator, relative to other companies in the industry. If property rights are weakly enforceable, competitors will duplicate an innovation, and any economic benefits from the innovation will be shared among customers and firms that control the necessary complementary assets. The innovation then becomes a strategic necessity.

In mature industries a large proportion of the complementary assets necessary for competitive innovations can be under the control of a few firms. Limited access to the necessary assets is an industry entry barrier, and coalitions of potential new entrants are likely to be created to circumvent this barrier and acquire a strategic necessity. An example is a regional ATM network established by several banks in Philadelphia to counter the competitive threat of a dominant bank's internal ATM network.[33] The system was implemented to assure a cost-effective means of providing ATM service (and preserving market share) by smaller banks when a major competitor launched a proprietary network. As more banks joined the cooperative service, costs dropped and the network became more attractive to current and potential customers. Economists refer to this situation as *network externalities.* Competing ATM services were wiped out, and their networks were absorbed by the cooperative system. The system later became the only ATM service in the region. This is an example of a cooperative system developed to gain access to a strategic necessity that also proved to be a competitive advantage for its members.

Second, *asymmetrical differences* in competitors' resources have been proposed as an explanation for competitive advantage and first-mover effects in both the strategic management and economics literature.[34] Proponents of this concept believe that a company can only gain greater than average returns on its strategic activities when the costs of resources required to implement and support these activities are less than the economic value of the resources. Companies create or exploit asymmetrical differences in resource values to achieve a competitive advantage. The differences can be attributed to a variety of causes, including *technological discontinuity,* changes in the regulatory environment, luck associated with underestimating the true future value of a strategy, constraints on growth, and timing of market entry. The principal thesis of this theory is that it is more possible to compete effectively by exploiting resources under an organization's control than by analyses of the organization's competitive environment.

These concepts can be illustrated using some common examples. American Airlines was one of a few carriers that had sufficient information processing power in place to handle the additional telecommunications volume associated with the placement of terminals in travel agencies in the 1970s.[35] As more and more agencies were automated, the minimum investment required to compete in the computer reservation business increased, erecting an industry barrier for smaller airlines. The same carriers that possessed sufficient processing power also had built up a technological and marketing experience base that was not easily duplicated by potential competitors new to the business. In this situation, the strategic resources that American (and United) Airlines preempted were the technological and marketing experience bases, not the technology itself. Deregulation proved to be a major external event (discontinuity) that precipitated the complex, information-intensive environment of the airline industry. Skillful use of IT combined with ongoing incremental improvements provided and supported American's competitive edge.

Merrill Lynch's complementary assets for the CMA account were the firm's retail presence and money market fund management expertise. The CMA product leveraged these assets by creating a new, large market that was not possible without their support. Deregulation of the banking industry was the discontinuity that provided the opportunity for the competitive advantage associated with the CMA account.[36]

For BZW's TRADE system, the principal complementary asset is BZW's coverage of the broadest range of securities on the London market. Without such coverage, it is unlikely that TRADE could be a competitive advantage, because the technology is not unique and there are other successful automated order execution systems in operation.[37]

When American Hospital Supply Corporation (AHSC) rolled out ASAP, its resource of relatively large market share in comparison to fragmented, regional competition enabled the company to gain significant first-mover effects quickly, outdistancing its direct rivals. Larger hospital supply companies did not respond to AHSC's activities until the company merged with Baxter Travenol Laboratories and became a distinct competitive threat. At that time, Johnson & Johnson, AHSC's principal large competitor, encountered another strategic resource of AHSC. AHSC had a centralized order entry system that served it well in the industry's competitive arena. Johnson & Johnson had to struggle to develop a similar concept because its divisions were highly decentralized.[38]

The lack of competitive advantage from McKesson's ECONOMOST system is likely due to the company's inability to preempt the necessary complementary assets. Other large drug distributors were able to provide equivalent services soon after the introduction of ECONOMOST. Technology and organization did not prove to be unique for McKesson. Customers have stated that McKesson's only unique asset in comparison with its major competitors was the higher-quality relationship that it maintained with them.[39] As previously discussed, ECONOMOST may have brought about concentration in the wholesale drug distribution industry and reduced the drug manufacturers' level of direct distribution. The resulting parity among the remaining companies created a strategic necessity for the industry.

STRATEGIC NECESSITIES

Although strategic necessities have been discussed earlier in this chapter, it is useful to summarize the concept and consider some additional aspects. *Strategic necessities* are difficult-to-obtain capabilities required by a company to compete effectively (or at all). Even though strategic necessities do not provide competitive advantage, they threaten the competitive position of a company and alter its industry's structure. Industry structure is characterized by the number and distribution of buyers and sellers, product differentiation, entry barriers, vertical integration, diversification, and cost structures, or the shapes of cost curves associated with scale and scope economies.[40] Therefore, these activities can be considered as strategic as competitive advantages. Other necessities that are mere requisites of being in business like telephones and copy machines have been defined as *routine necessities.*[41]

Strategic necessities are a form of strategic information system risk. In some situations, extensive hardware and software is required by all industry participants to support strategic IT applications. These systems can result in an extension of the current competitive situation at an increased level of cost.[42] As an example, a 1990 study found two applications that failed to deliver any competitive advantage in a survey of customer-oriented strategic information systems. The systems were continuing to be offered to customers to avoid a potential competitive disadvantage.[43]

A survey of the Australian banking industry in the 1980s did not find a single sustainable competitive advantage attributable to strategic information systems. The bank's customers received valuable improvements in the areas of product quality and delivery as a result of the implementation of various systems intended to provide competitive advantage, but the basis of industry competition remained unchanged.[44]

Another risk associated with the implementation of a strategic necessity should be considered. If an IT innovation is imitated and the innovator is unable or unwilling to maintain its lead over later entrants, imitators can offer comparable or better products or services at lower costs, resulting in a weakened position for the original innovator. A case in point is a manufacturer of commercial appliances that developed a system for translating a building contractor's specifications into recommended products and installation instructions. The system was installed on a mainframe, and an early-model computer could be used for data entry and preprocessing. The company then harvested the results of its increase in market share without further system development. A larger and more technically capable competitor followed with a more sophisticated system used to recapture and augment the competitor's former market share. The concept's innovator lost its competitive advantage and more.[45]

Electronic data interchange (EDI) systems appear to be an application of information technology that rarely provides competitive advantage. Evaluation of three case studies covering eight EDI systems conducted as part of MIT's management in the 1990s research program revealed that at least six of the eight systems were motivated by competitive necessity. Only one of the systems seemed to be capable of providing a significant competitive advantage through first-mover effects. The researchers concluded that suppliers who were partners in an EDI type of interorganizational system (IOS) must maintain a program of continual incremental improvement to differentiate themselves from competitors.[46]

While IOSs seem to offer limited competitive advantage among their members, they can be more than strategic necessities to the supporting organization as a whole. The cooperative ATM network described in the previous section on leveraging resources and capabilities proved to be the kiss of death for its competitors.[47]

Some IS scholars and industry leaders claim that all strategic information systems will ultimately become strategic necessities.[48] Max Hopper, champion of SABRE at American Airlines, stated that "In this new era, information technology will be at once more pervasive and less potent—table stakes for competition, but no trump card for competitive success. As astute managers maneuver against rivals, they will focus less on being the first to build proprietary electronic tools than on being the best at using and improving generally available tools to enhance what their organizations already do well.[49] He feels that managers will shift their attention from developing systems to using information in research on competitive advantage. Exceptional returns will be earned by those who excel in turning data into information that can be quickly analyzed to generate superior knowledge.

This is a familiar theme in the IS literature.[50] Several letters to the editor of the Harvard Business Review following publication of Hopper's views in 1990 pointed out that American Airlines continued to maintain its strong competitive position with SABRE, and the company already was working on another competitive advantage based on IT.[51] One of the letters was from Peter Keen, the prominent IS scholar and observer, who maintained that the management process in a company provided the competitive edge despite the ready availability of information technology to all participants in a market.

Keen labels the theory that all strategic IT applications degenerate into competitive necessities as "infopessimism" and argues that IT-based competitive advantages are sustainable by (1) preempting the market with a good product, (2) focusing on developing an effective IT platform, not just individual applications, and (3) being fortunate enough to have competitors whose management does not support similar IT infrastructure.[52]

From a marketing perspective, it may be that companies that try to lock in customers with single-source electronic sales channels are being left behind by an evolution toward unbiased electronic markets that offer the products and services of many suppliers. American Airlines' reservation systems list flights from other airlines, and the ASAP system carries products from several of Baxter Healthcare's competitors. Inventory Locator Service lists suppliers of aircraft parts in a database accessible to subscribers. The company sells information, not parts. Several retail shopping services have been established, including Prodigy and Comp-U-Card. Insurance Value-Added Network Services (IVANS) was established to support independent insurance agents by linking them with insurance carriers and other information sources.[53] The implications are clear: tomorrow's strategic information systems may be unbiased strategic necessities.

SUMMARY

In spite of the growing importance of information technology as a competitive factor, many companies have not achieved sustained competitive advantage from strategic information systems. The question of how to determine the difference between IT-based competitive advantages and strategic necessities before investing in a potential application goes to the heart of the problem. Even developing a usable measure of competitive advantage for SISs has proven to be difficult.

It is clear, however, that IT can support a sustainable competitive advantage under certain circumstances and neutralize a competitive disadvantage in other situations. The dimension of sustainability determines the strength and durability of a competitive edge. Sustainability in turn can depend on a number of factors.

Barriers to imitation by competitors is a classical method for achieving sustainability, but it has proven unsuccessful for protecting SISs. Being first to market with a product or service or executing a preemptive strike has been successful for a number of SISs. The key to their success has been a program of continual improvement after introduction to maintain the lead over competitors (if you are the lead dog, the view always changes).

An SIS may provide or leverage a competitive advantage that utilizes a company's strength in strategic resources and capabilities relative to its competitors. A number of IT-based competitive advantages and strategic necessities can be explained using this theoretical framework, and it may prove to be an extremely useful strategic planning tool.

Although competitive advantage through IT is possible, current evidence indicates that strategic necessity is the more likely outcome of SIS implementation. Strategic necessities are another form of SIS risk, because the companies that introduce them generally spend more and get less than the imitators that follow (contrary to Samuel Johnson's statement that "no man ever yet became great by imitation"). As a result, cooperative systems shared by competitors may be the predominant form of strategic information systems in the future.

REFERENCES

1. Maglitta, J., "It's Reality Time," *Computerworld* (Apr. 29, 1991): 81–83.
2. Maglitta, J., and Sullivan-Trainor, M. L., "Do the Right Thing(s)," *Computerworld Premium 100*, section 2 of 2 (Sept. 30, 1991): 6–12.
3. Porter, M. E., *Competitive Strategy: Techniques for Analyzing Industries.* New York: Free Press, 1980.

4. Woo, C. Y., "Evaluation of the Strategies and Performance of Low ROI Market Share Leaders," *Strategic Management Journal* 4, no. 2 (Apr.-June 1990): 123–35.

5. Rockart, J. F., "Chief Executives Define Their Own Needs," *Harvard Business Review* 57, no. 2 (Mar.-Apr. 1979): 81–93; IBM Corporation, *Business Systems Planning: Information Systems Planning Guide,* IBM Manual No. GE20–0527, 1981.

6. Clemons, E. K., and Weber, B. W., "Strategic Information Technology Investments: Guidelines for Decision Making," *Journal of Management Information System* 7, no. 2 (Fall 1990): 9–28.

7. Maglitta, "It's Really Time."

8. "American Hospital Supply Corporation: (A) The ASAP System," *Harvard Business School Case,* no. 9-186-005, 1986; "American Hospital Supply Corporation: (B) ASAP System," *Harvard Business School Case,* no. 9-186-006, 1988; "Baxter Healthcare Corporation: ASAP Express," *Harvard Business School Case,* no. 9-188-080, 1989.

9. Clemons and Weber, "Strategic Information Technology Investments"; C. Wilder, "Crandall Attacks Curbs on Reservation Systems," *Computerworld* (Oct. 14, 1991): 4.

10. Wiseman, C., *Strategic Information Systems.* Homewood, Ill.: Irwin, 1988.

11. Clemons, E. K., and Row, M. C., "The Merrill Lynch Cash Management Account Financial Service: A Case Study in Strategic Information Systems," *Proceedings of the Twenty-First Annual Hawaii International Conference on System Sciences,* vol. 4. Los Alamitos, Calif.: IEEEE Computer Society Press, Jan. 1988, 131–40; Wiseman, *Strategic Information Systems.*

12. Clemons, E. K., and Row, M., "McKesson Drug Company: A Case Study of ECONOMOST—A Strategic Information System," *Journal of Management Information Systems* 5, no. 1 (Summer 1988): 36–50.

13. Clemons, E. K., and Weber, B. W., "Barclays de Zoete Wedd's TRADE System," *Proceedings of the Twenty-Third Annual Hawaii International Conference on System Sciences,* vol. 4. Los Alamitos, Calif.: IEEEE Computer Society Press, Jan. 1990, 137–46.

14. Wiseman, *Strategic Information Systems.*

15. Coyne, K. P., "Sustainable Competitive Advantage—What It Is, What It Isn't," *Business Horizons* 29, no. 1 (Jan./Feb. 1986): 54–61.

16. Sullivan-Trainor, M. L., and Maglitta, J., "Competitive Advantage Fleeting," *Computerworld* (Oct. 8, 1990): 1.

17. Clemons and Row, January 1988, "Merrill Lynch Cash Management Account."

18. Margolis, N., "Look-and-Feel Suits: Not Just for Spread-sheets," *Computerworld* (Aug. 8, 1990): 85.

19. Petre, P., "How to Keep Customers Happy Captives," *Fortune,* Sept. 2, 1985, 42–46.

20. Harris, C. L., "Information Power: How Companies Are Using New Technologies to Gain a Competitive Edge," *Business Week,* Oct. 14, 1985, 108–114.

21. Synnott, W. R., *The Information Weapon: Winning Customers and Markets with Technology.* New York: Wiley, 1987.

22. Keen, P. G. W., *Competing in Time: Using Telecommunications for Competitive Advantage.* Cambridge, Mass.: Ballinger, 1988.

23. Clemons and Row, January 1988, "Merrill Lynch Cash Management Account."

24. Clemons, E. K., and Row, M. C., "Ahead of the Pack Through Vision and Hustle: A Case Study of Information Technology at Rosenbluth Travel," *Proceedings of the Twenty-Fourth Annual Hawaii International Conference on System Sciences,* vol. 4. Los Alamitos, Calif.: IEEEE Computer Society Press, January 1991, 287–96.

25. Hopper, M. D., "Rattling SABRE—New Ways to Compete on Information," *Harvard Business Review* 68, no. 3 (May-June 1990): 118–25.

26. Venkatraman, N., and Short, J. E., "Strategies for Electronic Integration: From Order-Entry to Value-Added Partnerships at Baxter," Working Paper No. 210. Center for Information Systems Research, Sloan School of Management, M.I.T., June 1990.

27. Clemons and Row, Summer 1988, "McKesson Drug Company."

28. Clemons, E. K., "Corporate Strategies for Information Technology: A Resource-Based Approach," Decision Sciences Working Paper No. 89-09-15, Wharton School, University of Pennsylvania, Aug. 1990.

29. Horwitt, E., "Would Muzak Improve over ISDN?," *Computerworld* (May 21, 1990):1.

30. Ricardo, D., *Principles of Political Economy and Taxation.* London: G. Bell, 1981; Schumpeter, J.A., *The Theory of Economic Development.* Cambridge, Mass.: Harvard University Press, 1934; Penrose, E., *The Theory of the Growth of the Firm.* New York: Wiley, 1959.

31. Grant, R. M., "The Resource-Based Theory of Competitive Advantage: Implications for Strategy Formulation," *California Management Review* 33, no. 3 (Spring 1991): 114–35.

32. Teece, D. J., "Firm Boundaries, Technological Innovation, and Strategic Management," in L. G. Thomas, ed., *The Economics of Strategic Planning: Essays in Honor of Joel Dean.* Lexington, Mass.: Lexington Books, 1986, 187–99; Teece, D. J., "Profiting from Technological Innovation: Implications for Integration, Collaboration, Licensing, and Public Policy," in D. J. Teece, ed., *The Competitive Challenge: Strategies for Industrial Innovation and Renewal.* Cambridge, Mass.: Ballinger, 1987, 185–219.

33. Clemons, E. K., "MAC—Philadelphia National Bank's Strategic Venture in Shared ATM Networks," *Proceedings of the Twenty-Second Annual Hawaii International Conference on System Sciences,* vol. 4. Los Alamitos, Calif.: IEEE Computer Society Press, Jan. 1989, 214–22.

34. Barney, J. B., "Strategic Factor Markets: Expectations, Luck and Business Strategy," *Management Science* 32, no. 10 (Oct. 1986): 1231–41; Coyne, K. P., "Sustainable Competitive Advantage"; Lieberman, M.B., and Montgomery, D. B., "First-Mover Advantages," *Strategic Management Journal* 9, Special Issue (June 1988): 41–58; Schoemaker, P. J. H., "Strategy, Complexity, and Economic Rent," *Management Science* 36, no. 10 (Oct. 1990): 1178–92; Spence, A. M., "Investment Strategy and Growth in a New Market," *Bell Journal of Economics* 10 (Spring 1979): 1–19.

35. Copeland, D. G., and McKenney, J. L., "Airline Reservations Systems: Lessons from History," *MIS Quarterly* 12, no. 3 (Sept. 1988): 353–70.

36. Clemons, E. K., and Row, M. C., "Sustaining IT Advantages: The Role of Structural Differences," *MIS Quarterly* 15, no. 3 (Sept. 1991): 275–92.

37. Clemons, E. K., and Weber, B. W., January 1990, "Barclays de Zoete Wedd's TRADE System."

38. Venkatraman and Short, "Strategies for Electronic Integration."

39. Clemons and Row, Summer 1988, "McKesson Drug Company."

40. Scherer, F. M., and Ross, D., *Industrial Market Structure and Economic Performance.* Boston: Houghton Mifflin, 1990.

41. Clemons, E. K., and Kimbrough, S. O., "Information Systems and Business Strategy: A Review of Strategic Necessity," Decision Sciences Working Paper 87-01-04, Wharton School, University of Pennsylvania, 1987.

42. Vitale, M. R., "The Growing Risks of Information Systems Success," *MIS Quarterly* 10, no. 4 (Dec. 1986): 327–34.

43. Reich, B. H., and Benbasat, I., "An Empirical Investigation of Factors Influencing the Success of Customer-Oriented Strategic Systems," *Information Systems Research* 1, no. 3 (Sept. 1990): 325–47.

44. Sager, M. T., "Competitive Information Systems in Australian Retail Banking," *Information and Management* 15, no. 1 (Aug. 1988): 59–67.

45. Vitale, "The Growing Risks."

46. Benjamin, R. I., De Long, D. W., and Scott Morton, M. S., "Electronic Data Interchange: How Much Competitive Advantage," *Long Range Planning* 23, no. 1 (Feb. 1990): 29–40.

47. Clemons, E. K., "MAC."

48. Seaton, W. B., "Information Sharing Is Vital for Smooth Sailing," Interview by J. S. Bozman, *Computerworld* (Sept. 30, 1991): 59.

49. Hopper, M. D., "Rattling SABRE," 118.

50. King, W. R., Grover, V., and Hufnagel, E. H., "Using Information Technology for Sustainable Competitive Advantage: Some Empirical Evidence," in K. C. Laudon and J. A. Turner, eds., *Information Technology and Management Strategy.* Englewood Cliffs, N.J.: Prentice-Hall, 1989, 50–63.

51. "Letter to the Editor," *Harvard Business Review* 68, no. 4 (July-Aug. 1990): 176–82.

52. Keen, P. G. W., *Shaping the Future: Business Design Through Information Technology.* Boston: Harvard Business School Press, 1991.

53. Malone, T. W., Yates, J., and Benjamin, R. I., "The Logic of Electronic Markets," *Harvard Business Review* 67, no. 3 (May-June 1989): 166–70.

9

Strategic Information Systems Risks

Denial ain't just a river in Egypt . . .

—From a Dire Straits' song

INTRODUCTION

Previous chapters have described different aspects of using information technology (IT) by companies to impact their competitive position in their industries. Information systems that accomplish this objective were labeled *strategic information systems* (SISs). Developing, implementing, and then using an SIS entails risks that go far beyond the conventional risks associated with any large and complex information system.

New systems always generated new problems. SISs introduce a class of risks that depart from those usually associated with information systems. They could lead to spectacular successes or to huge failures (and failures are like rabbits—you turn some of them loose and soon there's a bunch of them).

There is a paucity of documented cases of failed SISs, and for a good reason. Nobody likes to brag about a failure; furthermore, history is written by the victors. Unfortunately, it's the painful lessons of failed systems we don't know about that we are bound to repeat. Conversely, even for many successful SISs, not much is known about the obstacles and temporary hardships they had to overcome (as Joe Namath said, "when you win, nothing hurts").

This chapter addresses the risks of developing and implementing SISs. Risk is generally viewed as the deviation of realized from expected results of the system. Risks are measured in terms of the scope of contemplated change to the existing systems and the amount of resources required to implement change. The risks associated with developing any information systems also apply to SISs. These risks (intrinsic to a project) that are under the control of the organization implementing the system are distinguished from extrinsic risks, which arise from circumstances external to the organization. These extrinsic risks pertain to potential threats that may be triggered by the implemented SIS and prevent or detract it from helping its organization to gain a competitive edge or sustain it.

155

Intrinsic risks relate to a failed implementation of an information system. These depend on the size and complexity of the system, the degree to which the organization's users have information requirements that are stable, and finally, the familiarity of the organization with the IT underlying the application. Any one of these factors increases risk. Risk levels are highest when all these factors are dominant.

Extrinsic risks are unique to strategic information systems. In non-SIS applications, the information system carries only the risk of failed implementation. Once properly operational, non-SIS applications carry virtually no extrinsic risk. Although there is still some issue of the system's adaptability to future changes, this is purely an intrinsic technical risk related to the maintainability of the system. However, even a properly designed and implemented SIS risks the adverse impact of some exogenous factors. For example, a competitor may copy or imitate the system with better results. Another example is that the SIS may expose the firm's data to a rival firm. (It can be claimed that when it comes to extrinsic risks, any risk can be the unrecognized bearer of success. Furthermore, no system is ever a complete failure; it can always be used as a bad example.)

Thus, in the context of SIS, risk assessment of information systems becomes even more important. This chapter addresses the issue of both intrinsic and extrinsic risks characteristic of SISs. It starts by discussing the problems encountered by the Bank of America in developing their Trust Accounting System. The trust accounting system was intended to enable the bank to capture a large share of the trust accounting market. The system was a major failure, resulting in both financial losses to the tune of $80 million and much more in terms of lost potential revenues from the lucrative trust management business. The case provides a valuable example for addressing both intrinsic and extrinsic risks in the development of SIS.

After describing the Bank of America case and analyzing the causes of failure in light of the two categories of risk, airline reservation systems are briefly reviewed to highlight the intricate way in which risks play a role in the future of companies. The following sections describe SIS risks in more detail: The categories of risks, ways to measure risks, and strategies to reduce the effect of the risks. Wherever possible, real-life examples illustrate the effect of the risk on actual SIS applications.

BANK OF AMERICA TRUST ACCOUNTING SYSTEM

The Bank of America Trust Accounting System is a good example of management's failure to recognize both risk categories. It eventually led to a $80 million project loss, and much more when the loss of the trust accounting business is taken into account.[1]

Background

In the early 1950s, Bank of America was the world's banking technology leader. However, by the late 1970s, the bank had fallen behind the technology curve. Despite the gap in technology, in 1980 Bank of America had reported 58 quarters of consecutive profits and was considered a model of bank operations. In 1980 the bank had annual profits of $643 million and was the largest bank in the world. In 1981, the bank planned on spending $4 billion to leapfrog into state-of-the-art technology in computers and communications.

Trust departments act as managers of investment for individuals, corporations, unions, and government agencies. They are characterized by a diverse customer base, from small accounts to very large accounts, ranging from managing several thousands of dollars to millions and even billions for each customer. Although Bank of America had the largest trust department on the West Coast, it was still miniscule compared with the large trust banks on the East Coast. Trust operations are by and large for corporate, union, and government pension funds. They help individual money managers to complete the trade, record performance of the investment portfolios, gather income from investments, and pay beneficiaries. The trust business base in the United States is huge, amounting to trillions of dollars; annual revenues from fees for managing the trust accounts amount to several billions. This motivated Bank of America to develop an online trust management system.

A batch version of the system was previously designed by SEI corporation. Premier Systems, a company formed by former SEI employees, was contracted by the bank to provide consultation on the new system. A consortium of banks was formed to share the costs of developing a state-of-the-art online trust accounting system called MasterNet. Premier was chosen as the contractor to develop the system. Although the bank was using IBM mainframes, Prime computers were chosen by Premier as the hardware platform to host the new trust accounting system. MasterNet was originally slated to cost $20 million. It was designed to meet trust data processing needs of small- to midsized banks and to solicit major institutional trust accounts to be online using MasterNet. The system intended to provide monthly statements and online updating and querying with fast response times. MasterNet was intended to be a strategic system that would allow Bank of America to overtake the trust industry leader, State Street Bank and Trust Company of Boston.

The system was not ready for use by the original target deadline of December 1984. Although it did not cause immediate alarm, the system was delayed by two more years, and it finally grabbed the attention of Bank of America's senior management. Although the system was not operational in 1986, the bank held a lavish party for important clients to announce and display MasterNet. The system was slated for a June 1986 release. MasterNet was finally released in April 1987. The large system encompassed over 3.5 million lines of code. Unfortunately it was beset with problems. Approximately $25 million was spent to fix the problems, followed by an additional $35 million. The total cost amounted to approximately $80 million. In 1988, Bank of America decided to scrap MasterNet and indicated to its customers that it would shift 95% of its individual trust accounts to its subsidiary Seafirst Corporation, and the big institutional accounts to its competitor State Street Bank and Trust Company of Boston.[2]

Lessons Learned

The Bank of America failure can be attributed to many causes, but the foremost was the fundamental lack of understanding of the risks involved in developing the trust account-ing system. Risk assessment is not a one-time a priori activity, done prior to the start of an information system project. As this example illustrates, it should have been undertaken on an ongoing basis. In the Bank of America case, risk assessment should have been performed at each critical decision point in the system development life cycle. For example, when the system was not ready in December 1984, it should have been analyzed for causes of failure to meet the target schedule.

Bank of America—Intrinsic Risks

Three sources of risk that are clearly prominent in the case of MasterNet are the *size* of the project, Bank of America's *unfamiliarity with the information technologies* involved, and the low *degree of structuredness* of the system.

The project was poorly designed and managed. The system was large as evidenced by its software size (3.5 million lines of code). Although at the start of the project, one could not know precisely how large the system would be, Bank of America was aware that trust management systems are large. Size is one major factor that contributes to risk, because other things being equal, a larger system consumes more resources, people, capital, and time, and thus has more chances of going wrong than a smaller system.

MasterNet employed technology new to Bank of America (Prime computers as opposed to the IBM machines that the bank had experience with). This created the risk of developing an SIS on unfamiliar hardware. The risk was higher in this case because the organization was lagging behind the technology curve. There was another technological risk, in that although the bank had developed a trust accounting system, it was batch-oriented. Batch-oriented systems and online systems embrace quite different information technologies, and familiarity with batch does not imply expertise with online. These risks could have been easily eliminated by choosing a familiar vendor (IBM) and providing enough schedule slack to gain experience from migrating batch systems to online systems.

Developing an online system entails another source of risk that relates to the structure of the project. Precise definition of user requirements is critical in online systems where users have direct and immediate access to the information system. The very nature of the trust operations involves customers with varying needs. Creating a set of system requirements that satisfies all sets of its users is a very complex task. Poorly structured systems, as was the case with MasterNet, carry the risk of improper specification of the system.

The implementation strategy adopted was not suited to the type of problem that the trust accounting system represented. A significant schedule risk was not addressed in the beginning. Not allowing adequate time for design and not verifying the feasibility of design was a major risk.

The bank's lack of experience in the institutional trust accounting business merited a careful study of the trust accounting business with resources that had experience in the institutional trust accounting field. Bank of America chose Premier Systems, whose experience was with small banks. This was risky because Bank of America's objective was to capture a large share of institutional trust accounts.

The system development strategy adopted by the MasterNet project team was based on the *waterfall* model. The model assumes that the application being developed is relatively quite structured; that is, user requirements defined in the early stages of development remain fairly stable throughout the development effort. Therefore, the development can cascade from the definition stages to the design stages to the construction stages and finally to the implementation stages.[3]

In the case of MasterNet, however, this development strategy was risky, because successful implementation using a waterfall model can work only if the requirements are stable and well established. This was not the case with the trust accounting application. A more prudent strategy would have been to use a phased incremental approach, where the users get to view at least parts of the system as it was being developed and could provide feedback before the system was fully designed.

Bank of America—Extrinsic Risks

The nature and importance of the trust accounting business itself carries an inherent risk. Each transaction, particularly where large institutional accounts are concerned, must be error-free. This aspect of the risk was not well assessed by Bank of America. The task of technology advancement of the bank was assigned to Max Hopper, who was earlier the principal designer of SABRE, the computerized reservation system developed by American Airlines. The primary reasoning behind this decision was that operating a bank was similar to operating a reservation system. Therefore, several key individuals from the airline industry were trusted to advance information technology in the banking industry. The risks, however, are different. Losing a reservation is less costly than losing a transaction in the trust account business.

One of the risks undertaken by Bank of America was building an SIS without understanding the nature of customers in the trust account market. The lack of customer orientation was evident from the bank's insensitivity to customers. Customers in the trust account business do not have brand loyalty, and the low costs of switching to another bank carry the risk of easy loss of market share (as they say in banking, if you want loyalty buy a cocker spaniel). Bank of America also took a legal risk in venturing with the system. The important customers were not small individuals but large institutions with great legal resources. Because MasterNet changed the way customers dealt with the bank, mistakes could have led potentially to legal action by customers who had the strength to take on the big bank.

Choice of a poor supplier (Premier) highlights another risk taken by Bank of America. Committing to a single supplier in a large-scale information system is a big risk, because failure of the supplier is transferred to the customer (Bank of America, in this case). Choice of a low-quality supplier is a major risk when developing a workable system.

Bank of America did not understand the domain of the large trust accounting business. In this domain, the bank was competing with large and seasoned institutions with experience in dealing with large trust accounts. The system provided thus a strong potential for imitation by competitors who could easily improve on the bank's SIS, even if the bank successfully developed a working trust management system.

AIRLINE RESERVATION SYSTEMS

Airline reservation systems provide an example of extrinsic risks and of how risks interplay with one another. Airline reservation systems started with the objective of reducing processing costs. Their importance evolved from being mere substitutes for clerical services to becoming an integral part of controlling airline operations. As early as 1953, American Airlines initiated discussions with IBM to develop a computerized reservation system. It started as a vision: a record for every seat. C. R. Smith, then president of American Airlines, was the visionary who set his sights on a system that could match passengers to seats, speed communications among airlines, contain seat availability on all carriers, print passenger itineraries, issue boarding passes, have travel agents connected directly, and tie into overall airline operations. The technology at the time was not capable of performing all these functional requirements. However, with IBM's support, SABRE, a streamlined version of Smith's vision, was developed.[4]

In the mid-1960s, IBM developed a generic reservations system called Programmed Airline Reservation System (PARS). The motive was that airline carriers could develop their own specific reservation systems but most of the system-level functions such as hardware, communications, system software, and utilities would be common and provided by IBM. Eastern Airlines developed their system based on IBM's PARS. Eastern's reservation system was considered to be well designed and state-of-the-art. TWA and United Airlines developed their system in collaboration with Burroughs and Univac (these two computer vendors eventually merged to become Unisys). However, the systems developed were not well designed, because neither the airline carriers (TWA and United) nor the computer vendors appreciated the complexity of developing reservation systems.

In the early 1970s, the airline industry was heavily regulated with captive markets. Therefore, Eastern Airlines did not consider their successful reservations system to be of strategic competitive value and thus consented to sell their system to TWA and United. In light of the deregulation that followed in the late 1970s, Eastern was unable to compete and later ceased to exist. Eastern simply did not consider the risk of selling proprietary information technology to its competitors. This is a classic example of trading away strategic advantage for short-term gains. (Certainly, information technology was not mature in the early 1970s and the notion of using information systems to gain a competitive edge was not well recognized.)

In the early 1970s, American Airlines' reservation system was rendered obsolete by the introduction of IBM's System/360. American also purchased Eastern Airlines' reservation system and modified it to their needs. Developing the reservation system all over again was deemed risky, and therefore a strategy of acquiring existing technology was adopted. It upgraded the processors to IBM System/370 line, which had the computing capacity to allow terminals to be placed in travel agents' offices and provide them with online query capabilities.

Most carriers possessed stable reservation systems in the early 1970s. In 1974, American Airlines proposed a joint task force, comprising airline carriers and the American Society of Travel Agents (ASTA), to consider a joint industry computerized system (JICRS). Earlier, in 1972, ASTA had approached Control Data Corporation (CDC) and proposed a joint effort to develop a common integrated travel agency system. CDC's feasibility studies had indicated that such a system was technologically viable as well as economically attractive. The airline carriers offered ASTA members an additional 1% commission for participating in JICRS and delaying development of the CDC system. United did not favor the committee approach taken by JICRS and eventually dropped out, citing the high cost of such a system.

In late 1975, United offered its own system to ASTA members for delivery about nine months later. This forced American Airlines and TWA to follow suit. By becoming the first, United had inadvertently triggered a war to woo suitors for the reservation system business. American Airlines was better prepared for this move than United. United's move was very risky, because being the first exposed its move to its competitors. Furthermore, United's APOLLO system was far less advanced than SABRE. This gave American Airlines a significant advantage. In addition, American had the advantage of having built a strong rapport with ASTA members by its pioneering effort on JICRS. American adopted the strategies of constant innovation and top-down marketing, which resulted in capturing a significant share of the travel agents' market. United, on the other hand, felt it did not have to change the system. However, United still retained a major portion of the market share, far ahead of American Airlines, simply because of its greater breadth in the route structure. The airline deregulation act of 1978 prompted both United and American to intensify their efforts in enhancing APOLLO and SABRE, respectively. Other airlines like TWA simply had not evolved their reservations system and lacked resources to seriously compete with United and American. This forced such carriers to use APOLLO or SABRE, reflecting the risk of being a failure.

The use of computerized reservation systems expanded from simply the operational domain to the marketing domain. SABRE and APOLLO could be used, for instance, to assess the impact of fare changes. Even more important, through them, American and United could assess the business situation of their competition. As an example, they could track the competitor's fare assignments and monitor changes in city-fare market shares. They could then use this information to distort market signals to their competitors. They also had the advantage of charging fees to rival carriers using the systems. They also enjoyed the luxury of manipulating schedule displays on travel agents' screens, creating the potential of favorable advantage for some carriers over others. The large investments required to develop systems with the capabilities of APOLLO and SABRE provided a successful capital entry barrier to prevent other carriers from launching similar systems.

In 1982, the Justice Department began a preliminary investigation of allegations by several airlines and determined that sufficient evidence pointed to anticompetitive practices by American and United. The Civil Aviation Board (CAB) set a body of rules to provide for equitable use of the reservation resources and for setting fair tariffs. However, American and United, being large domestic carriers, simply dominated the schedule displays on travel agents' screens. This hurt the small domestic carriers. Furthermore, the uniform fee structure actually raised fees and significantly raised revenues for American and United.

In 1984, 11 domestic carriers concluded that APOLLO and SABRE were not just systems that provided competitive advantage but actually an anticompetitive weapon. They filed suit, charging that American and United possessed a monopoly in computerized booking to limit competition. The suit also alleged that American and United intended to require travel agents using their systems to become franchised dealers and restricted the travel agents' sales activity. American countered by stating that investing in SABRE was a very risky business to begin with, and thus that its success should result in significant profit commensurate with the risks undertaken. In addition to the antitrust proceedings, Texas Air separately initiated suits against both American and United alleging anticompetitive tactics.

While forcing the two airlines to somewhat modify their reservation systems, the courts have basically upheld United's and American's practices. In fact, in early 1992, while APOLLO and SABRE handled more than 70% of airline reservations in the United States, most of the carriers that brought suits against United and American have left or were forced to leave the industry.

RISK ASSESSMENT OF SISs

The examples provided in the previous two sections highlighted risks and lack of risk management that led to a significant monetary loss to the organizations involved. In the Bank of America case, it resulted in a loss of market share in the large account trust management business. The airline reservation story indicated the trade-offs between various forms of risks. This section discusses the nature of risk and the various forms of risks within the context of an SIS.

Strategic information systems, as defined in earlier chapters, provide a competitive edge. There are broadly two kinds of SISs: information systems of strategic intent (those designed with a SIS in mind) and systems that have strategic potential. The former are more costly, more risky, and more difficult to implement because the target is moving. Systems of strategic intent also are more difficult to evaluate in terms of their cost/benefits and economic feasibility, and it is harder to assess their performance. The key aspects of SIS can be studied by understanding the competitive environment in which the business operates (i.e., the relationships of the organization with respect to existing competition, potential competitors, suppliers, customers, and substitute products). Strategic business opportunities enabled by strategic information systems include changing the basis of competition, raising entry barriers for potential competitors, increasing switching costs (locking in) of customers, changing the balance of power with suppliers and customers, and developing new products.[5]

It was pointed out before that systems by themselves are not strategic. The business change that results from such systems is strategic. The implication here is that changes in key business processes must be identified, then leveraged by new information systems that will support the processes.

ECONOMOST—An SIS Example

Before understanding the risks associated with SISs, it is important to understand the motivation that leads organizations to develop them. ECONOMOST, an order entry and management support system, is chosen to illustrate the basic tenets of SISs. Developed by the McKesson Drug Company, it is a good example of a successful application of information technology to a competitive use.[6]

ECONOMOST affects four dimensions of revolutionary changes within McKesson: its competitive posture, impact on industry as a whole, impact on suppliers, and impact on customers. ECONOMOST provides retail drug sellers a simple method for ordering items. Each pharmacist simply uses a bar code device to record an order of items in short supply. A default reorder table provides the convenience of not specifying ordered quantities for each item. The bar code method eliminates potential errors in cross-referencing item numbers against the products actually ordered. The accumulated orders are transmitted by the retailer over an 800 WATTS line. About 99% of McKesson's orders come in an electronic form.

In addition, McKesson provides a wide range of management services based on ECONOMOST. It can provide retailers with a virtual franchise capability. McKesson distributes products carrying the brand name Valu-Rite. Retailers can simply stock only products that carry this particular name, thus reflecting the illusion of a franchise without the strict legal requirement to stock only a specific brand. McKesson also provides consulting services to help retail units choose location, and miscellaneous retail services like drug credit card systems, third-party claims processing, and pharmacy terminal systems. The customers of ECONOMOST (pharmacies) enjoy greatly reduced transaction costs, get volume discounts if orders are placed through ECONOMOST, and reduce the inventory holdings owing to quick turnaround on orders.

The strategic advantages realized by ECONOMOST went far beyond cost savings. The druggists got used to the McKesson salespeople. Even though switching costs between competitors were minimal, the intimacy with McKesson staff and McKesson's way of doing business deterred druggists from switching to other vendors. McKesson benefited from consolidated orders, fewer purchasing agents, and better bargaining power from its suppliers. McKesson also benefited from improved productivity of its staff, which directly contributed to increased earnings. The most significant effect on the industry was that potential entrants now needed significant investments in information systems to compete with McKesson. The ECONOMOST software alone cost between $20 million and $30 million when it was developed in the mid-1970s, and went through continuous evolution into the early 1980s.

Risks Taken by McKesson

Even with the strong positive strategic impact of ECONOMOST, there were some negative side effects of McKesson's creating an entry barrier with ECONOMOST. Competitors, who could not afford a similar investment, sought three alternative strategies:

1. Find a niche market.
2. Get acquired by competitors, thus making them more powerful (for instance, regional competitors formed wholesale buying groups to counter the bargaining power of McKesson).
3. Grow by acquiring new businesses.

Thus, even with the success of ECONOMOST, there were some undesirable effects for McKesson. This was one of the risks McKesson assumed when it installed ECONOMOST.

McKesson took even greater risks with ECONOMOST. Powerful suppliers could themselves get into the distribution business if they found the returns attractive. Powerful hospital chains could link up directly with manufacturers. The electronic order entry reduced the *distance* between customer and supplier, making distributors like McKesson vulnerable. For example, the very technology that provided McKesson's customers (drug retailers) with tools to facilitate order entry reduced the importance of McKesson's value-added management reports. Increasing use of POS terminals at checkout stands, for instance, could provide many of the same reports provided by McKesson. Independent pharmacists also were placed in a favorable position to bargain with McKesson because of low switching costs. One of McKesson's major rivals was Bergen-Brunswick. Both facilitated conversion of a pharmacy to their system in a day or two and allowed use of the competitor's codes and formats during the transition.

McKesson provides an example of a planned use of IT to gain a strategic advantage in the market. However, many SISs arise purely by accident. Olivetti, for example, launched one of the world's first electronic typewriters. This resulted in lowering the entry barrier to many companies. Any company that could assemble a few electronic modules could then enter the typewriter market. Major typewriter companies like IBM discovered that the electrical and mechanical typewriters had given way to electronic typewriters and word processors. Olivetti had thus (unwittingly) precipitated a change in the structure of the typewriter industry by the use of information technology.

Even SABRE, the powerful strategic weapon unleashed by American Airlines, did not start off as a strategic system. In fact, it began with a modest vision of a record for every seat. Even as late as the early 1970s, American was interested in forming a coalition with computer vendors, travel agents, and other airline carriers to develop a reservation system. Efforts by United to start their own system actually prompted American to launch SABRE as a strategic instrument.

DEFINITION OF SIS RISKS

Risk can be defined as the deviation from an expected outcome. It is a measure of variability in the occurrence of events. An SIS project can suffer from slippage in time, cost overrun, or technical shortfalls. This type of risk, common to all information systems projects, is an *intrinsic, technical risk*. An SIS project can be completed in time and within its planned budget, yet not meet its strategic business objective. This type of risk, unique to SISs, is an *extrinsic, strategic risk*.

Paradoxically, an SIS that is a huge technical success (i.e., completed on time and within budget and meeting all expected requirements) may turn out to be a huge business failure. For instance, an SIS was expected to increase a company's market share by 40%, yet, after an early gain, all new customers and many old ones switched to a competitor who easily replicated the SIS and added new customer-enticing features to it.

In the context of SISs, risk can refer to an information system that has unanticipated effects. In an SIS, information technology influences the interaction of the organization with competitors, suppliers, customers, and other environmental forces like government regulations. The uncertainty is much greater in SISs than in conventional information systems because more players are involved. Furthermore, an SIS tends to be novel in nature, and innovation always entails some risk. Advantages from using an SIS are sometimes transitory. For example, competitors may react with a more powerful SIS, resulting in a heated race for marginal market share to cover (by now) larger fixed costs. The real issue is the organization's level of tolerance of risk and whether the risk level is appropriate for the specific SIS in question.

To emphasize the difference between risks associated with non-SIS applications and SIS applications, all information systems carry some risk based on the type of system to be implemented. These are called intrinsic risks. In addition, SISs carry some risks not characteristic of other IS applications. These are extrinsic risks. This categorization separates technical issues that contribute to risk from the business issues of using an information system to gain competitive advantage.

There is yet another fundamental difference between intrinsic and extrinsic risks. Through good planning and proper management of the implementation of an IS project, the impact of intrinsic risks can be significantly reduced. In fact, intrinsic risks have also been called implementation risks.[7] Extrinsic risks, on the other hand, always result in a trade-off: reducing one form of extrinsic risk might actually increase another. For example, to reduce the risk of being easily replicated, a software vendor may intentionally complicate the design of the software package. The trade-off is the difficulty of making changes later in a complex software product that may be desirable to retain the competitive edge of the package.

The breakdown into intrinsic versus extrinsic risks is one of several ways to classify risks associated with SISs. Peter Keen, for instance, suggests six classes of risks associated with SISs[8]:

> *Market concept risk* refers to the sole criterion by which an SIS that seems sound and logically ought to succeed will be judged—customer acceptance and continued use.
>
> *Technology risk* is incurred when a technology is new or unproven in the context of intended use, users, volumes, and performance requirements.
>
> *Implementation risk* refers to problems in software design, project management, component integration, or vendor delivery that might impede turning SIS into a reliable product or service using an otherwise sound technology.
>
> *Economic risk* is the potential for the outcomes of an SIS to be other than what was optimistically forecast in terms of revenue, direct or indirect cost, or support.

Organizational risk refers to the possibility that a technically functional SIS will fail to secure buy-in, threaten key aspects of the firm's traditions, norms, management processes, or culture, or require skills that the organization does not have.

Regulatory risk refers to the potential for what appears to be a reasonable business use of IT to be blocked by regulation, government policy, social concerns, or interest groups.

The discussion that follows incorporates SIS risks under several categories. The next section describes the nature of intrinsic risks. It is followed by a description of extrinsic risks. Examples are provided to illustrate the presence of those risks in real-world SIS applications.

THE NATURE OF INTRINSIC RISKS

Intrinsic risks are associated with the development and implementation of an SIS project. A three-dimensional analysis of IS projects can be used for discussing intrinsic risks.[9] The three dimensions affecting the level of risk are the *size* of the project (e.g., in dollars or person-months), the *degree of familiarity* with the information technology involved (e.g., first time the organization is exposed to expert systems), and the *degree of structuredness* of the system (e.g., a payroll system is a highly structured because information requirements stay fairly stable from start to end of the project development cycle).

The three dimensions provide a framework for assessing intrinsic risks of information systems and are discussed later. In brief, intuitively, the larger the size of an IS project, the lower the degree of familiarity with the technology, and the lower the degree of structuredness—the greater the risks of the system's outputs and uses deviating from the expected.

The factors that lead to project failure can be classified under two major headings: planning and implementation. Planning deals with specifying the goals of the application, understanding its feasibility, and specifying a management approach for developing the system. Implementation deals with constructing the system, verifying that it meets its goals, and transferring it to the environment in which it will be operational.

Planning Risks

Risks of Poor Estimation.   There are several methods of estimating IS resources needed for a specific project. In all of them there is a common risk of underestimation or excessive padding. The former is more prevalent because lower estimated costs have a better chance of being accepted by the sponsor. The importance of a specific SIS may create the political environment for a "buy-in" (i.e., the tendency of not fully understanding the cost of developing the SIS). Although estimation is far from an exact science, it is important to make the best attempt at estimating resources to facilitate proper planning. The presumption here is that better estimates of needed resources lead to better planning, reducing the risk of project failure.

Risks of Schedule Compression.   The need date usually specifies the target delivery date. The risk is that the time required for the development of a system is not dependent on when the organization needs the system, but rather on the nature of the system, staff resources available, and familiarity with technology. Although there is some flexibility in manipulating available resources, there is little in the other areas. Thus, target delivery dates should not be just based on needs but on the nature of the system as well. This is particularly difficult for SIS projects, because timely development is critical to whether the project succeeds or fails. This poses a major risk to completing the project on time. Merely adding more personnel is not likely to solve the problem of developing the system faster.[10]

Inappropriate Set of Resources.   One major cause of project failure is the use of inappropriate resources. Bank of America's MasterNet failure illustrates a classic example of this risk, quite common in IS planning. The bank chose to implement their system using a software house whose experience was primarily in trust management systems for small banks. The fact that the nature of trust management business for small individual accounts is quite different from that of large institutional accounts was not considered in the planning process. This unwarranted risk could have easily been avoided by choosing the right resources for the job.

Implementation Risks

Development and implementation of SISs are usually prolonged, difficult, and expensive. The ASAP system developed by American Hospital Supply Corporation (described in chapter one), intended to provide modern materials management for hospital customers, took over six years to develop and two years more to see gains from the system. SABRE, the computerized reservation system developed by American Airlines, took over six years and $350 million to develop.

ANAQUEST (the company's name is disguised) illustrates how even a successful implementation strategy can trigger unplanned risks. ANAQUEST (a $100 million pharmaceutical firm in Wisconsin) marketed two well-accepted anesthetics, Ethrane and its successor, Forane.[11] It boasted a small but well-educated field sales force of 46, who generated sizable revenues (in 1983). The market was highly price-sensitive. The company decided on pilot testing a field support system on seven field service agents, including a sales manager. The pilot approach appeared to be highly risk-averse from several perspectives. First, the cost was very low, around $160,000. Second, the full spectrum of functions would not be needed to be implemented for the pilot. Third, the system development team would gain experience with the GRID software system underlying the project. Finally, the system would impact only a small percentage of the field force. Of course, ANAQUEST recognized some risk of failure. It would threaten the professional image of the compact sales force. It would also interrupt revenue generation, because ANAQUEST had only 46 field sales representatives. ANAQUEST's size and financial position appeared to mitigate the impact of the risks.

The system developed was based on application software running on a portable PC. The application software supported four functions: comparative pricing, clinical references, speakers file, and electronic mail. The comparative pricing application would allow the field sales agent to develop comparative costs based on the technique employed by a physician. The clinical references application would maintain a database of citations in the professional literature indexed by topics like type of surgery or drug used. The speakers file would maintain a database permitting a sales agent to locate a speaker on a specific topic. Although the system was behind schedule and had some shortcomings, it was unanimously endorsed by the pilot participants.

The overwhelming success of the pilot brought a new form of risk: the sales force could become overzealous and expand the project beyond the technical resources available at ANAQUEST. This is the risk of suboptimal implementation. There is yet another risk that was not obvious with the pilot project. Success with 7 field sales representatives does not necessarily imply success with the entire field sales staff of 46. Fortunately for ANAQUEST, it had prior experience with pilot tests and overcame these risks. The strategy adopted by ANAQUEST was to transfer some of the risks by using contract labor, extensively field-testing the production system using hypothetical test cases with medical staff providing consultations, and providing extensive training to the field sales representatives.

Implementation risks are both technical and political. The following section describes the characteristics of implementation risks that can potentially lead to the failure of SISs.

Technical Risk.   Technical risk can result from the incorrect choice of technical architecture. For example, the system and its expected capabilities may be unfeasible with current technologies. One way to mitigate this risk is to choose a proven technology. This may not always be appropriate. First Boston Bank, faced with massive programming enhancement needs and low programmer productivity, decided to use Computer-Aided Software Engineering (CASE) tools despite immaturity of CASE technology at the time. A second way to reduce technical risk is to scale down the activity to match the current level of technology maturity. The SABRE airline reservation system, when originally planned in 1953, far exceeded the capacity of the technology available at the time. A scaled-down approach and support from IBM paved the way for the early versions of the system. Technical risk can also result from the sheer size of the SIS. By their very nature, SISs tend to be large and thus carry all the risks associated with implementing large-scale information systems. One way to mitigate this is to use incremental development strategies such as modular development.

Lack of familiarity with the technology can result in technical risks. The three major areas of lack of technical familiarity include

- Hardware familiarity (computers/networks)
- Software familiarity (examples: computer language used, operating system)
- Database familiarity (data collection and data management experience as it relates to the specific SIS under consideration)

A simple strategy to mitigate this risk is to team up with vendors who have the specific technological expertise lacking in the firm developing the SIS. In the early 1960s and

1970s, airline carriers teamed up with computer vendors to develop airline reservation systems. The Fireman's Fund Insurance Company purchased a software company called ARC Automation Group that used to develop information system applications for insurance agents. This alleviated Fireman's risks in developing a massive software-intensive agent application.

Project Risk.   The size or complexity of the SIS or both could be beyond the organization's technical skills. It may be possible to reduce this risk by outsourcing or bringing in consultants.[12] Of course, this introduces a new type of risk, because the firm now depends on the supplier's capabilities. Bank of America's MasterNet is an example of how SIS can fail when the system development exceeds the resource capabilities of the implementing organization. SIS systems are particularly difficult to control because requirements are at best fuzzy and constantly changing. One way to overcome this problem is to have constant top management involvement and guidance.

Functionality Risk.   The firm may implement the system to the specified design but still fail to realize the anticipated benefits because of the following:

- The design was wrong and systems analysis failed to accurately assess user needs, possibly because of lack of user involvement and incorrect feedback.
- The system design was no longer appropriate. The long lead times of developing SISs often result in a situation where the system meets original design goals but those goals themselves are rendered obsolete because of changes in the business environment. A strategy to mitigate this risk is to involve users in the system development process. Another strategy, in addition to early user involvement, is to use prototyping methodology so that the system can evolve to meet the changing needs, while constantly providing feedback to users as prototyped modules are presented to users.

Organizational Risk.   An SIS can be undermined by vested interests who may perceive a threat to their position. This may result in low motivation among staff and cause them to be uncooperative, which slows down implementation. Some factors that contribute to this risk are listed below[13]:

- Lack of a good change management.
- Launching new technology without adequate experimentation and training of employees.
- Lack of a good performance evaluation system. A common problem is basing implementor evaluation on short-term results of the SIS without taking into account long-term benefits. This may force implementors to take shortcuts that increase the risk of successful implementation.
- Lack of cohesion. A team that has built a successful system in the past can be believed to be cohesive and pose less risk than a newly assembled team. The

motivation here is that an SIS is a people-intensive project and cohesive teams provide a greater chance of meeting goals.

- Lack of team incentives. This is a big problem in information system development—teams are encouraged but incentives are still based on a prima donna concept.
- Choice of inappropriate SIS project leader. This can pose risks for SIS systems, particularly if an SIS is deemed a technological difficulty and a technical guru is chosen as the leader. In that case, the extrinsic risks of SISs (discussed in the next section) may get downplayed, which may prove detrimental to the organization.

Lack of Sound Economic Feasibility Study.   The lack of a sound economic feasibility study can pose a risk. The effect, again, is that an SIS project could be rejected because of near-term benefits that fail to take into account long-term benefits. Of course, the reverse of this also embodies an economic risk. An SIS may get launched by simply looking at the short-term benefits and ignoring the long-term impacts not included in the analysis. This risk applies to all information systems but even more to SISs, because it is very hard to estimate/quantify benefits owing to the strategic value they contribute. A way to mitigate this risk is to quantify benefits of an SIS based on assumed strategic value (i.e., adding the *cost of not launching an SIS*). The argument here is that some SISs may be a "do-or-die" for the company. Two examples of this risk are the IMNET and Allegis cases.[14]

International MarketNet (IMNET) was a joint venture by IBM and Merrill Lynch to provide stock quotations to users with IBM PCs. Monchik-Weber, a software house specializing in securities, won the contract to develop the software. Merrill's motivation was to eliminate the fees it paid to the Quotron service for use of its stock quotation system. The venture failed mainly because of the following:

- Cost of $70 million failed to provide real benefits commensurate with the costs and risks.
- Poor management of the venture.
- Inadequate systems design of the user interface (users had to juggle disks/modems, etc.).

Allegis, known prior to 1987 as United Airlines (UAL), Inc., acquired Hertz and together with UAL and the Westin hotel chain, planned to develop a system to provide complete traveler's needs. They planned on pouring over $1 billion into UAL's APOLLO reservation system to develop synergies among the three strategic business units. This strategy failed and eventually Hertz and Westin were sold. The main reasons were the following:

- Investors became impatient when delays were experienced in realizing the proposed benefits.
- Benefits were not carefully studied.
- Customer price/convenience sensitivities were not properly analyzed and accounted for.

The Risk of Not Being Familiar with the Application.   The lack of domain familiarity is a major cause of information system project failures. Bank of America's lack of familiarity in managing institutional trust accounts was not taken into account by management when it launched MasterNet. One way to mitigate this risk is by sharing domain experience. Kroger Company, a supermarket chain, joined with Capital Holdings, an insurance company, to develop an SIS in support of its entry into a completely new market of selling insurance, money market funds, and IRAs in its stores. Kroger had no domain experience in the insurance field. Without this alliance, it would have been very risky for Kroger to venture into the insurance-selling business.[15]

The Risk of Outsourcing.   Outsourcing carries some trade-offs in risks. From a risk perspective, the advantage of outsourcing is the transfer of risk from the organization developing the SIS to the supplier in charge of implementation. However, this introduces other risks:

- Choice of a poor supplier will result in poor implementation. This may render the SIS ineffective. For example, an excessive delay in development changes the timing of introduction of the SIS. This could be critical to its success.
- Choice of a single source increases dependency on the supplier. Bank of America chose this as their implementation strategy for MasterNet, with disastrous results. This risk can be mitigated by having more than one supplier, but at the expense of increased overhead caused by the need to keep track of multiple suppliers and to coordinate their inputs into a single SIS.
- The organization may get locked in with a supplier. The need for constant modifications of the SIS may increase the organization's dependency on a specific supplier, who may start taking advantage of the captive customer.
- The supplier gains information about the organization's strategic plan. Developing an SIS invariably involves an intimate understanding of the organization's business strategy. This information may be sought from the supplier by rivals. Not sharing strategic information reduces this risk but creates the risk of poor implementation, because the supplier may fail to understand the functional requirements of the SIS.

THE NATURE OF EXTRINSIC RISKS

Two levels of impact of extrinsic risks may result from an SIS. The first level stems from external environmental risks such as unanticipated response from competitors and government bodies. The second stems from SISs that may so radically change the business environment that all previous assumptions about prevailing market conditions, economic analysis, market share, and growth are rendered obsolete.[16]

The Risk of Being First

The risk is simply the threat of competitors to replicate or improve the system introduced by the pioneer. The newspaper industry in the United Kingdom (UK) provides an illustration of such a risk.[17] In the UK, the trade unions had successfully delayed the introduction of information technology in the newspaper business to thwart potential loss of jobs. The newspaper industry was burdened with manual processes that resulted in highly inefficient and expensive production systems. The newspaper *Today* was launched in 1985 with the strategy of using information technology to provide a massive competitive edge by reducing production costs. The success of the paper in winning the battle over the unions by introducing information technology caused competitors to attempt to maneuver the trade unions into accepting IT into their production process. *Today,* which started with the intention of using IT to gain a significant cost advantage over competitors, thus forced the competition into adopting IT as well. This evaporated *Today's* advantage. Because *Today* had less news content than its competitors, its survival became questionable. The result was that a competitor actually took over the newspaper.

One way to reduce the effects of this risk is to build complex and sophisticated systems that are hard to replicate. However, this inherently increases the risk of implementation because a more complex system carries a higher intrinsic risk. Another implication is that sustaining the advantage carries a risk, because it requires constantly upgrading the SIS. As systems are changed, their maintainability becomes difficult from a technical point of view; at the same time, from a business point of view, it becomes harder to maintain the edge, because competition will catch up sooner or later. One risk mitigation strategy is to design maintainable systems, use methods (such as object-oriented design) to minimize technical maintainability risk, and constantly change/enhance the features provided to maintain a competitive advantage.

The Risk of Changing the Basis of Competition

In many cases, SIS changes the very nature of competition. If the race to stay competitive becomes a technology race, the basis for competition shifts from who sells, markets, or manufactures the best to one of who has the best technical ability. Michael Vitale of the Prudential Life Insurance Company (and formerly a professor at the Harvard Business School) provides an illustration of such a risk.[18] A manufacturer of commercial appliances (Company A) offered contractors the capability to mail in specifications, which the company would translate to products and instructions on site preparation and installation. In 1981, Company A developed a set of computer programs on a mainframe and early microcomputers to automate the process. The contractors would still send the specifications by mail, but the company would feed the requirements to a mainframe computer that would then generate the product list and instructions. Contractors were encouraged to enter specifications on a microcomputer with Company A–supplied software. The microcomputer itself was not powerful enough to generate the product and instruction list but checked the consistency of the specifications input by the contractors. This gave Company A a market advantage and it started capturing a bigger share of the market.

Over time, microcomputers became cheaper and more powerful. One competitor, Company B, who had a more progressive information systems staff, developed a similar system, but both the specification checker and the product list–generation software ran on more powerful PCs. This meant no delays in getting mailed-in specifications and mailing back the product and instruction list. The software was offered by Company B to the contractors at no charge. Although Company A had done nothing at the time to take advantage of the lower-cost PCs, Company B had entered the market with a better product that would not cost the contractors any nonrecurring software expense. Company B more than recaptured its market share lost initially to Company A. Conclusion: "If the other side has bigger guns, don't start a fight."

The Risk of Losing Proprietary Information

The advantage of a fast linkage to suppliers, by allowing them access to the firm's inventory database, carries the risk of suppliers potentially accessing the organization's proprietary information and selling it to a competitor. The same applies when customers are allowed access to the organization's product information with the intention of providing instant access to the firm's products and services.

The point is that such linkages may make information too easy to get or may make information accessible to competitors. Strategic information systems deal with both data and functions. Sharing data in an alliance may lead to a disadvantage if competition can use them for their own benefit. The strategy to mitigate this risk is similar to dealing with any information that needs to be secured, that is, include the SIS in the company's information system security plan. However, there is no free lunch; achieving the necessary level of management involvement and acceptance of security measures and costs may be extremely difficult.[19]

The Risk of Unintentionally Lowering Customers' Switching Costs

American Hospital Supply Corporation (AHSC) provides an example of such a risk. As described in chapter one, AHSC has an online system called ASAP that allows online ordering of medical and surgical supplies and has an installed base of over 3,000 U.S. hospitals. The system identifies substitutes for out-of-stock items and provides the user (hospital) flexibility in specifying several delivery options. Although some of AHSC's competitors have developed similar systems, they have been unable to keep up with AHSC. A major risk in this approach, however, is the risk of a system developed by a supplier that initially introduces a customer to advanced information technology and thus allows the customer to switch to another supplier's system without incurring high switching costs. The computerized order system of AHSC provides an example of how to deal with this risk. As Vitale comments:

> Why not develop a master system that would take data from hospitals and pass it to suppliers? The hospitals could retain advantages of a single system, and might get lower prices as well since the master system could shop amongst the suppliers for the best price. If American had not continued to develop and enhance ASAP, this danger might be very real today. In fact, the company has taken the system well beyond the order entry stage. Later versions of ASAP allow a hospital to order based on its own stock numbers, as well as American's; to create and store files of frequently ordered items; and in other ways to

personalize ASAP to the hospital's own environment. It would be extremely difficult for any master system to keep up with these ongoing developments. By continually adapting ASAP to its customer needs, American has preserved the competitive advantages of the system and minimized the risk of being bypassed.[20]

The Risk of Potential Legal Intervention

There are two basic threats to companies using SISs, grounded in the legal system:

- The government initiating a lawsuit for potential violation of antitrust regulations.
- Competitors filing lawsuits contending unfair business practices facilitated by the SIS.

An earlier section has described the attack on SABRE and APOLLO by both the government and small airline companies. Baybanks of Boston filed suit against the five largest New England banks, contending they had conspired to form an ATM network excluding the small banks. SIS victims are not the only ones using the legal suit as a weapon. Merrill Lynch obtained a patent to protect the software running its Cash Management Account (CMA) system and threatened to sue companies who infringed on the patent. It actually sued and won against the Dean Witter brokerage house.

Dealing with this risk is difficult, mainly because there are uncertainties due to a lack of well-established rules and few procedures available on record. Organizations are seeking innovative ways to deal with this risk, however. One way is to team with one's competitor. For example, American Airlines (owner of SABRE) offered United Airlines (owner of APOLLO) support in litigations against United Airlines. Another example is that competitors of American Airlines offered travel agents legal support as an incentive for them to switch over if American sued them for breach of contract.

The Risk of Nonacceptance by Customers

The timing of when to introduce an SIS is strongly impacted by customer acceptance. Introduction of SISs and the scale of introduction pose risks because of the inherent changes in the information systems infrastructure required to implement the SIS. The customer may be reluctant to invest in the necessary infrastructure and hence reject the SIS. The trade-off here is that delaying the introduction of an SIS based on an unfamiliar new technology could incur the risk of a competitor beating the firm. On the other hand, introducing technology too soon entails the technical intrinsic risk of "bugs" that may also be detrimental to the firm. Reducing one form of risk can be only at the expense of the other.

McKesson provides an example of this form of risk. McKesson wholesales nondurable consumer goods (ethical and proprietary drugs, toiletries, sundries, wine and spirits, industry and special chemicals, etc.).[21] After their success with ECONOMOST, they developed a computerized merchandising program and a computerized order entry system. A corporate strategy of differentiation (see chapter four) led to the formation of McKesson Chemical, which used the same underlying order entry know-how. The success of a new prescription drug claims–processing system led McKesson in 1983 to form a new business unit, which acted as intermediary between the consumer (patient) and service provider (insurers). It processed over 27 million claims from over 45,000 pharmacies from a customer base of over 6.5 million.

In 1983 McKesson joined with Action Industries (a company selling household hardware) and acquired SKU, a microcomputer software distributor with annual sales of $25 million. SKU's leading competitors were Micro-D, with sales of $28 million, and Softsell, with sales of $75 million. The cost of acquisition was $8 million. The strategic objective of the acquisition was to expand the scope of McKesson's business by entering the software distribution industry. The idea was to tailor McKesson's order entry and adapt it to the software distribution industry. This strategy failed, primarily because the software market was not mature in 1984. In addition, software is not a commodity; its buyers are more sophisticated and value-conscious compared with pharmaceutical buyers, whose customers are less sensitive to price/value ratios.

One way to mitigate this risk is to use pilot tests, test market area, and get customer feedback during implementation. Of course, the ANAQUEST case, described earlier, demonstrates that pilot-testing an SIS carries other risks.

RISK ASSESSMENT AND MANAGEMENT

Any process of risk management includes the stages of risk identification and assessment, selection of appropriate risk treatment tools and solutions, and then the constant monitoring of the program of risk treatment. The last stage should involve an organizational body that is in charge of implementing the risk treatment device, collecting statistics about the impact of the implementation, and taking corrective actions if necessary.

For example, one factor that creates an intrinsic risk is project size. The solution (risk-treatment device) may be a modular development and implementation of the project. Another cause of an intrinsic risk may be the organization's unfamiliarity with the information technology underlying the SIS project. The solution here may be to hire an expert consultant familiar with the technology or to outsource the project development to an expert provider. In both examples, somebody in the organization must monitor the solutions.

When the risks are extrinsic, they involve business rather than technical threats (such as not locking in customers or being subject to litigation). The solutions are, therefore, usually business rather than technical solutions. For example, a company ready to launch an extensive SIS project may have too limited resources. The solution in this case may be to forge an SIS alliance with a big rival, or customer, or supplier. Obviously, there are cases when an SIS involves both intrinsic and extrinsic risks. In such cases the solutions need to be both business and technical ones.

Coping with Extrinsic Risks

Assessment of business risks should be included as part of the SIS evaluation process, where the project costs and benefits are evaluated prior to making a decision. Vitale suggested a simple framework for understanding the potential risks that can result from an SIS that has an initial success.[22] Such risks can include the following: being forced to "stay the course" with continued investments in information systems to remain competitive; becoming vulnerable to competitors that have underutilized information systems resources; raising entry barriers that can also raise exit barriers; launching very successful SISs that cause competitors to claim unfair practices and lobby for government regulation; increased dependencies on SISs that open up vulnerabilities to software and hardware suppliers.

To assess these and other risks, Vitale developed a quadripartite framework based on the *strategic impact framework* (both frameworks were described in chapter three). The current impact of ISs is mapped against its future competitive importance (Figure 9.1).

The risk-assessment framework is intended to help managers focus on the options and consequences of SIS choice. For example, a successful proprietary system that moves a firm and the industry from a high-current-impact/low-industry-importance position to a high-impact/high-industry-importance position (quadrant *c* to quadrant *d*) may bring on governmental action.

The current competitive impact of ISs identifies how important they are to the firm now and how widespread is their use within the organization. The future competitive importance of ISs to the industry should be assessed by the firm according to competitors' capabilities in ISs and the impact of the planned SIS. For industries with limited technological expertise, being in quadrant *a* is a major risk if the importance of the information system is increasing (illustrated by the shift from quadrant *b* to *a*). This implies that organizations not willing to make a sustained commitment to information systems should refrain from changing their importance. In the case of Olivetti, for instance, shifting from the mechanical typewriter to electronic typewriters led to a great disadvantage to the firm, because competitors (particularly IBM) had a tremendous advantage in information systems over Olivetti.

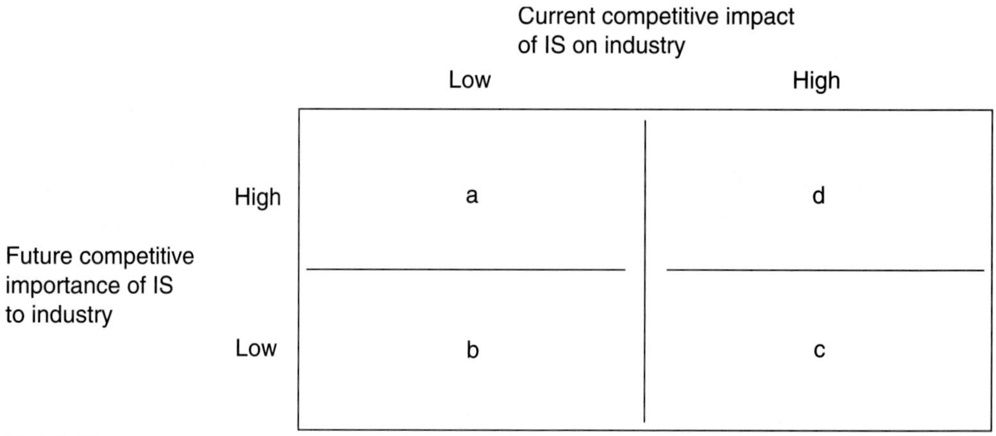

FIGURE 9.1   Risk assessment grid

An organization on the right-hand side of the grid has considerable investment in ISs already, because the impact of ISs is high. However, it should observe industry trends, particularly those that shift the importance of ISs from high to low (a shift from quadrant *d* to *c*). This would imply that the competition may be seeking means other than information technologies to gain a competitive edge. In such cases, the organization should be risk-averse: an SIS project that at one time was deemed acceptable should be rejected to mitigate the risk of eventually falling behind the competition.

Coping with Intrinsic Risks

Once intrinsic-technical risks have been identified, tools can be selected to reduce or eliminate them. The selection must be judicious; all tools have explicit or implicit cost elements and may be appropriate for certain risks or inappropriate for others. For example, hiring an expert consultant involves fees and can reduce the risk emanating from using an unfamiliar information technology. When an SIS project is lowly structured (namely, the information requirements and outputs are not well defined), appointing a functional manager as the project leader rather than an IS professional may reduce the risk of a failure. In that case, however, the implicit cost is the time of the manager who is not performing regular duties as a functional manager.

A helpful classification of tools for managing intrinsic risks is the following:

- *External integration tools* that include organizational and communication devices that link the project team's work to users (for example: selection of a user as a project leader, creation of steering committees, distribution of progress reports to users). These tools are very appropriate for SIS projects that have low structure.
- *Internal integration tools* include a variety of devices that ensure that the project team operates as an integrated unit (for example, frequent team meetings, managed low turnover of team members). These devices are appropriate for highly structured projects based on a familiar technology.
- *Formal planning tools* help in formalizing the schedule and budget of a project and in estimating the timing and cost of needed resources (for example, feasibility studies, milestone phase selection). These devices can be used in a highly structured project that involves a familiar technology.
- *Formal control tools* help managers evaluate progress and take corrective actions if necessary (for example, formal walk-throughs, periodic status versus plan reports). These tools are highly appropriate for projects that are large, have low structure, and involve an unfamiliar technology.[23]

Again, the contribution of each tool to reducing intrinsic risks varies widely according to the project's characteristics. A contingency approach, by project type, is merited—there is no universally correct way to manage all SIS project risks (as the saying goes, there are many ways to skin a cat).

Recognizing the Need for Considering Trade-offs

The various forms of risk described in earlier sections are not independent of one another. There is always a need to trade off one risk against the other. In many cases these trade-offs are not very obvious. First Boston embarked on using a Computer-Aided Software Engineering (CASE) tool that was very risky from an intrinsic perspective. First Boston was in the securities and banking business, not information technology. The CASE technology was new, the project large and not well defined. This would indicate a very high intrinsic risk. Still, First Boston decided to go ahead with the development tool because they recognized the trade-offs. Not implementing the tool meant that programmers at First Boston had to do massive conversions in a rapidly changing application environment without the benefit of automating some of the conversion processes. This method carried the greater risk of making changes in a lower-productivity programming environment. The CASE tool provided the opportunity to enhance programmer's productivity by supporting the automation of the information system's environment. In fact, the CASE tool implementation was so successful that the bank started to sell the application to outside clients.

Another area where the trade-off is necessary has to do with the balance between intrinsic and extrinsic risks. In many cases, these may share a contradictory relationship. For example, size risk and risk of imitation share a contradictory relationship: larger systems are more difficult to be imitated. Another example is that to avoid the risk of being left behind, major technical risks may have to be undertaken in an SIS project, as evident from the SABRE example. Creating this balance is nontrivial. For example, the risk of low structure (not well-defined requirements) probably implies that customer needs are not well understood. This could lead later to nonacceptance by the customer.

CONCLUDING REMARKS

Any IS development project carries with it intrinsic (technical) risks that the project will be a failure when implemented. The implementation risks have to do with budget overruns, time slippages, and/or failure to meet users' information requirements adequately. IS project characteristics that lead to such risks are usually associated with project size, degree of inherent structuredness, and degree of newness of information technology used by the system.

SIS projects are likely to be large, reflecting the growing complexity of the business environment. They will often be the first in an application area, with little previous structure to draw on. Many of these systems will be based on an information technology that is new to the firm. This suggests that high intrinsic risk will accompany information systems designed to provide competitive advantages.

As SIS may technically "succeed," thereby creating potential negative strategic impact for the company implementing it. We refer here not to the SIS project's failing but to the extrinsic risks of competitive disadvantages arising from unanticipated effects of the SIS on industry structure and the competitive position of the implementing firm.

There is little agreement on where the responsibility lies for SIS risk management. Leaving it to the implementors may cause the business factors (extrinsic risks) to be ignored. On the other hand, leaving it to business managers may cause the planning and implementation factors (intrinsic risks) to be ignored. It has been well observed that we tend to blame our failures on somebody else, as with the story of the man with a bad limp who complains that the national ballet company didn't hire him as a dancer because he didn't carry a party card.

SIS risks can be managed by understanding and assessing them and taking appropriate action to prevent, reduce, or control them. The following guidelines may be of help:

1. Evaluate the impact of SIS at the firm and industry level before a decision is made to proceed. Consider the firm under a scenario in which the proposed SIS is technically successful and one in which it is not attempted.

2. Reduce the risk of being bypassed by continually adopting and adding features to meet additional or changing customers' needs (let the competition play catch-up).

3. Consider the IS resources and capabilities of current and potential competitors.

4. Create policies to assure that end-user–developed SISs match corporate objectives.

5. Promote a technical partnership between general management users and SIS implementors.

6. Verify commitment and support of senior management. An SIS changes the way you do business and this is why senior managers must be involved. Their involvement can assure that internal policies for resource allocation do not rule out SIS opportunities.

7. Reduce risks by being a follower rather than a leader of a new SIS.

8. Verify that the firm's culture provides for willingness to experiment, to entertain innovative ideas, and to learn from mistakes and misses.

9. Build on internal IS knowledge, capabilities, and systems and only then extend this platform externally with SISs.

10. Do not try to win over IS-wise customers.

11. Perform a thorough review of the potential impacts of the SISs before they are developed and again before they are installed.

12. Standardize an SIS management checklist that covers overview of the SIS, effects of SIS failure, and special unique circumstances like laws, regulation, and government policies (when all else fails, read the checklist).[24]

REFERENCES

1. Ahituv, N., and Neumann, S., *Principles of Information Systems for Management,* 3rd ed. Dubuque, Iowa: Wm. C. Brown Publishers, 1990.

2. As mentioned later in *Computerworld,* Apr. 9, 1990, the newly appointed CIO, Michael Simmons, promptly ended the MasterNet system development and shifted IS focus within the bank to emphasize cost control and improve operations efficiencies.

3. Boehm, B., "A Spiral Model of Software Development and Enhancement," *IEEE Computer* 21, no. 5 (May 1988).

4. Copeland, D. G., and McKenney, J. L., "Airline Reservations Systems: Lessons from History," *Management Information Systems Quarterly* (Sept. 1988).

5. McFarlan, W. F., "Information Technology Changes the Way You Compete," *Harvard Business Review* 62, no. 3 (May–June 1984).

6. Clemons, E. K., and Row, M., "A Case Study of ECONOMOST: A Strategic Information System," *Proceedings of the Twenty-First Hawaii International Conference on System Sciences.* Los Alamitos, Calif.: IEEE Press, 1988.

7. Ginzberg, M. J., and Moulton, R. T., "Information Services Risk Management," Case Western Reserve University, Weatherhead School of Management, Working Paper No. 90–01, Jan. 1990.

8. Keen, D. G. W., *Shaping the Future: Business Design Through Information Technology.* Boston: Harvard Business School Press, 1991.

9. McFarlan, W. F., "Portfolio Approach to Information Systems," *Harvard Business Review* 59, no. 5 (Sept.–Oct. 1981).

10. Brooks, F. P., Jr., "The Mythical Man-Month, *Datamation,* Dec. 1974.

11. Vitale, M. R., and McGee, J., "ANAQUEST: The Professional Services Project (A)," Harvard Business School Case, 9-186-275, 1986; "ANAQUEST: The Professional Services Project (B)," Harvard Busines School Case, 9-186-301, 1986.

12. Clemons, E. K., and Weber, B. W., "Strategic Information Technology Investments: Guidelines for Decision Making," *Journal of Management Information Systems* 7, no. 2 (Fall 1990).

13. Ibid.

14. Wiseman, C., *Strategic Information Systems.* Homewood, Ill.: Irwin, 1988.

15. Ibid.

16. Clemons and Weber, "Strategic Information Technology Investments."

17. Jackson, C., "Building a Competitive Advantage Through Information Technology," *Long Range Planning* 22, no. 4 (1989).

18. Vitale, M. R., "The Growing Risks of Information Systems Success." *MIS Quarterly* 10, no. 4 (Dec. 1986).

19. Moulton, R. T., *Computer Security Handbook: Strategies and Techniques for Preventing Data Loss or Theft.* Englewood Cliffs, N.J.: Prentice-Hall, 1986.

20. Vitale, "The Growing Risks."

21. Wiseman, *Strategic Information Systems.*

22. Vitale, "The Growing Risks."

23. Cash, J. J., Jr., McFarlan, F. W., McKenney, J. L., and Applegate, L. M., *Corporate Information Systems Management: Text and Cases,* (3rd ed.). Homewood, Ill.: Irwin, 1992.

24. Ahituv and Neumann, *Principles of Information Systems.*

10

Organizational Requirements
for Introducing Strategic
Information Systems

I would say to the House, as I said to those
who have joined the Government, I have
nothing to offer but blood, toil, tears,
and sweat.

—*Winston Churchill*
House of Commons, May 13, 1940

INTRODUCTION

This chapter discusses the organizational environment for a successful implementation of
a *strategic information system* (after all, God gives the nuts, but does not crack them). Toward
this end, two types of organizations are investigated—those that successfully implemented an SIS, and those that did not meet the same level of success. The investigation
reveals two distinct sets of characteristics, each shared by one of the two types of organizations. In addition, the investigation identifies a number of important processes used
by successful organizations. If properly implemented, these facilitate the introduction of
a strategic information system (SIS).

The resulting sets of characteristics concern required personnel, organizational culture, and the way of doing business. The personnel include key positions in an organization like the CEO, and prominent players such as *champions,* who do not occupy a formal
role in the introduction of SISs but carry out essential informal functions of overcoming
organizational hurdles. The organization's characteristics are either required attributes,
such as flexible information systems (ISs) management, or changes in organizational
policies, such as development of a strategic plan. The characteristics are classified as either
barriers or catalysts. Barriers like inflexible IS management should be eliminated; catalysts, such as strong technical expertise, must be encouraged.

Many of the issues raised in the chapter may be viewed from two distinct points of view, those of the organization and departments other than the IS group, and those of the IS group. For example, when the issue of tolerance is reviewed, it will be discussed from both points of view. Decision makers should consider both points of view when attempting to introduce an SIS into the organization.

The chapter is divided into six sections. The second section, following this introduction, includes a number of pertinent definitions. The definitions fully specify the environment, the scope of the SIS, and the terminology used. They are intended to prevent confusion that may arise from using ill-defined or vague terms, such as *management support.* The definitions are not limited to this section; several others are included throughout. In general, the chapter attempts to define terms when best suited. For example, a great deal has been written on the importance of the *SIS champion.* However, there is no agreed-upon definition of the term; it is invariably used to describe the role of the CEO, the CIO, as well as SIS sponsors. When discussing these roles and players, the chapter provides a definition of each.

The term *SIS introduction,* which is central to the chapter, encompasses recognizing the organization's need to change, the belief in an SIS as the most suitable vehicle for change, the activity associated with the introduction of an SIS into an organization, identification of an appropriate SIS, and its development and implementation.

The third section is devoted to the discussion of vision. *Vision* describes the organization's transformation to a technology-based one (some have claimed there is a lot of discussion about vision because people do not see the future clearly anymore). Vision signals the determination of management to move toward a technology-based system. A full section is devoted to vision to underscore its importance and to fully define it.

The fourth section discusses the roles of important players, including the CEO and CIO, who are together the driving force behind the organization's change process. The players are either identified by their official titles, such as CEO or CIO, or by the role they play, such as champion or sponsor. This distinction represents the belief that different people may play several roles, and that what is important is to recognize the tasks each player performs in the successful introduction of an SIS.

The fifth section continues the coverage of the required characteristics. However, it shifts the focus of the fourth section from individuals to departments and to the organization as a whole. It investigates the barriers, catalysts, and enhancers of SIS introduction.

The sixth section reviews the processes required to facilitate the introduction of an SIS, for instance, developing partnerships between the IS department and the rest of the organization. Although the importance of these processes is identified in other sections of the chapter, this section is concerned with how to implement them.

A brief conclusion summarizes and underscores major issues, and paints a clear picture of organizational requirements for the successful introduction of SISs.

One underlying theme must be clearly stated and understood. There is no unique answer or magic formula to insure the successful introduction of an SIS. Moreover, as Machiavelli said in *The Prince:*

It must be remembered that there is nothing more difficult to plan, more doubtful of success, nor more dangerous to manage than the creation of a new system. For the innovator has the enmity of all who would profit by the preservation of the old institutions and merely lukewarm defenders in those who would gain by the new ones.

The chapter includes findings from research projects, from case studies, and from field studies of organizations. Many of these findings deal with behavioral issues. A quick survey of social science research reveals that no two organizations are completely alike. Even if they are similar in terms of industry and size, they may be different in terms of maturity, and surely they will be different in terms of personnel and informal structure. One popular concept in ISs is fit. *Fit* deals with the question of whether a system matches the organization in terms of culture, norms, and other factors. It seems that the concept of fit was articulated to suggest that organizations are as unique as they are alike, and that it is the responsibility of management to choose among various alternative systems based on their fit with the organization and its culture. The manager contemplating the introduction of an SIS into the organization can use the insights and examples in the following sections to develop the necessary steps appropriate to the environment and to the fit of his or her organization, and then to implement them.

DEFINITIONS

SIS became one of the buzzwords in trade publications and academic research articles in the late 1980s. As is often the case, the preciseness of the term and associated activities has been lost. The following set of definitions clarify and limit the scope of SISs. The definitions pertain to two major questions: (1) what are strategic information systems, strategic systems, and systems with strategic potential? and (2) what is the difference between information and information technology?

Strategic Systems and Systems with Strategic Potential

The term *strategic information system* has been loosely used to describe a number of information technology (IT)–based applications. Although some information systems are defined as strategic by many writers, the same systems appear to be described ad nauseum. The term *strategic* has also been used to reflect cost or complexity of the system and not its *critical importance.* However, very rarely can a conventional inventory system, for example, be considered strategic, regardless of cost or complexity.

Information systems can be differentiated by the purpose of their development. Systems designed for strategic purposes, and those designed for operational and management purposes, may both be strategically useful. Information systems designed for strategic purposes include "those that are designed to bring about product or service differentiation, cost reduction in production for competitive purposes, or concentration on a particular market niche."[1] These include systems developed to support an intraorganizational strategy, a military strategy, or an electoral strategy. On the other hand, information systems with strategic potential include systems for operational and management purposes, such as an airline reservation system or an online customer order system, designed primarily to cut costs, that later evolve to create strategic advantages.

The latter type is prevalent in organizations, while few if any examples exist of the former. The dearth of strategic systems initially designed as such may be due to the difficulty of building them, the lack of practical experience, the high cost of these systems, and the difficulty of evaluating their impact.

A further issue significantly contributes to the rarity of truly strategic systems. A change of strategy results in a change in the organizational structure and work processes. This adjustment of structure and process is a dynamic process that occurs over time. A strategic system requires a level of knowledge of both the organizational structure and work processes. However, because both elements are expected to change, it is difficult to design a system based on future, and yet undetermined, changes.

The difference between strategic systems and systems that become strategic after development was noted by Max Hopper, American Airlines' IS senior vice president. Hopper stated that leaders became visionary after the fact, and that during the development of American Airlines' computerized reservation system, SABRE, "I was not trying to be visionary; I was trying to solve our business problems and the travel agent business problem." Indeed, American Airlines' computer-based frequent-flyer program was the result of a lunch discussion on how to improve customer service when an IS executive suggested combining two existing computerized tracking systems into the frequent-flyer program.[2]

The purpose of the above discussion is to include both *strategic systems* and *systems with strategic potential* under the SIS umbrella. It also underscores that most of what is labeled *strategic information systems* today started as operational or managerial control systems with some strategic potential.

Organizations going through a first-time introduction of an SIS should limit their activity to systems with strategic potential. To undertake the risk and cost of building a complex strategic system may prove to be detrimental to their efforts. It is also important to ensure that the system fits the organization. One cannot risk developing a system that would be rejected by the organization. Finally, the system developers must gain experience in developing strategic systems. It may be tempting to promise the moon, but it will be a disaster if nothing is delivered.

Another critical, albeit implicit, corollary of the discussion is the ability to identify some of the prerequisites of the SIS development process, discussed in a later chapter in greater detail. One such prerequisite is that the system developers must have a good understanding of the business. Almost all companies have systems for operational and managerial controls; hence, a legitimate question to ask is why some systems evolve to possess strategic importance while others do not. The answer to this question is simple— successful systems have a level of flexibility that allows users to identify systems' potential and designers to modify them to utilize a strategic potential. A good example is American Airlines frequent-flyer program, which was initially based on two tracking systems developed for other purposes. This level of system flexibility depends on the level of understanding of both the designers and developers of an SIS.

There is a difference between using information systems to create a *competitive advantage* and their use as a *strategic necessity.* The first type of utilization is aimed at achieving a sustainable competitive advantage to allow the organization a strategic advantage over its competitors. The second simply allows the organization to compete in the marketplace without giving it an advantage over competitors (i.e., it keeps the organization on a par with its competition).

This distinction, discussed in chapter eight, is subtle and dynamic. For example, early automatic teller machines may have been considered a competitive advantage, but today the same systems are no more than a competitive necessity. The strategic advantages of early systems are usually twofold: they have to do with the organization's reputation among its customers and its image as perceived by its employees. The reputation as a technology leader attracts customers who appreciate the flexibility generated by the new technology and it differentiates the technology leader from its competition. In addition, new technology can sometimes lock in customers to the organization. The organization's image as a technology leader can attract higher-caliber employees and also assist in stressing a culture that fosters innovation and technical solutions to complicated problems.

More important, this distinction plays a critical role in determining system success. The previously discussed concept of fit requires the system to fit the organization. If the organization's culture does not foster innovation, it may not be possible to successfully introduce an innovative system based on leading-edge technology. It may be preferable to limit the organization's effort to a system that only better fits the organization and allows it to stay competitive.

Use of Information versus Use of Information Technology

There is a distinction between information and information technology. *Information* is data processed for some use, whereas *information technology* is the hardware and software configuration used to collect and process the data. For example, American Hospital Supply Corporation used information technology to support their strategic use of information resources. The terminal in the customer's office tied them together, because the same information could have been collected by other means. On the other hand, information allowed Denny's coffee shop chain to successfully implement its guarantee of serving breakfast and lunch in fewer than ten minutes or giving it for free. Of course, an organization may use both. For example, American Airlines utilized both—software and hardware installed in travel agencies and the yield information collected by the SABRE system to support decisions about routes.

This distinction is extremely important when adopting the best vehicle to achieve a corporate objective. Denny's first and unsuccessful attempt to produce point-of-sale systems did not consider the cost of information technology.[3] Its second, and successful, attempt concentrated on using a fairly standard platform (i.e., IBM PC/AT). The use of the standard platform facilitated the software development, allowed for potential future migration of software to more advanced machines, and kept system cost low.

Another reason for the distinction is that each may strategically support different functions of the firm. In a 1989 survey, companies were asked to identify the various areas of applications where information and information technology might be strategically used.[4] The first area for both was customer service. Subsequent areas differed, with strategic information assisting in market segmentation, and information technology playing an important role in cost competitiveness. Henceforth, when we discuss introducing strategic information systems to an organization, we are not suggesting the latest hardware or software platform but a combination of hardware and software that best suits the organization.

VISION

Most IS scholars agree that *vision* is the most important characteristic for the successful introduction of strategic information systems.[5] Vision is defined as "a statement of how someone believes the future will be or how he or she wants the future to be."[6] For example, Boeing's vision in 1966 was "to get the right part in the right place at the right time."[7] In the 1980s their vision evolved to "creating an enhanced information stream." It is absolutely essential to have a vision. There is a tale in *Alice in Wonderland* about the caterpillar who asked Alice where she was going. When she said she did not know, the caterpillar said, "Then any road will take you there." And indeed, vision determines the road map by defining the destination.

To limit the definition of vision to a simple statement suggests a grave misunderstanding of both vision and SISs. A *corporate vision* is the go-ahead given by senior management to all concerned to transform the organization to a technology-based enterprise where information is perceived as an organizational resource. Similarly, an *IS vision* shows how IS will implement the corporate vision. Although the two may be different, the IS vision must guide the implementation of the corporate vision. For the transformation process, sometimes called *reengineering,* to succeed, the corporate vision must stand for a great deal more than a statement. Vision is a new climate in the organization that informs everyone of the need to change and fosters the appropriate changes. Vision is a new way of thinking, a new organizational structure, and a set of norms, culture, and procedures for a *specific organization.* Norms and culture are the unwritten laws; procedures are the written ones. The term *specific organization* is emphasized because the vision must take into account the available capabilities and characteristics of a given organization.

Vision signals the beginning of the transformation of the organization to one that is open for new ideas. It is *prospective* in that it reflects the organization's intention to survive using all possible tools. It is *anticipatory* in the sense that the organization is actively searching not just for solutions to existing problems but also for new technologies to provide it with advantage over competition. Finally it is *participatory* in that it is based on a team approach where all employees are invited to participate in either generating ideas, assessing approaches, or developing solutions empowered by the vision.

It must be stressed that if the vision does not *fit* the organization or is difficult to understand, it will not succeed. The important question is how to manage the change process so that the existing organization and the above characteristics fit.

IS vision includes the identification of an information systems–related problem area of a major concern to the organization. For example, when the U.S. Navy and the CEO of USAA (United States Automobile Association), a large automobile insurer, separately adopted their *paperless* office visions, both had in mind more than just the statement. For the navy, excessive documentation was a real problem. There are a great number of manuals and written procedures on board ships, as well as paper documents exchanged between ships and shore, and between the various departments. Documentation caused unnecessary waste of precious ship space and time consumed to retrieve a document.

To solve this problem, the navy embarked on an internal effort and sponsored external research projects. More concrete results have been achieved by USAA. The company introduced imaging technology, which required new partnerships. One partnership was developed with IBM to insure that the implemented solution becomes an IBM standard. The second partnership, within USAA, was among its departments to facilitate the assimilation of the new technology and insure that systems meet user requirements.

Vision is not creativity. Vision must be understood in terms of supporting the strategic use of information and the ability to identify opportunities. For example, Boeing's problem in 1966 was shortage of parts that affected airplane production—around 2,500 to 5,000 missing parts per month. That number was reduced to fewer than 100 by the middle 1970s.

Vision does not specify the solution to the problem. When Boeing developed their vision, or when the navy and USAA adopted "the paperless office" vision, no solutions were offered. Vision solicits a solution from others in the organization. In the environment of the early 1990s, use of computers is a foregone conclusion—the main reason why visions must be translated into strategic information systems.

It may be worthwhile to reflect, in conclusion, on what some call the *vision that changed the world.* Since the development of atomic weapons, the balance of power in the world has been based on a simple, albeit horrifying, concept: mutual assured destruction guaranteed that no superpower could launch a first strike without being destroyed itself. In other words, each superpower stockpiled enough weapons to insure it could survive a first strike and launch its own attack to destroy the enemy (and possibly the world).

This balance continued until President Reagan announced a new vision. Instead of limiting strategy to the destruction of the enemy, he sought to insure the safety of the country (i.e., its ability to defend against any incoming missiles). The new vision, called *Strategic Defense Initiative* (SDI) by some and *Star Wars* by others, changed the balance of the competition.

In an era characterized by scarce funds, SDI meant long-term reduction in the funds required to sustain the mutual assured destruction concept. It also presented new challenges to the other superpower to keep pace with the possible technological breakthrough expected from this concept. It changed the relations between the various branches of the military, and between the U.S. military and friendly forces. The list of effects is fairly long, but the result is simple. SDI meant a new type of superpower, new internal structure, and external relations.

Vision, again, is a signal that suggests the beginning of a change; it also states where this change should start.

Who Creates the IS Vision?

Vision must transcend its creator. Tying the vision to one person will simply result in its demise if the person leaves the organization. Vision affects the organization's structure and processes. As such, regardless of who creates the vision, it must be supported by and communicated to the organization by top management.

This does not necessarily mean that top management has to develop the vision. In certain cases, the chief information officer (CIO) is in a better position to assess the technology, future developments, and how the technology can support the organization. Knowledge of technology, however, is a necessary but insufficient condition for creating an IS vision. A thorough understanding of the business and its problems is mandatory. The vision creator must first be knowledgeable about the business, the organization, and industry trends. The technology expertise is secondary in that the vision must be achievable; in other words, the technology must be available to allow the vision to be implemented.

Executives outside the information system group may be able to create the organization's IS vision if they have the required technical expertise, either individually or as a group of executives. The OTISLINE system, the SIS implemented by the Otis Elevator company (described in chapter five) was guided by a vision created by a non-IS executive: "When elevators are running well, people do not notice them. . . . Our objective is to go unnoticed" (Bob Smith, executive VP and CEO, Otis Elevator North American Division). In other cases, an outside consultant may be better prepared to assist in creating the vision. Outsiders are not besieged by the business problem and may offer a fresh look at problems.

The vision creator must be credible, be able to convince others of the organization's ability to implement the vision, be able to explain the vision and technology, and be able to sell the vision to superiors, peers, subordinates, as well as the rest of the organization. As Roger Smith, General Motors's CEO, once contemplated, "I sure wish I'd done a better job of communicating [my vision] with GM people."[8]

It doesn't matter who the vision creator is as long as the vision is supported by top management. What is important is the creator's knowledge of the business and the technology. Another lesson repeated throughout this chapter is that there is no one correct way to follow. The determining factors include the culture and norms of the organization, the relations among its various executives, and other behavioral factors.

How to Create a Vision

Visions may be created by studying the present or forecasting the future. Studying the present involves studying the organization, identifying weak links and areas of possible improvements, and discussing possibilities with others inside and outside the organization. As areas of possible improvements begin to emerge, the vision creator develops approaches for changes and discusses these approaches with technical staff. In other words, vision is not a revelation, it is a revolution in the making. In the words of Max Hopper, "creating a vision simply means solving a business problem."[9]

Forecasting the future involves studying trends in information technology, as well as business trends. It also involves studying shifts in these trends. As trends materialize, alternative visions can be developed to deal with and support the organization's objectives.

How to Implement the Vision

Whatever means are used in creating the vision, the next step is to sell it to the organization. Although the issue of selling an SIS is discussed in greater detail later, a number of points are worth considering here. The first is that selling is an art. If you don't feel able to do it, find a better salesperson. Selling means negotiating and forming alliances. The art of bartering is as old as humanity, and it is prevalent in selling. Finally, to believe that people will immediately accept what one may consider the most important vision is a mistake. Sometimes, an initial failure is just one step toward success.

Second, a successful sale is just an early milestone that must be followed by a great deal of effort. The organization must translate the vision into a set of systems, a new culture, and a number of organizational changes. It must overcome procedural, behavioral, and structural obstacles. The translation process includes the definition and development of the necessary SISs and the management of the organizational change. Boeing's "to get the right part in the right place at the right time" was translated into more than 15 major IS projects as well as a number of organizational changes.

Managing organizational change is a difficult task. It covers identifying new work processes, selling them to employees, and implementing them. As J. Singleton, vice-chairman of Security Pacific National Bank in California and CEO of its IS unit commented in 1991, "The first thing a bank can do is to stop automating obsolete manual processes. You can't take an existing paper-processing method and simply automate it."[10] To suggest that developing new ways of doing business is easy skirts the issue. It is easy to propose transplanting approaches that succeeded in other organizations, or even other countries. However, such a recommendation disregards the important concept of fit. There is a difference in cultures between organizations and in work force homogeneity. The change must fit the organization (contrary to the adage, grass is greenest where it is watered, not in the neighbor's yard).

To sum up, vision implementation entails a great deal of effort. Within that, three activities are of paramount importance—selling the vision, developing appropriate SIS applications, and managing organizational change. The remainder of the chapter revisits these processes, after first identifying the key players in the SIS introduction process.

MAIN PLAYERS

The successful introduction of an SIS to an organization requires the support of major players who perform critical tasks. Players may be classified in terms of their system role or in terms of their organizational position. Sponsor, champion, and opinion leader are examples of system roles. The CEO and the CIO are examples of organizational positions.

Overlap can exist between the organizational positions and the system roles. Several roles may be played by one person and such a person may occupy different positions in different companies.

The Chief Executive Officer (CEO)

The CEO is a major player in the introduction of an SIS. He or she must not only approve the IS vision but also support the expected organizational transformation. Supporting the vision means agreeing that information must be treated as a resource, that a certain SIS is the best possible vehicle to support the IS vision, and that the problem identified is a major business problem. It also means understanding and supporting the organizational changes that will result from the introduction of the SIS. The IS literature has plenty of examples of failed systems owing to lack of management support. One should stress that lack does not necessarily mean disapproval; mere indifference is sufficient reason for failure.

Need for support of top management is evident in almost all system implementation studies. However, no clear definition is given for what support means or entails. For instance, there is a distinction between executive involvement and participation.[11] *Involvement* is concerned with how the executive feels, or believes in the importance of an issue to the organization. As such it is a perception, but it is not a description of how actively the executive participates in the process. *Participation,* on the other hand, is concerned with actual behavior and time spent on the activity. It seems that while executive involvement is sufficient for successful introduction of conventional systems, participation is required for the SIS introduction.

As previously mentioned, the introduction of an SIS in an organization requires a change in culture, norms, and work processes. The executive support of these changes is of vital importance. To change a culture of an organization requires more than mere words. An example is the state of shock the military inflicts on conscripts by shaving their heads and other policies that expose them to the new life-style. Although we do not subscribe to introducing the same measures in organizations, top management must clearly stand behind the cultural changes (albeit some executives are born to companies they cannot change).

The CEO is in a position that allows her or him to insure that the vision is developed and executed. More importantly, the CEO is responsible for choosing the right person(s) to carry out this task. In some cases, the IS manager may not be well equipped for the job. A 1990 survey of Booz, Allen and Hamilton suggests that as "Chief executive officers are waking up to the strategic imperative of information systems . . . they will find many IS organizations embarrassed and unprepared." Only 30% of CIOs and CEOs surveyed in the study shared the same understanding of one another's position, role, and viewpoint to function together as a team.[12]

As a CEO who was once a successful CIO in a major utility once remarked, the criteria normally used for choosing an IS manager do not support the desire for change that must characterize the right person for implementing an SIS.[13] The same notion is supported by research that shows IS people are not inherently qualified to develop strategic information systems, because they are too entrenched in traditional data processing activities (sort of "we have met the enemy and they is us").[14]

The Chief Information Officer (CIO)

The CIO is a fairly new title that has replaced the title of director or manager of information systems in some organizations. Some organizations have developed other titles or kept the old ones. As the head of the IS group, the CIO is responsible for much more than managing conventional or even strategic information systems developments. Scanning the environment to determine new technologies that may benefit the company, testing the various possibilities, and selling to top management promising projects are some of the new responsibilities of this position. More than selling to top management, the CIO is responsible for educating top management and the organization. The CIO is the catalyst who insures a smooth transition into the information age.

In addition, the CIO must work on positioning the IS function as a proactive technology partner (provided, of course, that the notion that like all true professionals, the CIO is often wrong but seldom in doubt, is erroneous). IS must participate by suggesting new systems, instead of limiting its efforts to developing requested systems. This requires a deep understanding of both the existing and future technology and the business. Furthermore, the CIO must develop partnerships with the rest of the organization. The CIO is a powerful means for ISs to understand the business and for the organization to understand the technology.

Finally, the CIO is responsible for ensuring that the required infrastructure is available in the organization. Technologies such as networks, personal computers and large mainframes, telecommunications, and others are needed for the SIS development. More important, a good infrastructure of conventional information systems is a must. Conventional systems play two important roles: they introduce computers into organizations, and they are the data collection points for SISs.

Some observers have suggested that the CIO role will be eliminated in the future. The 1990 survey mentioned above suggested a more actively involved non-IS senior executive serving as a CIO.[15] In the same survey, the CIOs expressed their belief that their position would evolve in the next decade to a chief technology officer or would be absorbed by the ranks of line managers.

In any case, the role of a CIO must exist in one form or another, because the CIO, or a similar player, must assist in the organization's growth in the IS area. Organizations develop incrementally, not through acts of nature or mutation. The CIO is the gatekeeper and the educator for smooth growth, whatever the change in job description, as elaborated by Vincent Swoyer, vice president of corporate systems at Sara Lee: "The CIO role is changing from a technology-oriented position to a business-driven one. We used to look for ways to apply technology; now we look for business problems and then seek to solve them."[16]

Some organizations have not separated the IS function and the technology development and introduction function (i.e., the IS group is responsible for all computerized systems in the organization). The information systems group responsibility may then extend to the development of an SIS. Organizations find this role of an IS group to be incompatible with the introduction of an SIS.

A CEO with IS background, reflecting on the traditional role of the head of information systems group, noted, under what he called "managerial discontinuity":

> Many IS managers are confused about what is expected of them and why they can not succeed in today's environment when they have been successful in the past. . . . IS managers have traditionally dealt with highly structured ideas, e.g., systems and logic, and structured things, e.g., computers and programming languages . . . we have selected our IS managers according to their ability to deal successfully and consistently with a relatively structured environment, and only secondarily according to their ability to deal with people. . . . we have rewarded them when they have brought order from chaos. Now we expect these same people to suddenly jump to handling complex, unstructured business problems, command them to address such esoteric concepts as strategic advantage of information.[17]

The traditional image of the IS group may hinder the proper execution of the role. Some organizations have separated the activities of traditional system development and SIS introduction into two separate groups. The new group has been given different names such as *technology transfer, information technology unit, emerging technology unit,* and the like.

SIS Champions and Sponsors

An important player in the successful introduction of strategic information systems is the SIS champion. *SIS champions* are "managers at fairly high levels of the organization who take on the responsibility of shepherding an information technology innovation project through the development process. They differ from sponsors in that they lack the funds and authority to accomplish their goals."[18] Champions are able to work around the organizational problems that may develop owing to changes introduced by the IS project. They also are able to cut through the bureaucracy of reviews and rational investment decision processes. In a way, the IS champion can do things the CIO alone cannot, in terms of the shoemaker's (CIO's) kids running around barefoot.

Champions fight for the introduction of the SIS and should be supported by the IS group. However, this support is not always forthcoming. Champions tend to seek change in IS priorities to alter the allocation of personnel or equipment (e.g., postpone other IS projects for the sake of their own, or bypass standard procedures like project evaluation). The next section discusses the causes of the rift between champions and the IS group.

SIS sponsors may be information systems champions who control a budget and have the requisite authority to expend it. However, in most organizations, a similar title denotes those who have control over the budget without necessarily playing the champion role. The distinction between a champion and a sponsor is important. Having the funds and the authority to support the development of an SIS does not make a sponsor a champion. To play this role, the sponsor has to convince the rest of the organization of the importance of the SIS project. This includes overcoming resistance to change and fostering the required change in culture.

Opinion Leaders

Opinion leaders actively participate in forming the organization's opinion of an information system. They are normally outside the IS group, respected by their peers, and play a role in developing the perception of the system by users. A positive perception may give a poorly developed system greater tolerance, and a negative perception may give an excellent system no chance of survival.

Because of the importance of their role for the success of the system, the SIS developers must actively seek opinion leaders who are supportive of their effort. Opinion leaders should be involved in the project development phase. Their involvement, more often than not, will result in their blessing and in turn their support.

End Users

Operators and managers at all levels constitute an important yet either forgotten or misunderstood factor in SIS development. It was argued earlier that vision is not creativity. Vision sets the stage on which others develop ideas on how to implement it. James Martin remarked, "End Users with information center tools need to be encouraged to explore how they can use computing strategically."[19]

End users are an important source of ideas to translate the vision into reality. They are also the main system utilizer; on their acceptance hinges its success or failure. Research, as well as actual case studies, suggest that end users and new employees who are not bogged down with constraints and apprehensions generate more creative ideas than senior managers. As an example, the IS manager for a major talent agency revealed that the idea for the agency's SIS came from an unknown temporary employee.[20]

Most of the discussion in this section has concentrated on the characteristics of the individuals needed for the successful development and implementation of an SIS. It has been observed that during organizational changes and upheavals, the tasks and roles of each position change. New positions are created, existing individuals require new tasks, while others change their roles. The process of identifying appropriate individuals who will play roles during the expected organizational change is no easy task. Care should be exercised in looking for the individuals' characteristics instead of their positions in the organization.

BARRIERS AND CATALYSTS

Real-life attempts to introduce SISs into organizations provide helpful insights in identifying several factors that either support or hinder the effort. These factors, labeled here *barriers* and *catalysts,* are organizational characteristics that enhance or reduce the possibility of system success. They cover behavioral as well as technical aspects and pertain to the organization, departments within it, and individuals. The previous section dealt with the required characteristics of individuals. This section focuses on the existing departmental and organizational characteristics. Before reviewing barriers and catalysts, we discuss a class of characteristics unique to some organizations.

Enhancers are characteristics of organizations that are, or strive to be, leaders in their fields. It is unrealistic to suggest that all organizations should be leaders. Leadership is a function of an organization's size and culture. However, because of the importance of the enhancers, at least as characteristics to develop over time, some of the major ones are briefly reviewed.

Four important organizational enhancers are openness, future orientation, anticipation, and participation. *Openness* stands for the organization's acceptance of new ideas from internal and external sources. It also describes the ability to the organization to scan the environment in search of new technology and potential problems. *Future orientation* stands for the organization's belief that it continuously changes because the market changes, the competition changes, and the technology changes. As such, decisions made by a future-oriented organization deal with current problems as well as future conditions.

Anticipation refers to an organization that does not wait until conditions change. It actively seeks solutions to anticipated problems and searches for new solutions. This sometimes entails experimentation with new and unproven technology. Finally, the organization must be *participatory*. This characteristic refers to a team approach as the organization's way of doing business. It also includes encouraging new ideas from all sources. Finally, it includes training of all employees in various aspects of the business.

The remainder of this section covers barrier and catalyst characteristics. These may pertain to the IS department, to other departments, or to the organization as a whole. The distinction is important because the appropriate attempts to affect each characteristic may differ by department. For example, when addressing resistance to change, there is the IS department's resistance to change, as well as the organization's resistance to change. The IS resistance to change may be reduced by searching for outside support, such as consultants or outsourcing. The organization's resistance to change may be remedied by greater participation.

Climate

The introduction of an SIS in an organization entails the implementation of radical changes. For an organization to accept changes, there must be a realization of the need to change. This realization normally exists during crises or similar situations. At such times, resistance to change is minimal and the organization is open to new ideas. Recent years have seen increased competition, massive layoffs, and cost-cutting mechanisms. All these conditions present opportunities to the organization to start the change process.

Technical Expertise

The IS department's technical expertise is a strong facilitator, and its absence is a strong inhibitor. The IS group, assuming that there is no environmental scanning group, is responsible for environmental scanning to identify new technologies and their potential advantages to the firm.

One example underscoring the importance of the IS department's expertise occurred in a large construction firm. The firm was one of the first to acquire an IBM system 38, a system built around relational database technology. The hardware system acquisition meant conversion of existing applications, which were designed to use traditional flat files. The lack of database experience within the IS group resulted in a conversion effort that kept the flat file approach, as well as duplication of data elements.

One possible mitigation of this barrier is to hire outside expertise to assist in training the IS group or developing systems. Another is encouraging current IS employees to pursue professional education. A third is developing a partnership with a university IS program to supervise strategic systems development. More than once in this chapter it has been suggested that new ideas come from users. Hence, it is important to ensure that employees are familiar with new developments.

Relations Between the IS Department and the Organization

As was previously mentioned, the IS department is the most technically qualified group to develop an SIS. Technical qualification is a necessary but not a sufficient condition for introducing an SIS. Technical competence is required for the actual development effort but does not play an important role in the processes that take place before development, or during implementation.

The interpersonal relationships among the CIO and other top officers are extremely important. For the organization to accept the system, the CIO must have excellent relations with other members of senior management. Questions such as whether the CIO is considered part of top management or an outsider, or even questions such as how the organization perceives the title of CIO are important. A 1988 study found that the title creates animosity in the organization.[21] It was disliked by the CIO, who considered it pompous, and by other business managers, who tried their best to "turn his life into misery."

Prior to the actual development of an SIS, a vision must be created and accepted by the organization. It is also important to choose an appropriate problem(s). In order for the IS department to assist in these activities, it must be accepted by the organization. Acceptance depends on a number of factors including the quality of the previously developed systems; the knowledge by the IS group of the business; the interpersonal relations between the IS group and the rest of the organization; the image of the IS group and its political clout; and whether the manager of the IS department is considered by top managers to be one of them.

Researchers identified three types of IS departments based on the probability of a successful introduction of an SIS, the characteristics of each type, as well as the prevalent characteristics of the CIO.[22] *Exploiters* are IS departments with a culture open to the introduction of SISs. The CIO is one of the "in" managers, with a tenure of at least ten years in the organization, who knows the business well. The same is true with regard to the reputation of the IS group. Knowledge of the business creates trust between the IS department and the organization. It also allows for much stronger interpersonal relations between the individuals in the IS and in the rest of the organization, which in turn facilitates the transformation process.

Competitors are IS departments that are not leaders in the field but are not far behind. The CIO tenure is shorter than in exploiters, over five years, and he or she does not know the business well. This type of IS group should not attempt to develop an innovative SIS without careful planning.

Participants have CIOs with an extremely short tenure, who are not familiar with the business. This type of IS group should not attempt to introduce an SIS without assistance from experts or before developing other important programs to gain acceptance, such as partnerships with other functional departments.

Acceptance is a cultural issue, not a professional assessment of the IS department. Several organizations have attempted to insure the acceptance of the IS group by forming partnerships with various departments and by developing programs of rotating IS employees in other departments and non-IS employees in the IS department. Nissan, Boeing, and DuPont developed such programs that not only increased the IS group's understanding of the business but also created the type of interpersonal relations that was paramount for the success of their SISs.

One catalyst for the success of an SIS is an organization's climate—an awareness among employees that a change is needed when an organization faces problems. Some researchers argue the importance of climate for the success of SIS; others state that the IS department's maturity can substitute for climate.[23] *Maturity* is thorough understanding of the business environment. This issue was recognized by practitioners as well as researchers.[24]

The Intolerance to Change

Intolerance to change applies to the IS department as well as to the rest of the organization. Intolerance on the part of the IS group is important because this group is responsible for scanning the environment to identify new technologies and for developing the system design. The intolerance of the IS group may leave the organization in the dark until it is too late to catch up with the competition. It also may cause the system failure not only because of poor design but also because of lack of support, and of negative perception of the new system by other departments.

Introducing any information system to an organization results in a number of changes. At the very least there should be changes in the way of conducting business. Without such changes, the new information system becomes an additional expense with no benefits. Intolerance on the part of the organization is manifested in its resistance to meeting the changes mandated by the requirements of the new information system. There is no doubt that several factors other than intolerance may result in the same level of resistance to change. These can include bureaucracy, size, culture, and the like.

Cost–Benefit Issues

The organization's focus on short-term profits is often translated into little or no concern for long-term information systems benefits. SIS development is a commitment that may not be justified using the conventional cost–benefit analysis. A successful SIS entails organizational changes and includes added flexibility that may be difficult to quantify. Additionally, sometimes the benefit of the SIS is achieved after the organization has had a chance to use the system. This was the case in two of the most widely publicized SISs—American Airlines' SABRE and American Hospital Supply Corporation's ASAP system.

A second factor that hinders the development of an SIS is the charge-back system often used by IS departments. Frequently, IS is unwilling to develop without a sponsor; simultaneously, sponsoring departments are not willing to invest unless there are immediate or short-term paybacks. An SIS benefits the whole organization and should be sponsored by the organization instead of by individual departments.

To resolve these issues, several organizations have set aside special research and development budgets earmarked for the IS group. Other organizations have developed unique approaches. For example, in one organization, the IS group is responsible for the development of a pilot study and then the system is sold (or not) to other departments.

Excessive Rationalism and Bureaucracy

Rationalism in this context means erecting barriers to the development of innovative systems.[25] To require cost–benefit analysis of a new SIS covering uncharted territory, or even one that adds flexibility, may mean an early death of the system. At some point, the organization should agree to experiment. Some IS industry observers suggested that a better measure of SIS effectiveness should be the degree of its alignment with business objectives.

Bureaucracy exists in all organizations and departments. This is true for the IS department as well as the rest of the organization. As mentioned earlier, champions who play an important role in the successful introduction of an SIS cut through the bureaucracy to push their vision forward. But this can cause a problem with the IS group. Research found that in the majority of systems, IS planning and project selection procedures were either purposely circumvented or ignored.[26]

Inappropriate Incentives

Inappropriate incentives can become a barrier to the development of an SIS. Creative or complex systems take a long time and cost more, while most employee incentive systems are based on quarterly, annual, or other periodical schemes. This disparity discourages IS professionals from working on long-term projects in favor of the shorter and more rewarding ones.

Incentive is but one side of the equation. Creative SIS projects are risky and may fail. If the organization does not support innovative personnel who stumble, it is likely that few will try. Merrill Lynch's executive vice president DuWayne Peterson underscored the importance of this point when he observed in 1991 that "the worst thing is a culture where people who fail are killed and thrown out the door."[27]

A separate but related point concerns the disposition of personnel who may be affected by a system success. If success adversely affects the livelihood of peers and co-workers or demands more from them, fewer ideas may be generated. Classical time-

and-motion studies reflected workers' apprehension about performing, owing to misconceptions as to the outcome.

Planning for SIS

SIS planning is as important as the end product. Planning covers several elements—vision implementation, problem selection, project development, project implementation, and personnel training. Denny's initial attempt to introduce point-of-sale equipment failed because of poor planning. As John Wooden, the famous UCLA basketball coach, said, "failing to plan is planning to fail."

The organization must plan for the priority and sequence of SIS projects. To suggest that one can develop all systems simultaneously taxes the organization's limited resources and may result in failure. The initial problem must be small enough to insure successful implementation and an improved IS image. Yet it must be large enough to benefit the organization. Finally, it must be important enough to improve the IS. Another possibility is to divide a large problem into smaller ones, start with one, and finish the rest later.

Planning must fit the organization's culture and characteristics. For example, if the organization is informal in structure or in its general planning activities, then insistence on a very formal planning process may prove to be a mistake.

As part of the planning, whether formal or informal, a group must be established that is responsible for scanning the environment and examining new ideas that are not part of the formal IS plan. *Environmental scanning* is scanning the environment to identify available technology, as well as business trends, to identify potential problems and opportunities. The new ideas may also be generated by end users. The scanning group may also assist SIS champions in their endeavors.

Management Support

Active involvement and participation of the organization's management is vital. As previously mentioned, strong support with active involvement without looking over the IS department's shoulders is the best environment for success. Lack of support may cause the system's demise. A 1990 case study compared two SIS development efforts in two similar financial service organizations developed by two technical groups that were very similar.[28] The outcomes of the two efforts were completely opposed. Lack of management support and the negative political climate in one organization caused the system to fail. In the second organization, strong management support overcame the various obstacles introduced by stakeholders and the system succeeded.

Power and Politics in the Organization

This inhibitor is considered by both IS and functional managers to be one of the most important barriers to implementing strategic information systems. An SIS will change the way organizations do business. It will result in power shifts, in eliminating positions, and in redefining work processes. The previously mentioned example, regarding the introduction of database technology based on an IBM system 38 in a construction firm, can be used as a case study for power and politics within an organization. One of the main objectives of a database system is to consolidate identical data elements into one, thus ensuring the integrity of the elements. However, several of the applications used by the firm were sponsored by different departments. Each department insisted on keeping its own data files and did not accept the notion of other departments accessing them. As a result, the data administration group had to develop a computer program to update the scattered copies of the various data elements across applications. Each evening, the program, which took few hours to run, updated every copy of each data element. An SIS cannot survive intrigues. It is the responsibility of top management to ensure that the strategic system is supported and accepted by the organization.

Clarity of Objective

Earlier in the chapter, it was clearly stated that the vision must be communicated to the organization. This statement is reiterated here with the additional emphasis that clarity is an important factor in the success or failure of a strategic system. Clarity is not only simplicity and applicability of the vision; it extends to all the activities discussed in this chapter. Clarity is also making sure the organization knows that top management supports the project and the resulting changes.

PROCESSES

Throughout this chapter, several recommendations have been presented without any guidelines on how to implement them. This section defines and explains some guidelines. The issues discussed include how to measure the cost of an SIS, how to build a partnership with other groups in the organization, how to support the SIS champion, and how to sell the SIS approach to management.

The Economic Justification of an SIS

One cannot measure the feasibility of an SIS with conventional methods. Information and strategic information systems are organizational resources supporting corporate objectives and must be treated as such. The organization must measure the benefits realized from the resources. They should be measured in terms of business objectives supported by the SIS.

After measuring the value of the business objectives, the next step is to measure how the investment in an SIS supports the achievement of the objective. Attaching the SIS to business objectives makes it easier to review the investment as part of the normal review process of the various business functions.

The notion of measuring the benefit of business objectives versus system's cost is not new. In previous studies of investment in information systems, the most successful companies in technology utilization were those that aligned the information system's objectives with the business objectives.

Partnerships

Vision is not sufficient to insure that investments in strategic information systems will yield significant organizational benefits. Failure to achieve goals is often the result of the inability to integrate the technological infrastructure into the mainstream of the firm.[29]

One frequently used method to overcome this barrier is building intraorganizational partnerships. Partnerships between IS and other departments are a common approach to achieving several objectives. They reduce organizational resistance to change by involving other departments in the system development; they improve system quality because knowledgeable business and technical experts are involved in the design of the system; they increase the understanding by the IS department of the business and by the organization of the technology and SIS. In addition, a partnership is a good source of new and creative ideas for vision implementation and a prelude to the team-based approach discussed earlier.

Both DuPont and Boeing developed an extensive training program to involve non-IS personnel in IS classes and activities. Nissan has developed a similar manager rotation program. IS project development teams in a number of Japanese companies include representatives from various pertinent groups in the organization.

Partnerships can also be formed between the organization and the outside, which allow the organization to concentrate on its strong points while soliciting assistance from other organizations in their fields of expertise. On a larger scale, for an excellent example of partnerships one may examine the coordination among the various armed forces from the countries that took part in the 1991 Gulf War. If a partnership between countries seems farfetched for some, maybe the 20,000 partnerships IBM has with various businesses may drive the importance of the point closer to home.

How to Support the SIS Champion?

In spite of the important role played by champions, many IS managers see them from a different perspective. Champions, who are cutting through the organization's bureaucracy, disrupt IS plans and schedules. They may ask IS to postpone some projects in order to support theirs, or give up computer time and capacity for their own favorite applications. This interference is sometimes aggravated by the personal characteristics of those IS managers who are accustomed to structured problem solving and to dealing with machines and technical issues as opposed to people.

The IS manager is faced with the important decision of whether to support champions or to become an obstacle in the way of introducing an SIS. This question is more rhetorical than it initially seems. An SIS must be introduced for the well-being of the organization. Few individuals, whether SIS champions or IS managers, can do it alone. Cooperation and coordination among concerned individuals are of utmost importance, and their absence may cause more harm to the future of the organization. In other words, the IS department should be the incubator for the champion's vision. As such, the question should be how to support champions without degrading the quality of IS outputs.

Champions require three categories of resources to perform their innovative work: *information*—to evaluate, choose, and sell an innovation; *material resources*—to obtain the necessary information; and *political support*—to guarantee both the information and material resources.[30] Various means can be used by the IS department to support champions.

IS managers can assist champions by explaining how information technology in general, and the specific SIS in particular, will help the organization. They can also assist by explaining what the benefits, costs, risks, and expected changes associated with the introduction of SIS are, and how to investigate and test various approaches. It is also important to describe to the champions the existing IS application portfolio and the data gathered by the various applications. A final point in the first category, *information,* is sharing with the champion the experience of the IS department in introducing new systems to the organization—what cultural and organizational hurdles need to be tackled, what approaches have succeeded in the past, and the like.

Under the second category, two support mechanisms are important—hardware and software—and technical staff to assist in assessing the various alternative configurations. Finally, the IS department should legitimize the role of the champions by supporting their claims about the technology.

One question for which there is no single answer is how the IS department can identify legitimate champions. One company's experience may assist IS managers in finding an answer. Aetna Life and Casualty, the big financial services company, has a corporate Technology Planning Group responsible for identifying breakthrough IS projects, that is, projects with at least 100% performance increase.[31] The group sponsors workshops for end users and publishes papers on specific technologies. Their goal is to identify projects and associated champions.

Potential Applications Portfolio Management

The diversity of SIS applications and an organization's attempt to simultaneously introduce several of them may result in duplication of effort. Furthermore, the chapter has suggested that the IS department will benefit from uniting SIS champions and users. One approach to achieving these objectives is to build a centralized repository of SIS applications and their stakeholders.

The repository should include data on current as well as past attempts to develop applications. The term *applications* includes all suggestions and requests from end users, user-developed applications, experimentation with technologies, as well as acquired applications. For each, the repository should include a list of sponsors, champions, potential users, developers, type of technology used, disposition, and reasons for the disposition. In other words, the repository represents a computerized organizational memory.

How to Sell an SIS to Top Management

There are several reasons for the lack of top management support for strategic information systems (one may claim that "war is too important to be left to the generals"). These include lack of awareness or lack of familiarity with information technology and its capabilities. Top management normally understands and observes traditional systems as opposed to strategic systems. There also may be a credibility gap. Top management may not believe that computers can play a strategic role. The IS manager is usually perceived as a technical expert, not a business expert. Top management may not view information as a business resource. They also may demand a financial justification using traditional methods such as cost–benefit analysis. Finally, top management may be action-oriented, with preference for immediate instead of long-term developments.

To overcome these problems, top management must be convinced of the importance of strategic information systems. Training sessions, whether organized by an outside agency or by the IS group, are one method to achieve this objective. Another idea is to advertise the achievements of the IS group. Actions speak louder than words, and if the IS group has a good track record, it must be marketed. Besides marketing the achievements of the IS group, an attempt can be made to add a business image to the group image. Finally, potential users of the SIS must be involved in the selling. Support from users, champions, and sponsors must be sought. An alliance of the IS department with important potential stakeholders could be formed to present a unified approach.

It is also important to use the success stories of other companies to underscore the need for strategic systems in order to stay competitive. In addition to successes, it is helpful to note the demise of competitors who did not develop and use information as a competitive resource.

CONCLUSIONS

Eddie Cantor once said it takes 20 years to make an overnight success. This chapter has outlined what it takes to succeed in introducing an SIS into an organization. The pertinent factors may be individually appreciated, but all must be considered to succeed. Furthermore, they are not autonomous but individual pieces in a jigsaw puzzle. Without seeing the total picture, one will not be able to efficiently piece the puzzle together.

An organization must have a vision, which must pertain to two issues—the first shared by all enterprises, the second organization-specific. First, companies must start using information as a resource. In today's environment, with the availability of information technologies, this resource must be provided by strategic information systems. The utilization of this resource adds flexibility and ability to change in order to meet changing market demands. The flexibility is created because of reduction in the number of human communication channels or middle-level management, and because of the redesign of the work processes to benefit from the information.

Second, vision must improve the company's current position. Not only will the company reap financial benefits and stand to compete better with other firms but will also convince its employees of the importance of the vision. The difference in vision shared by USAA and the U.S. Navy is subtle but fundamental. To USAA it meant a better way of doing business. To the navy, the benefits were not as drastic because the problem was not a basic business problem; a paperless office does not improve the fighting capability of the navy.

Vision creation demands a thorough understanding of the business by those who are IS-knowledgeable and comprehension of IS concepts and technologies by corporate managers. The importance of this prerequisite cannot be overstated. Information is a resource;

all must understand how to manipulate and benefit from it. Information system specialists must be knowledgeable about the business. More and more organizations are recruiting CIOs with backgrounds in other than ISs. Few IS trade publications today are void of familiar management terms such as Porter's value chain and other frameworks.

Vision implementation is the first step in the organization's change process. The vision must be supported by top management and communicated to all the organization. When Roger Smith, General Motors's CEO, regretted his inability to communicate his vision, he was identifying one cause for GM's problems. Communication is just one aspect—visions must be simple enough for all to understand, and important enough for all to believe in.

When terms such as *business experts* or *IS-knowledgeable* are used, they do not refer to senior personnel only, nor to veteran employees of the organization. Creative and innovative solutions, more often than not, originate from those who are not bogged down by the organization's culture. The implementation must include all possible personnel. These must have a vehicle to express their ideas and be aware that the organization is unmistakably searching for and is open to SIS ideas.

The next step is the search for the applications. An SIS is not a solution searching for a problem. Business problems exist; the question is which problem should be tackled next. Whether it is the paperless office, the right part in the right place at the right time, or any of the other visions discussed earlier, the problems are there. If the organization does not start implementing the solution, it will end up on the losing end.

SIS applications cannot be developed using solely prevailing work processes but must develop new processes. These must be built around information as a resource. They also must consider the linkage between the organization and the environment. Finally, they should not be limited by frameworks that constrain the imagination. Although this is easier said than done, when the organization's survival is at stake, everything else is secondary.

This chapter contains a great deal of do's and dont's, and recommendations that may cost precious dollars. It suggests that the organization must change but does not guarantee that change will benefit the organization. It does ostensibly violate the adage, "If it ain't broke, don't fix it." Recent history suggests that something is amiss in this adage and that a better one may be, "If it ain't broke, why not improve it?" The experience of the steel industry and automobile manufacturers in the late 1980s presents evidence that stagnation is costly. It is possible that the same adage was used by steel industry executives when they refused to adopt new technology developed in-house, while selling the same technology to other countries, thus assisting in their own demise.

REFERENCES

1. King, J., and Kraemer, K., "Implementation of Strategic Information Systems," in K. Lauden and J. Turner, *Information Technology and Management Strategy.* Englewood Cliffs, N.J.: Prentice-Hall, 1989.

2. Rifkin, G., "IS Executives Must Put Their Vision to Work, Speakers Urge," *Computerworld* (May 27, 1991).

3. Krause, C., "In Depth: Denny's POS Effort," *Computerworld* (May 27, 1991).

4. King, W., Grover, V., and Hufnagel, E., "Using Information and Information Technology for Sustainable Competitive Advantage: Some Empirical Evidence," in K. Lauden and J. Turner, *Information Technology and Management Strategy.*

5. See, for example, Primozic, K., Primozic, F., and Leben, J., *Strategic Choices.* New York: McGraw-Hill, 1991.

6. McNurlin, B., and Sprague, R., *Information Systems Management in Practice,* 2nd ed. Englewood Cliffs, N.J.: Prentice-Hall, 1989.

7. "Creating a Vision and Selling It," *I/S Analyzer* (Sept. 1988).

8. Primozic, Primozic, and Leben, *Strategic Choices.*

9. Rifkin, "IS Executives Must Put Their Vision to Work."

10. Singleton, J., "Technology Gets Top Priority at Security Pacific: An Interview with John P. Singleton," *The Bankers Magazine* (May–June 1991).

11. Jarvenpaa, S., and Ives, B., "Executive Involvement and Participation in the Management of Information Technology," *MIS Quarterly* (June 1991).

12. Anthes, G., "CEOs Catching Strategic IS Bug," *Computerworld* (July 9, 1990).

13. Umbaugh, R. E., *CIO Crisis in the Making,* unpublished memorandum, 1989. Mr. Umbaugh was CIO of Southern California Edison.

14. Feldman, R., "MIS May Take Back Seat When SIS Vision Arrives," *Management Information System Week* (Aug. 29, 1988).

15. Anthes, "CEOs Catching Strategic IS Bug."

16. Ibid.

17. Umbaugh, *CIO Crisis in the Making.*

18. Beath, C. M., and Ives, B., "The Information Technology Champion: Aiding and Abetting, Care and Feeding," *Proceedings of the Twenty-First Annual Hawaii International Conference on System Sciences,* Hawaii, 1988.

19. Feldman, "MIS May Take Back Seat."

20. Nash, J., "IS: The Hottest Thing to Hit Hollywood Since the Phone," *Computerworld* (Dec. 24, 1990).

21. Tom, P. L., *Managing Information as a Corporate Resource,* 2nd ed. New York: Harper Collins, 1991.

22. Janulaitis, M., "Commentary: Barriers to Developing Competitive Systems," *EDP Analyzer* (Oct. 1986).

23. Kwon, T., "A Diffusion of Innovation Approach to MIS Infusion: Conceptualization, Methodology, and Management Studies," in *Proceedings of the Eleventh International Conference on Information Systems,* Boston, Dec. 1990.

24. Bozman, J., "Carmaker Turns Over Career Tracks," *Computerworld* (Mar. 11, 1991).

25. Janulaitis, "Commentary."

26. Beath, C. M., "Supporting the Information Technology Champion," *MIS Quarterly* (Sept. 1991).

27. Rifkin, "IS Executives Must Put Their Vision to Work."

28. Editor's comments: "The Management Difference: A Tale of Two IS Projects," *MIS Quarterly* (Sept. 1990).

29. Henderson, J. C., "Plugging into Strategic Partnerships: The Critical IS Connection," *Sloan Management Review* (Spring 1990).

30. Beath, "Supporting the Information Technology Champion."

31. McNurlin and Sprague, *Information Systems.*

11

Identifying Strategic Information Systems Opportunities

Cowards die many times before their deaths.

—*Shakespeare, Julius Caesar,* II, 2

INTRODUCTION

Once the top management of an organization is convinced it is possible, and perhaps necessary, to use information systems to gain competitive advantage, their next step will be to search for strategic information systems opportunities. They will soon find out that no standard search methodology works for all organizations and that the best approach is to combine parts of available frameworks that are most relevant to the organization's particular circumstances.

Do companies achieve competitive edge by luck? Is there some conceptual process or framework that can be utilized to translate information technology (IT) into corporate strategy? A 1986 survey of the Society for Information Management (whose members are mostly CIOs) found that 55% of companies surveyed had either an irregular process or no formal approach at all for identifying strategic uses of information systems (ISs).[1] What is the decision-making process of managers who want to employ a strategic information system (SIS) to gain a competitive advantage? Who are the parties involved? How formal should the process be? These types of concerns are addressed in this chapter.

Chapter three, specifically the section titled SIS Opportunity-Seeking/Identifying Frameworks, reviewed SIS frameworks and addressed them in terms of specific uses, scope, advantages, and disadvantages. Many frameworks presented there are used for two general purposes. The first is to search for SIS opportunities; the second is to assess the impact or value of existing or potential SISs. The reader is well advised to review chapter three when a reference is made in this chapter to a certain framework (such as Michael Porter's value chain or Charles Wiseman's strategic thrusts).

The next section discusses the plethora of SIS frameworks. Section three provides several examples of SIS opportunity search processes in practice, as a background to the conceptual discussion of these processes in section four. The last section suggests an SIS opportunity search process that incorporates major concepts and frameworks used in this book.

THE PLETHORA OF SIS OPPORTUNITY SEARCH FRAMEWORKS

Various frameworks and models are useful for thinking about how to search out SIS opportunities. Examples of competitive strategies and cases can also be very helpful. However, there is no "cookbook" solution to the search for competitive information systems applications. There are no copyright laws when it comes to competitive advantage and no way to patent or otherwise protect a good idea. Innovation and ideas cannot be preengineered. Most of the time they are spontaneous and unplanned.

Idea generation comes from a mixture of hard and soft data, hunches, facts, brainstorming, formal planning, computer analysis, and intuition. It is less likely to come from IS professionals, for it is the functional business managers who know best the products, the customers, the suppliers, and the competitors. Therefore, most of the SIS ideas are likely to come from the functional managers. A variety of techniques have been used by companies in the search for SIS applications. The following is a compilation of some.[2]

- *Foster Corporate Education.* The starting point for SIS planning is often a series of "awareness" sessions prepared for top management and other senior business managers. This may be done by inside people or by outside consultants. The purpose is to promote a better understanding and sharing of the vision of information technology as a competitive force.
- *Establish New Alliances.* Ally the IS people with customer contact people. IS people need to be directly connected to those who deal with customers—product managers, marketing people, strategic planners. These people will generate the new ideas; they only need the enlightened support of the technology experts.
- *Conduct Market Research.* Marketing research studies reveal what customers need and want and why they buy given products and services. Armed with these data, SIS planners can find ways to create new or substitute products, and/or enhance and differentiate existing products/services by adding value with technology.
- *Collect Competitive Intelligence.* Find out what competitors are doing right. Exploit competitive weaknesses, search for opportunities, head off threats, and attack competitive strengths with better strength. Knowing the competition is critical to competitive IS planning.
- *Fund Corporate IS Research and Development.* If granted funds from the R&D pool, managers are free to pursue SIS ideas with corporate funds without risk to their budget. This encourages entrepreneurship while fostering riskless (to the manager) information technology initiatives.
- *Establish an SIS Group.* Form a stand-alone group whose sole purpose is to nurture and encourage ideas. Anyone can suggest an idea to this group, and they will pursue

it independently until it flies or dies. This is another form of corporate R&D, except here the funds go directly to the group. Eastman Kodak has one called the office of innovation. Other companies have units called emerging technologies, which consider opportunities for the use of new information technologies.

- *Promote Integrated Planning.* Corporate and information planning should be an integrated process, with information systems people involved proactively with business planners during the planning process, not reactively after the planning process is completed. If this is done, technological trends and directions can be considered up front, as well as technological options, feasibility, and cost. Hence, SIS planning can then be made a deliberate part of that process.

- *Conduct Brainstorming Sessions.* Form groups to brainstorm ideas for SIS. The idea is to come up with as many ideas as possible, without comment or criticism, under the leadership of a facilitator for further consideration after the brainstorming session. A planning model can be used as a framework for generating ideas, running each product or service through the model's various strategies. The most worthy ideas can be ranked for further investigation. Repeating the brainstorming process with different groups can produce a plethora of SIS ideas to pursue.

- *Do Informal Planning.* One-on-one planning between a business manager and a CIO, for example, can be a very effective search strategy. Informal discussions often lead to a number of ideas worth pursuing.

- *Practice Incrementalism.* Many of the most competitive systems evolved over time. Starting with an internal application system aimed at productivity, IS planners have often been able later to add new functionality in the form of new information services or product enhancements that have competitive value.

- *Create "Trojan Horses."* The Trojan Horse strategy involves transferring IS people into user organizations to open the gates to SIS planning. By seeding business units with technically trained people, over time there will be a stronger natural interest and inclination to promote technology initiatives.

These are but some ideas of leading companies to search out and exploit competitive uses of technology in the firm. The important thing to remember is that SIS planning is not done in a vacuum. Nor is it done only once. It must be an ongoing collaborative effort that brings the vision of diverse groups to bear on the objective: the use of IT as a competitive weapon. Any planning strategy, method, or technique that helps to accomplish that goal is useful.

The two well-known and most widely used frameworks for identifying SIS opportunities are Michael Porter's *value chain* and Charles Wiseman's *theory of strategic thrusts.* These frameworks (reviewed in chapter three) underlie most search processes used by companies, as reported in the following sections. Triggered by the paucity of information on the implementation of SIS frameworks, a 1990 field study compared the value chain and the strategic thrusts frameworks as aids to identifying SIS opportunities.[3]

Each framework was used by ten different medium-sized firms. Criteria for comparison were (1) number of worthy ideas generated; (2) estimated costs of the ideas;

(3) estimated time required to implement ideas; (4) organizational level of the SIS application (i.e., senior-, middle-, or low-level management); and (5) cross-classification ability (i.e., could an application generated by one framework be classified on the other?).

The study found both methodologies to be valuable and productive in identifying SIS opportunities in medium-sized companies. Although there were few overall differences between the value chain and strategic thrusts frameworks, certain characteristics might lead an organization to choose one over another. Companies in stable environments looking to gain a competitive advantage through changes in their internal processes, such as innovation in production, might choose the value chain framework. Companies that face a turbulent environment might prefer the strategic thrusts framework to gain a better competitive position within this environment.

The search for relevant SIS ideas can be classified in two types:

- Problem-based SIS search—where the organization directs the search toward solving specific problems within the organization's product or service chain. The evolution of AHSC's ASAP system (chapter one) illustrates this type of search.
- Opportunistic SIS search—where the search is directed toward a general understanding of IT and its potential benefits to the organization. This type of search may often identify potentially new business strategies, which in turn may lead to the development of new products or services. Merrill Lynch's Cash Management Account is an example.[4]

Some organizations have appointed task forces responsible for identifying SIS opportunities. These task forces consist of several key personnel in each different functional or organizational unit corresponding to different product lines or service offerings. In some organizations the task force is a permanent fixture of the IS unit and consists of IS personnel only. It is natural for an organizational unit task force to concentrate more on a problem-related search in their area of expertise and responsibility and less on an opportunistic SIS search. On the other hand, in the IS unit task force, more effort should be devoted to opportunistic than to problem-based searches. The organizational unit task forces should address issues likely to have an impact on the organization. The IS unit task force, with its technical expertise, should be responsible for scanning the IT environment for promising technological opportunities with potential competitive advantage to the organization.

Despite (or because of?) the plethora of frameworks, identifying the best methods and the best areas for strategic information systems remains a tough job. Porter's *value chain* and *competitive forces* frameworks provide an understandable structure for assessing candidate areas for SIS. They also seem to have had the widest direct and indirect use in designing SIS applications. However, other frameworks could help guide the process of SIS idea generation, provided they are enriched by a very clear sense of the specific industry and organization being considered, coupled with a good understanding of the power of IT. In other words, a contingency approach is recommended, in which a framework would be chosen on the basis of its congruence with factors such as level of uncertainty in the company's environment, corporate strategy, and management of IS resources.

SIS OPPORTUNITIES SEARCH PROCESSES IN PRACTICE

It is not the intent of the following examples to advocate the processes reported here or any other particular methodology. They demonstrate, however, that search processes used by organizations combine parts of available frameworks that they deem to be relevant to their particular circumstances.

Searching for SIS Opportunities at a Toy Supermarket Chain

In 1986, the management of a 134-store network of toy supermarkets went through a formal planning process to discover strategic applications of information technology. The process, led by the vice president of MIS, followed the annual planning process that produced four baseline plans: two half-year operating plans (spring and fall); a one-year capital budget to support operating plans: and an annual strategic plan to address long-term issues. Functional plans, such as the MIS strategic systems plan, were linked to the baseline plans. Most planning was performed by line managers invited to executive committee meetings, rather than by staff.[5]

The corporate strategic plan defined the company's mission; highlighted strengths, weaknesses, opportunities, and threats; and identified three *critical success factors:* increase sales per store, increase the number of stores to increase leverage from overhead and support expenses, and convert more sales dollars to profit. Information systems applications were explicitly identified in support of these issues. Each issue was refined into two or three strategic targets supported by about 30 clearly defined tactics for integration into the two operating plans and the capital budget.

The vice president of MIS decided to adopt the information technology management (ITM) methodology as the basis for the MIS strategic systems plan. ITM is an AT&T-sponsored process to identify and evaluate strategic IT opportunities.[6] The ITM process combines industry and competitive analysis, based largely on the frameworks developed by Michael Porter of the Harvard Business School (see chapter three on Porter's frameworks), with a structured search for IT applications that would achieve competitive advantage. ITM also included $SIX+^{SM}$, a strategic information exchange planning service that used an AT&T proprietary computer model to match information technologies with business information flows.

The first phase of the process is a description of the company's business and an industry analysis. The latter uses Porter's *five forces* model and attempts to quantify the impact of each force (suppliers, new entrants, existing rivals, buyers, and substitute products). The second phase is a strategic analysis that leads to summary statements of the company's strategy and competitive scope. Individual elements of the strategic environment—target markets, product policy, cost position, and the like—are analyzed in more detail.

The third phase includes an analysis of the company value system and value chain, again using frameworks of Michael Porter. For the toy vendor, the value system included several entities and their linkages: suppliers (e.g., Fisher-Price), then the company itself, then channels (e.g., the company's trucks), then the company's retail outlets, then the customers.

The toy vendor's value chain included primary and support activities and their linkages. Primary activities included inbound logistics (e.g., storage of incoming merchandise from suppliers); operations (e.g., ticketing of merchandise); outbound logistics (e.g., advertising); and after-sale service (e.g., repair and parts supply). The support activities included procurement of assets used by the primary activities; technology development (e.g., installing point of sale terminals for the sales activity); human resource management (e.g., training repair technicians); and infrastructure support activities (e.g., accounting, finance, personnel).

Phase four of the ITM identifies and prioritizes strategic opportunities for IT. The first step identifies internal and external linkages of activities outlined in the value chain that could have strategic potential for the company. Next, the *opportunities* associated with these linkages are described in detail and their probable *impacts* are assessed. For instance, a strategic opportunity for the toy vendor may be *electronic shopping aid*—provision of an automated in-store shopping directory to suggest selections based on attributes of a child. The impact can be *increased store sales.* Each strategic opportunity can be mapped to a linkage in the value system. From the same example, electronic shopping aid concerns *internal store operations.* At the end of this phase of the ITM process, recommended opportunities are presented to corporate management.

In this case, the toy vendor decided during that time to sponsor additional study based on AT&T's SIX+^{SM} Planning Service. SIX+^{SM} is a tool to help customers of AT&T exploit new technology opportunities for effective information exchange. The planning service began with a series of workshops over a period of two days that identified about 300 information flows within various functions of the company. Each flow was profiled in terms of over 100 qualitative and quantitative information requirements. This was fed into a computer model. In addition to assessing the support quality of then existing technologies for these information flows, the computer model matched the flows with new and emerging information technologies that presented potential new opportunities to enhance the company's external and internal information exchange. For the toy vendor, one example of the technology proposals resulting from this study was a recommendation for establishing a centralized inbound/outbound communications center. The SIX+^{SM} method can be focused on a business unit or function, can be restricted to the most important flows, can consider hypothetical flows, and is designed as a supplement to an existing SIS opportunities search process rather than as the complete process.

Searching for SIS Opportunities at GTE Data Services

GTE, the large international telecommunications and electronics company, decided in 1983 to consider SIS opportunities systematically. They used a five-phase process for uncovering strategic system opportunities in their largest division, their domestic telephone operations division (TELOPS). The division had its own IS unit, GTE Data Services (GTEDS). The process moved from an initial dissemination of SIS ideas and identification of opportunities to a final acceptance by members of the senior management team. The last phase of the process resulted in a portfolio of SIS applications earmarked for implementation.[7]

In phase one, the head of information systems planning of GTEDS introduced his president to the SIS concept through a series of informal meetings and memos. The purpose of this phase was to win the president's endorsement to proceed.

In phase two, a two-day idea generation meeting was held off-site. It involved middle managers and systems analysts from GTEDS. The meeting began with a tutorial on the approach the participants would be using to uncover SIS opportunities—the *theory of strategic thrusts* suggested by Charles Wiseman of Columbia University (see chapter three). The approach begins by identifying the *target* of the strategic system. Is it to be aimed at suppliers, customers, or competitors? Next, the approach continues to determine how IT might be used to pursue a strategic thrust. A thrust can be used against the target offensively (if it seeks a competitive advantage) or defensively (if it seeks to reduce a competitor's advantage).

One thrust is *differentiation*—distinguishing a product from others. A *cost* thrust may lower a firm's costs or may raise costs for a competitor. A third thrust is *innovation*—doing something new that may change the competitive structure of the industry. A fourth strategic thrust is *growth*—expanding the customer base. The fifth thrust is forming *alliances*—with other companies. The theory of strategic thrusts maintains that companies often choose a combination of these thrusts when formulating a strategy, and that information systems can play a key role in making a competitive strategy possible. The tutorial thus provided attendees with an analytical framework with which they could identify SIS opportunities and threats.

Following the tutorial, participants analyzed some 20 actual SIS cases, drawn from a variety of industries, and learned how to identify strategic targets and thrusts. Then the information management planning staff of GTEDS described to the participants GTE's competitive position—its markets, business strategy, products, suppliers, customers, competitors, strengths, and weaknesses. By understanding these elements, attendees were in a position to consider how information technology could be used to support or shape strategic thrusts aimed at TELOPS's strategic targets.

Next, the group divided into teams of five to eight participants and each brainstormed for different kinds of SIS opportunities. One group looked at opportunities relating to suppliers, another studied customers, some searched for opportunities related to competitors, some looked at existing information systems, and others looked for new systems. Each team completed a short form describing the idea, the intended strategic target and thrust, and the specific competitive advantage. The ground rule in the SIS idea-generation sessions was that criticism of ideas must be suppressed so that creativity was not inhibited.

Following the two-hour brainstorming session, each team presented its ideas to the entire group. Duplicate ideas were eliminated and others were classified. Again, criticism was prohibited. Then the ideas were ranked by degree of competitive advantage, cost to develop, feasibility, and the likelihood that the idea would provide a sustainable competitive advantage. Applying these criteria, SIS ideas were classified into four categories:

- *Blockbuster* (potential for strategic dominance)
- *Very high potential* (but not blockbuster)

- *Moderate potential* (worthy of further consideration)
- *Low potential* (not worthy of further consideration)

In the final step of the two-day idea-generation meeting, the group concentrated on refining and recording the SIS blockbuster ideas.

In phase three, a similar idea-generation meeting was held off-site, involving the top information management executives within the local telephone companies and GTEDS. The meeting resulted, again, in several SIS blockbuster ideas. The meetings in phases two and three uncovered many of the same opportunities, and each reached a consensus on the blockbuster idea.

In phase four, the successful completion of the first three phases led to a meeting between GTEDS's president and TELOPS's top business executive. The latter was introduced to the SIS concept and told of the SIS opportunities already discovered at the previous two phases. The purpose of the meeting was to gain approval for a third SIS idea-generation meeting with TELOPS's corporate business planners, those responsible for initiating the business's strategic thrusts.

Phase five thus involved marketing and strategic planning managers in an off-site two-day meeting similar to those in phases two and three. This meeting also produced consensus on the SIS opportunities. The entire process identified some 100 SIS ideas. Of the top 11 ideas, 6 were rated as blockbusters and 5 were classified as having very high potential. Funds were allocated to develop the blockbuster ideas. TELOPS has subsequently added a SIS module to its long-range plan.

Searching for SIS Opportunities at E.I. duPont's Polymer Products Division

DuPont's polymer products division in 1985 investigated the use of information systems for competitive advantage. The division had at the time sales of some $3 billion a year. It produced and sold plastics and films, which it manufactured in plants around the world.[8] In the summer of 1985, the division decided to experiment with a formal planning process that would help them systematically uncover potentially strategic systems.

They chose a strategic information planning methodology developed by Arthur Andersen and Company, the large international accounting and consulting firm. The methodology contains nine activities; the first five of which lead to developing an information technology strategy; the remaining four lead to developing an implementation plan. The five phases are aimed at answering the following questions: What is the scope of the study and how should we organize it? Where do we now stand? What are our competitors doing? What are our information technology opportunities? What is our information systems strategy?

The methodology advocates that an SIS search project will look three to five years into the future and that it should have a sponsor (or several sponsors) from executive, user, or IS management. In the initial phase, the consultants (Arthur Andersen) and the sponsor prepare a plan for the chief executive officer or the executive steering committee. The plan defines the objectives and scope of the project, the schedule, the organization, and so on. This initial planning phase takes from one to two weeks.

The majority of the work is performed by a planning team, which is formed after the initial planning phase has been completed. The team is composed of people from the business function that is undertaking the study, plus one or more people from the information systems group and the consultants. These are all full-time participants. Typically, the team is led by a functional manager, with the Arthur Andersen consultants playing a comanagement role. Two steps are then undertaken in parallel. One step looks at information systems and the other looks at the business.

The information systems members of the project team investigate the business unit's current use of information systems. The assessment is both by quantity and quality, because it is important to find out how much experience the firm has in using new technologies. The team looks not only at the applications but also at the types of information gathered, the technologies used, and the computing infrastructure. Where possible, these are compared with what competitors are known to be doing. At the same time, other members of the team look at the competitive environment of the business. They study what competitors are doing, what the business environment looks like, and what the critical success factors for the business are.

With the two assessments of the current status in hand, the team focuses on identifying information technology opportunities, using Porter's frameworks. They start with the external view and look at Porter's five competitive forces—rivalry among competitors, threat of new entrants, power of buyers, power of suppliers, and substitutes. Often they add a sixth competitive force—the regulatory environment. The analysis then concentrates on the value chains of specific products or services.

Arthur Andersen recommends forming two types of groups to help in this discovery phase—advisers and focus groups. *Advisers* have expert knowledge of a specific area, and they advise the planning team in that area. A *focus group* is a group of people from one business unit who work in different parts of that organization—engineering, finance, operations, marketing, and so on. These groups help uncover strategic opportunities.

The focus groups are introduced to the analysis techniques and the company's current status. These groups then use value chain analysis to study the activities in their business, searching for those activities that are critical to customers. They delve into ways to improve these activities through information systems. Once the opportunities have been identified from these various sources, the planning team creates an information systems strategy to present to management.

To try out the Arthur Andersen methodology, DuPont's polymer products division studied two different products in one SIS search project. One product was mature, in a highly competitive market, and made little use of information technology. The other product was less mature, but it was highly dependent on information technology. By studying two products at once, they hoped to uncover ways to provide information systems support for marketing many types of polymer products.

The project team consisted of two full-time product managers who led the four-month project. Each team leader had extensive knowledge about one of the two products. The team also had two full-time Arthur Andersen consultants. Their role was to facilitate the process and educate the team by leading them through the methodology. Members of the information systems department were on the team to address technology issues. The team was to think expansively, rather than be concerned with whether an idea was technically possible. In most cases, the ideas were well within the state of the art. About 25 other people were also involved through focus groups.

Using the Arthur Andersen methodology, the team studied the major steps in each product's development and production. They developed the value chain for each product; that is, they noted each major activity that added value to the product. For each one they asked, "How can information systems have an impact on this activity?" They were trying to uncover what new services would make the product more valuable to the customer at each phase in the development and production process.

The team also invited a number of customers to participate in several advisory groups; they focused on similar questions. These customers provided DuPont with many insights. For instance, they described the kinds of information that would help them make better use of the DuPont products. These customer advisory groups played an important role in helping the team identify strategic opportunities. From the study, the division identified several possible new offerings supported by information technologies.

Strategic Application Search at IBM

IBM's own search process for new uses of IT, with the specific aim of beating the competition, has been developed under the name *strategic application search* (SAS) It is a series of linked activities involving a briefing, preparation, a structured planning meeting, and a follow-up action.[9] The essential elements of the process are listed below.

1. A briefing meeting for up to a dozen key line and IS executives and a planning consultant to
   a. Explain the SAS process.
   b. Bring the management team to a common level of understanding of competitive forces and value chain concepts as defined by Michael Porter.
   c. Describe some of the ways in which IT is used to obtain competitive advantage in various industry sectors.
   d. Allocate preparation tasks (previously agreed with the chief executive) to two- or three-person teams chosen from the group.

2. A *market analysis* phase in which the selected team members, using Porter's competitive forces model, research specific elements of their competitive environment to determine likely future trends and evaluate their own corporate strengths and weaknesses, threats and opportunities. This phase takes three to four weeks of elapsed time—a consequence of the fact that SAS lays great stress on understanding both the competitive and the technological environment, which takes time and effort. The market analysis is performed by senior managers.

3. A two-day workshop, attended by the participants in the briefing meeting of phase one, during which

a. The results of the market analysis carried out by each team are presented.

b. The competitive threats and opportunities are discussed and prioritized.

c. The main elements of corporate competitive strategy are agreed on in light of the threats and opportunities exposed by the market analysis.

d. The team is restructured into small groups and each is given the task of investigating a specific approach to using IT in support of the chosen strategy. The different approaches are in essence

Automation of individual information-intensive activities (to reduce cost or save time).

Creation of electronic links (internal or external) to optimize trade-offs between different value chain activities (by moving information-processing work from one point to another in the chain, for example).

Use of existing information in new ways to add value (by repackaging it and making it available to customers as an additional service, for example).

These three recommended approaches are not necessarily mutually exclusive; they can and often do lead to very similar conclusions about IT usage. The point is that they require each team to start from a different position, thus ensuring that a broad range of ideas is brought up for consideration.

e. The ideas generated by this process are presented to the whole team prioritized in accordance with their perceived strategic impact.

f. A follow-up plan is agreed on.

4. A six- to eight-week follow-up phase involving designated functional and IS executives. The feasibility and risk associated with implementing the ideas brought up during the previous phases are evaluated. The value and sustainability of the competitive advantage likely to be obtained are assessed.

5. The SAS process culminates with a follow-up meeting attended by the participants in the briefing meeting and in the workshop (senior management, senior IS managers, and a planning consultant). In this meeting decisions about future SISs are made and action plans for implementation are agreed on.

PROCESSES FOR DISCOVERING SIS IDEAS

Several processes can be used in discovering strategic systems. The *top-down process* uses a group of people assembled for a brainstorming session. Preferably, these people are familiar with a specific product/service, its customers, and its distribution channels. The purpose of the meeting is to generate ideas on how to enhance the competitiveness of the product through information technologies. A tutorial—focusing on a particular framework and many examples—can help the group to generate SIS ideas. The process adopted by GTE Data Services is a variation of the top-down process to search out competitive systems. Most of the idea-generation processes in use are illustrative of the top-down model.

There are circumstances when the top-down–based methods for identifying strategic applications may be unsatisfactory.[10] First, overall corporate strategy may not exist. The absence of an explicit strategy will preclude either mapping IS plans to long-range organizational plans or altering organizational plans through IT. Second, corporate strategists may be uninformed about IT. Without sufficient knowledge about IS possibilities and capabilities, corporate strategists will have a difficult time considering the potential strategic application of IT. Third, the environment may be turbulent. Considerable changes in the IS environment (changes in products, customers, competitors, suppliers, etc.) may reduce the appropriateness of strategies formulated using a top-down process in achieving competitive advantage.

The *bottom-up process* for uncovering strategic systems involves developing the skills of many employees. This process requires a large educational effort and a means for allowing the best ideas to "bubble up" to the top of the organization. Although this approach may cause some organizational changes, it is likely to provide a greater payoff in the future.

Using the bottom-up process, a company encourages its employees to acquire and experiment with new technologies. It aims at developing computer literacy throughout the organization—literacy in the uses of technology. This process requires top management to encourage an entrepreneurial spirit—to explore the new uses of technology. Technical specialists will be needed to answer technical questions, and internal consultants are needed to pursue promising ideas and act as intermediaries between technicians and users. This approach is longer-term than the top-down approach.

A process close to the bottom-up approach is the *adaptive process.* Unlike the top-down process, it deals less with predetermined corporate goals and strategies, and more with evolution and incremental and subtle changes. The adaptive approach appears to offer potential value for the identification of competitive applications in organizations facing considerable environmental turbulence or in which senior strategists are relatively uninformed about IS resources. Five organizational roles can help support this adaptive approach.[11]

Wizard.   Wizards are the corporate technology experts judged to have potential strategic impact on the firm. Wizards are also aware of the organization's own strengths and weaknesses relative to information technologies. They should maintain example applications of IT, including applications within or external to the organization.

Marriage Broker.   One or more senior IS executives might be designated to act as intermediaries between user-managers with interesting ideas and the wizards. They are charged with responsibility for seeking out and encouraging new ideas for competitive applications, ensuring their technical feasibility, and nurturing budding systems.

Rich Uncle.   Money is needed to acquire experimental technologies that appear to have some potential merit. The rich uncle provides the seed money for prototype applications that might not otherwise pass the organization's investment hurdles.

Weed Puller.   Prototypes and experimental applications may take on fascinating lives of their own that far exceed their utility to the organization. Periodically, such projects must be reexamined and their current utility assessed. The weed puller must be in a high enough position in the organization to avoid the pressures of special constituencies. He or she also has a responsibility to ensure that the persons associated with such projects are not branded as failures but rather are viewed as temporarily unlucky.

Teacher.   System analysts, wizards, and others within the IS unit must learn more about the organization's products, customers, competitors, suppliers, and distribution channels. The teacher provides an environment for this learning and also educates users about the possibilities presented by the various technologies. The presentations need to succinctly introduce the technology, with most emphasis placed on existing applications and the identification of potential applications. Teachers need high levels of credibility with their intended audience. External experts and consultants may frequently fill this role.

The "Accidental" SIS

The IS literature of the 1980s has emphasized formal planning techniques (mostly top-down) for identifying strategic IT applications. However, many well-known SISs started out as accidents, rather than as the result of a well-planned process. ASAP, the system launched by American Hospital Supply Corporation (AHSC), started as a localized response to a customer need (see chapter one). Because of difficulties in serving a hospital effectively, the manager of a local AHSC office gave prepunched cards to the hospital's purchasing department; the ordering clerks could then transfer the information on the cards expeditiously through a phone terminal. From the local ad hoc solution to a particular problem, the idea gradually emerged of linking all the hospitals in the same way through touch-tone telephones, bar code scanners, teletypes, and eventually PCs. The rest was history (one can say that AHSC made history while some of its rivals became history).

SABRE, the pioneering computerized reservation system built by American Airlines, was not originally conceived as a biased distribution channel to create entry barriers for competitors while locking in travel agents. In fact, it began as a relatively simple inventory-management system addressing a specific need that had nothing to do with ensuring a competitive advantage. On the contrary, it was supposed to address an internal inefficiency: American Airlines' inability to monitor the inventory of available seats and to link passenger names to blocked seats.

These and other most frequently cited SIS successes tell the same story. SIS ideas are not necessarily explored top-down or introduced in one shot; rather, they are the result of tinkering and prototyping.[12] This approach requires allowing and even encouraging tinkering by people close to the operational level so that they can apply known tools to solve new problems. Systems like ASAP originated in this way. The value of tinkering lies in the fact that it keeps the generation of an SIS idea close to the competencies of the organization and to ongoing fluctuations in local practices.

Although formal SIS search processes are thorough and systematic, their benefits come at the expense of considerable time—a luxury that many organizations cannot afford. In contrast, managed incremental learning and idea generation, particularly among line managers, can yield strategic application far more rapidly. (As Ann Landers said, opportunities are usually disguised as hard work, so most people don't recognize them.) Examples from case studies conducted in numerous organizations share several common elements:

- The source of the SIS idea was a line manager, not a staff planner, general manager, or IS manager.
- This line manager was a hands-on computer user.
- A manager at a higher level recognized the value of the new idea, promoted it, and provided resources to keep the idea alive during critical stages of its development.
- Initial expectations concerning the idea were modified over time through a process of incremental, experimental learning.
- The innovative idea led to organizational changes, many of which were not foreseen.[13]

The following example describes the introduction of a new IT-based marketing channel and the *champion* role played by a senior manager. An editor at the McGraw-Hill publishing company used a spreadsheet package to prepare statistical analyses and to communicate with other PC users via electronic bulletin boards. This led to his idea of listing his division's computer-related books on a national bulletin board. A senior editor, who saw the application, recognized a new marketing channel targeted at customers with an interest in computers. This manager pushed for the *electronic bookshelf* to be developed into a full-scale advertising and ordering system.

The electronic bookshelf idea arose outside of a formal process. Details of the idea emerged as the editor experimented with the PC. Idea generation and prototyping occurred simultaneously. The senior editor played a critical role: he saw the value of the innovative idea and promoted it to influential others in the organization. He ensured the transition of the ideas from small-scale prototype to complete system.

The top-down, *rational* approaches to SIS idea generation assume that an orderly, rational process is the best route to identifying SIS applications. Many case studies suggest, however, that a disorderly, incremental process also plays a large part in the identification of SIS opportunities. A proposal for a managed incremental process that minimized business and technical risks comprised four steps.[14]

In step one, *IT literacy* is attained, including awareness of IT possibilities, hands-on computing skills, and an ability to identify technical and business risks (e.g., faulty database designs). Step two involves *idea generation* by middle managers and their subordinates. Users are encouraged to seek out ways of performing key tasks, supported by their newly acquired IS skills. In the McGraw-Hill case, an editor identified a new way to sell books.

In step three, *value analysis,* ideas are assessed by potential senior management sponsors. Inexpensive PC-based prototypes can be used by users and sponsors to explore the features of a proposed application. Value analysis also assesses the technical risks of a proposed system (see chapter nine for a discussion of these risks). Step four, *implementation* of the most promising prototype into full-scale systems, involves all levels of management.

THE SEARCH FOR SIS OPPORTUNITIES—CONCLUSIONS

Corporate management, functional management, and IS management must be involved in the process of identifying SIS opportunities. The search for competitive applications of IT will be fruitful in an environment characterized by information-intensive processes or products. Several unique industry factors influence the likelihood of strategic IT potential:

- The presence of significant information content in key relationships with buyers or suppliers.
- The presence of competitive pressures within the industry (due, for instance, to deregulation, technological innovations, foreign competition).
- The industry's product/service life is limited (perishable products or services) (for example, in the airline industry, flight seats that are not sold; in the hotel industry, rooms that stay vacant).

If the firm's objective is to identify strategic applications of IT, active involvement from functional and general management is necessary. There must be a desire to use IT for competitive advantage and a vision of how this will be done. Delegating this responsibility to IS management will rarely achieve effective results. General managers and IS managers have to share the concern about the strategic opportunities of IT.

Figure 11.1 illustrates a methodology for identifying SIS opportunities. The SIS search process incorporates concepts and frameworks used in this book (e.g., generic corporate strategies, competitive forces, value chain, strategic thrusts [reviewed in chapter three], and SIS risks [reviewed in chapter nine]).

A preliminary stage to the process is the review of the firm's value system. During this stage, the organizational body responsible for carrying out the process (e.g., an ad hoc committee, a dedicated SIS section of IS, a consultant) analyzes all the critical areas in the primary and support activities (and the linkage between them) of the firm's value chains, buyers' value chains, suppliers' value chains, and the competitors' value chains. The analysis can pertain to a strategic business unit of the firm (e.g., a major product or service) and not to the firm as a whole. The results of this analysis provide inputs, ideas, and insights for stages one and two.

Stages one and two are conducted simultaneously, with feedback between them. They focus on a range of strategic targets and the corporate strategies supported by IT that can be used to impact the targets. The targets include buyers, suppliers, possible new entrants, existing rivals, and substitute products and services.

The process should generate the largest possible list of strategic targets. It is from this list that the firm can select those that are deemed suitable for attack (or defense) by strategic strategies supported or shaped by IT. These strategies comprise cost leadership, differentiation, focus, growth, alliances, innovation, and the like. A corporate strategy and its associated SIS can be used to attack multiple targets. A target can be impacted by more than one strategic SIS.

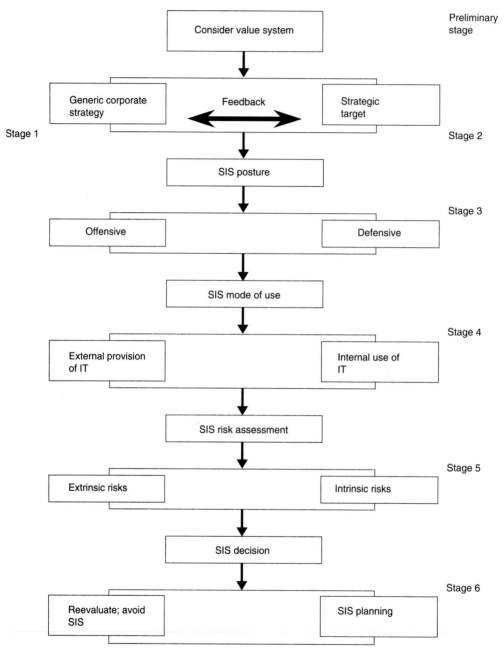

FIGURE 11.1 SIS opportunity identification process

Once a given strategy aimed at a given target is selected, stage three deals with the SIS posture. It can be used defensively, to reduce a competitive edge held by a target, or offensively, to increase an edge. The SIS selection can, for instance, create high switching costs for the firm's buyers to defend against a new entrant; alternatively, the firm can join an SIS alliance in order to expand the firm's market.

In stage four, the firm has to consider whether the offensive or defensive SIS is to employ an IT to be used internally or externally, by providing it to the target. For example, for a buyers' target, with a niche (focus) strategy and an offensive posture, the direction of the SIS is external if terminals and an inventory management system are provided to the buyers to lock them in. For a cost leadership strategy aimed at buyers, with a defensive posture, the SIS selected may use CAD/CAM technology internally to reduce costs of product development and manufacturing.

Stage five deals with the assessment of intrinsic and extrinsic risks (chapter nine). The intrinsic risks are evaluated by focusing on the size of the selected SIS, on its degree of structuredness, and the familiarity of the firm with the relevant IT. From this evaluation, the firm can select tools to deal with such risks (e.g., formal planning and control techniques, use of external consultants, a steering committee). In addition, assuming that the SIS is successfully implemented, the extrinsic risk implications of an initial success must be evaluated.

Finally, a decision has to be made whether to endorse the SIS being considered. The firm can decide to completely avoid the project or to modify it and then reemploy the SIS opportunity identification process to evaluate the modified SIS. A positive decision requires incorporation of the selected SIS into the master plan for IS and the ensuing annual IS plan.

The process described above raises important organizational implications for general management and IS management: Who should be responsible for SIS identification and development? Should the IS function create a unit responsible for SIS identification and development? Should the IS function create a dedicated SIS group? Should new SIS skills be created internally or hired? Should there be an ongoing SIS planning process? Some organizations, for example, have established a special unit within IS to monitor the environment and identify ITs that may lead to competitive advantage.

REFERENCES

1. Stahl, M. J., *Strategic Executive Decisions*. New York: Quorum Books, 1989, 129.

2. Synnott, W. R., *The Information Weapon*. New York: Wiley, 1987.

3. Bergeron, F., Buteau, C., and Raymond, L., "Identification of Strategic Information Systems Opportunities: Applying and Comparing Two Methods," *MIS Quarterly* 15, no. 1 (March 1991).

4. Ewusi-Mensah, K., "Developing a Competitive Intelligence System for IT," *Long Range Planning* 22, no. 5 (1989).

5. Vitale, M. R., and Gilbert, A. L., "Child World, Inc.: Information Technology Planning," *Harvard Business School Case* 9-188-002, Harvard Business School, 1987.

6. Sullivan, C. H. Jr., and Smart, J. R., "Planning for Information Networks," *Sloan Management Review* (Winter 1987).

7. Wiseman, C., *Strategic Information Systems.* Homewood, Il: Irwin, 1988.

8. "Uncovering Strategic Systems," *EDP Analyzer.* Bethesda, Md.: United Communications Group, Oct. 1986.

9. Lincoln, T., ed., *Managing Information Systems for Profit.* New York: Wiley, 1990.

10. Vitale, M. R., Ives, B., and Beath, C. M., "Identifying Strategic Information Systems: Finding a Process or Building an Organization?," in K. C. Laudon and J. A. Turner, eds., *Information Technology and Management Strategy.* Englewood Cliffs, N.J.: Prentice-Hall, 1989.

11. Ibid.

12. Ciborra, C. U., "From Thinking to Tinkering: The Grassroots of Strategic Information Systems," *Proceedings of the Twelfth International Conference on Information Systems.* Dec. 1991, New York.

13. Gogan, J. L., and Cash, J. I., Jr., "IT-Based Innovation: Managing a Disorderly Process," *Proceedings of the Twenty-Fifth Hawaii International Conference on System Sciences.* Los Alamitos, Calif.: IEEE Computer Society Press, 1992.

14. Ibid.

12

New Technologies for Strategic Information Systems

The most profound technologies are those that disappear. They weave themselves into the fabric of everyday life until they are indistinguishable from it.

—*Mark Weiser*[1]

INTRODUCTION

Imagine creating a system that would electronically link your organization to its customers, allowing you instantly to understand and service their needs and wishes. Imagine that it would handle all delivery and billing details without cumbersome paperwork, while being so effortless and effective for your customers that they have no incentive to consider competing products. Imagine that the technology you use is so beguiling that it lures your customers as much as the products you sell. Imagine that your system would feed customer response to your products directly back to the product design teams, where expert design systems would help your staff refine old products and rapidly create new ones. Imagine that it would advise how to set prices based on product cost and market intelligence.

Is such an enticing fantasy of using advanced technology for competitive advantage really possible?

Some technologists believe that technology no longer provides a competitive edge, if it ever did, and that it is a solution in search of problems. Max Hopper, who built SABRE, American Airlines' pioneering reservation system, asserts that technology alone cannot provide an enduring business advantage.[2] Timothy Warner even describes information technology as a competitive *burden*.[3] In an era of vigorous international competition, diminishing and high-cost resources, and heightened executive caution, many CEOs no longer believe that information technology can provide a sustainable advantage. At best, it is a strategic necessity. At worst, they believe that rapidly advancing technology can erode competitive advantage.[4] Today's competitive advantage can easily become tomorrow's liability.

Advanced technology by itself has probably never been the golden egg that its most enthusiastic advocates would like us to believe. Often, the more advanced the technology, the more difficult—and risky—it is to use. The timing of new technology introductions can be more important than the technology itself. Sometimes, technology delivers an unneeded or little understood service. Picture telephones appeared nearly 30 years ago but languished as a curiosity item. Only recently has a variant of that idea—teleconferencing— become a commercially viable product. New technologies often require no more than second-generation development with improved quality or lower cost to gain acceptance. But when a technology reshapes our social fabric, acceptance depends as much on social change as on technological wizardry.

These barriers should not deter us from seeking new technologies for strategic information systems. Most systems that can provide competitive advantage, or can satisfy strategic necessity, will depend on advanced technologies. Despite a weak economy in the early 1990s, interest in new technologies remains strong.[5] New technologies are being developed at an unprecedented rate, so there should be rich opportunities for the adventurous to exploit them. Put another way: if you can imagine a system for your business, it probably can be built.

The goal of this final chapter is to review the new technologies that are likely to unfold during the next decade and assess how they might be used for competitive advantage. Are some technologies more likely than others to provide competitive advantage? How can these technologies provide advantage? How might an IS manager select technology to fit a particular strategic thrust?

TECHNOLOGY USED IN STRATEGIC SYSTEMS

At first glance, many landmark strategic information systems (SISs) appear to rely on conventional, readily available technologies. Often, they are extensions of existing transaction processing systems, or use excess system capacity. Competitive advantage was obtained not by exploiting advanced technology but by addressing a business problem with existing technology. New applications software may have been required, but the technology was "off the shelf." Success came from being the first, or from being the largest, or from having the most savvy knowledge of the market. Sometimes attention to details made the difference: McKesson stored information about how a pharmacy organized its display shelves, and shipped packages that allowed easy shelf placement.[6] The first implementations of OTISLINE (a system developed to enhance Otis Elevator Company's responsiveness to elevator maintenance customers) used straightforward applications of existing database technology.

A close examination of successful SISs, however, reveals that many use advanced technology. The full implementation of American Airlines' original design for SABRE took 20 years to complete, as their ideal system design waited for network, computing, and storage technology to catch up.[7] Many of the technologies that made SABRE possible—enormous online mass storage and widespread telecommunication networks— are not flashy, like supercomputing graphics or multimedia, but improvements in bandwidth and storage capacity. They were the hard-core technological advances that underpin the more visible advances we love to marvel over. In this way, SABRE is like most of the other landmark strategic systems. Although it depended on advanced technologies, these technologies played a supporting rather than a starring role. Although American Airlines' passengers benefited from SABRE, it was travel agents—a distribution channel—that dealt directly with the technology.

The business and technology environments have changed since American Airlines first implemented SABRE. As Max Hopper observed, such *home run* systems may no longer be possible.[8] But if they are, constructing one that depends on new technologies will require not just technical foresight and skill but the ability to create new models of information exchange and processing in a business context.

Viets relates an instructive anecdote about using technology for competitive advantage. While visiting Florida, he rides in a cab driven by the aging owner and sole employee of Sonny's Taxi Company. When Jacksonville had deregulated the cab business in 1984, this driver had bought both a cellular phone and a display pager. When you called for a cab from Sonny's, you spoke with Sonny, who also was your driver. No more dispatcher cost, no more messages lost or garbled by a middleperson. Sonny had contrived a system that cut costs while improving service.[9]

This tale teaches five lessons. First, size is no barrier to using information technology for competitive advantage. Given the difficulties of managing large systems, the small player may have a better chance of using new technology strategically than a multinational corporation. The second lesson is that unusual combinations of technologies and organizations can obtain great advantage. The independent taxi business in a medium-sized city hardly seems the place to find telecommunications innovations, but it was. Third, although Sonny got the jump on the market, his approach would be very simple to copy. So unless you can protect your new technology through secrecy, patents, or insurmountable cost barriers, you surely will be soon copied. Fourth, Sonny's ongoing success depends as much on the quality of service that he provides as on his portable technology. Cellular phones and pagers pay off only if Sonny delivers what they promise. Finally, most future SISs will depend—or at least use—telecommunications.

The vulnerability of Sonny's system to copycats points up the most challenging aspect of employing new information technologies for strategic advantage. No matter how advanced the technology a firm exploits, a competitor is surely working on a similar or competing technology. Last year's competitive advantage could become this year's liability. Although every industry has a different technological base, few industries are immune to rapid technological change. Constant environmental scanning is essential. Table 12.1 plots the information technology experience of an organization (vertical axis) against the technological sophistication of its industry (horizontal axis). Although a given firm could fall anywhere on this continuum, four general roles highlight the opportunities and threats presented by the competitive use of technology.

Trail Blazer

A trail blazer is a firm that has found an industry-unique way to exploit technology for strategic advantage. Being a trail blazer may sound enticing, conjuring images of pioneering, leadership, and industry domination. However, images of increased risk,

TABLE 12.1   Relative position of firms using technology for strategic advantage

		High	TRAIL BLAZER	HOLDING YOUR OWN
			Best chance for sustained competitive advantage from technology	keeping pace—at best, can be leader for brief periods
			moderate risk of complacency—threat from new Trail Blazers in industry	uses technology as strategic necessity
Degree of successful experience using advanced technology strategically in your Organization				fairly high risk of complacency
			BUSINESS AS USUAL	LAGGARD
			competitive advantage comes from some other source	better have another means of sustaining competitive advantage
			low risk, but vulnerable to Trail Blazer moving into industry	high risk of never catching up to industry in adopting technology
		Low		may make costly mistakes trying to catch up

Low   High

Degree to which advanced technology is used strategically in Industry

uncertain and frustrating system development, failed experiments, and false starts should also be kept in mind. Despite these drawbacks, being a trail blazer offers the best chance of creating sustained competitive advantage through advanced technology. Once a dominant new system is established, complacency becomes the major threat. If the new technology overwhelms the competition, litigation may also arise from disenfranchised competitors. Being a trail blazer is a long-term commitment. Once a company takes the lead, it must continue to embrace new technologies to sustain its advantage. Otherwise, it may quickly fade, as more ambitious competitors leapfrog it to the next generation technology. Given the staff, the resolve, and the capacity, being a trail blazer can be highly beneficial to both market share and bottom line.

Holding Your Own

A company that keeps pace with industry leaders in the use of technology is holding its own. It uses technology out of strategic necessity. Holding your own does not entail as much risk as being a trail blazer, but with enough effort it can still yield a profitable niche to an enterprising company. Holding your own, however, seldom yields the higher profits of sustained market leadership. And just as with the industry trail blazer, complacency can leave a firm vulnerable to ambitious upstarts willing to take the risks needed to become a new trail blazer.

Business As Usual

A company without new information technology in an industry without any technological innovation is the most extreme case of conducting business as usual. It may be that advanced technology has no obvious application, or *tradition* has blinded industry participants to the advantages of technological innovation. Competitive advantage comes from factors other than technology. However, very few industries are completely immune to the advantages of advanced information technology. The clever application of a relatively modest dose of new technology can spring a company free from the pack. If you do not want to become such a trail blazer yourself, staying alert for aggressive new players can allow you to defend yourself strategically if one enters your industry. Only a small distance separates business as usual from industry laggard.

Laggard

A laggard firm competes in an industry where technology is widely used as a competitive weapon and either has no technological tools or consistently lags behind the leaders in adopting new technologies. Laggards that don't have some other significant competitive edge such as price, quality, or reputation usually don't survive for long. Catching up can be extraordinarily hard. The effective use of new technologies requires organizational maturity in the use of technology. An inexperienced firm that tries to make up for lost time can make costly mistakes from which there is often no recovery.

A STRATEGIC FRAMEWORK

A simple framework helps link specific technologies to corporate strategies. For convenience, the technologies are organized into four groups: processing/storage, interface, information access, and telecommunications. These technologies can support different corporate strategies, such as cost leadership, differentiation, innovation, growth, and alliance, as they may affect different targets, such as suppliers, customers, rivals, and the organization itself (enterprise).

Although fanciful speculations can be fun, they seldom help the line manager find a technological solution to a strategic problem. So our discussion will be limited to plausible future technologies (while heeding Oscar Wilde's admonition: "I never make predictions, especially those concerning future events"). Ideally, an IS manager should be able to take these ideas and create working systems within five to ten years. These technologies extend the information technology trends that have unfolded over the past three decades:

shrinking sizes

decreasing costs

increasing storage capacity

increasing processing/transmission speed

increasingly sophisticated interfaces.

All five factors interact. For instance, shrinking devices allow more power in a given package, and more powerful and faster devices can combine to form far more sophisticated interfaces.

Processing/Storage: Downsize, Down-cost, and Power-up

Downsizing has been a relentless trend throughout the history of computing. As sizes have shrunk, power has grown. Computing power that used to fill a large air-conditioned room now easily fits in a briefcase. Data General has advertised "100 MIPS mainframe power in a pizza box." Magnetic disk sizes continue to shrink, so that where once 2.5 megabytes were stored on a disk larger than a frisbee, now IBM engineers fit 1 gigabyte nicely on a 1-inch-square platter. A University of California researcher has patented a laser device that can store up to 6.5 terabytes of data on a sugar-cube-sized chunk of polysty-rene.[10] Even as the number of active devices on a single chip increases, chip packaging is becoming more compact through surface mount technologies. Sun Computing predicts desktop workstations that can sustain 1,000 megaflops (million floating point operations per second) with 1,000 megabytes of memory connected to a 1 gigabit network by 1994.[11]

Costs have shrunk along with size. Memory chips have long been a commodity item. Personal computers are becoming—or may already be—commodities. The cost for a given amount of computer power decreases by half every three years.[12]

These technological trends provide never-ending opportunities for those seeking strategic advantage through technology. Change occurs in three domains. Downsizing enables technologists to put inexpensive power and data storage at the disposal of the end user—to put *supercomputers* on every desk. Thus most computation-communication tasks can be done faster and in more locations than before. Parallel-processing computers from Teradata are used by firms like K-Mart, Citibank, Boeing, and American Airlines to sift through the mountains of data produced by their transaction processing systems to discover trends that can affect pricing and product decisions.[13] As recently as 1987, Batterymarch Financial Management could only consider minicomputers to optimize its investment portfolios. Even then, the process would take eight hours.[14] By mid-1991, these same computations easily could be handled by an inexpensive workstation in less time. What was once a monthly or weekly task could now be done daily. Inventories can be reduced, market trends rapidly identified, and innovative products developed. *Empow-ered* workstations could enable other computing architectures that reduce traffic on over-burdened networks.

By putting more power at the hands of skilled workers, more relevant data informs decisions more frequently. Increasing computer power is changing the ways probabilistic statistics can inform managers. Resampling, or the *bootstrap,* allows statisticians to determine more accurately the reliability of numeric data analysis. Resampling can often solve problems that were too difficult using traditional formulas.[15]

In industries where product design is laborious, complex, and time-consuming—from aerospace to pharmaceuticals—desktop supercomputing would enable firms to reduce product development times by orders of magnitude.[16] Complex tasks can be broken into pieces and distributed to skilled workers, each equipped with a networked super-workstation. The computers could even cross-check work on various tasks. Designs can be tested in simulation, avoiding the cost and time of building models.[17] Product innovation and product line expansion become easier, even for smaller organizations.

Increased processing power has made computer-generated graphics cost-effective for motion picture producers.[18] Before 1990, digitally produced special effects seldom comprised more than a small portion of any theatrical film. Reduced computing cost and increased power make feasible plans to produce a feature-length film consisting entirely of digital animation.

Thus, increased computing power can be harnessed within the enterprise in a variety of industries for innovation, growth, cost control, and differentiation. A single, low-cost system can leverage all four strategic thrusts.

Miniaturized, low-cost computing can reshape white-collar work. It can help create a new work environment for teams of knowledge workers by replacing computers with *information appliances.*[19] One scenario, called *ubiquitous computing,* uses computers that are as commonplace as small electric motors are today. A single room might have a hundred or more computers dedicated to different tasks. A single worker might have five or six intelligent screen *pads* active at a time, in much the same fashion that we now spread out multiple documents on a desktop. The current size and clutter limitations of the *desktop* metaphor in graphical interfaces could be swept away by such devices. This environment provides many new information channels and computing resources for workers; combined with *smart* blackboards and employee badges, it could improve work group productivity.[20]

Another major result of shrinking size and cost is the proliferation of portable devices. The sales of laptops, palmtops, and other portables has exploded to the point where current trends show them comprising 70% of computer sales by the year 2000. Other portable technologies, like cellular telephones and portable faxes are experiencing similar growth.

Portables already have enabled competitive innovation. Sales representatives use laptops for sales presentations where product complexity makes static presentations unacceptable, or where multimedia presentations could boost customer response, or where customized presentations are desired. Portables are used to sell life insurance,[21] assist elevator service calls, and provide input devices for waiters.[22] They can optimize schedules and routes for field personnel.[23] They can provide *smart,* graphical access to service manuals and support documentation in the field. Hand-held devices for inventory and order entry have become nearly essential in high-volume retailing and wholesale operations. Frito-Lay Corporation rolled out one such hand-held computer system in the mid-1980s. Input from 10,000 of these devices was transmitted to host computers to monitor daily sales trends. Product mix decisions were decentralized to the regional and even the sales-force levels.[24] Thus product distribution can be tailored to individual markets.

Field workers can use portable computing to access the massive central databases while simultaneously collecting more data for storage in those same databases. Critical market intelligence becomes instantly available for further analysis.

Downsizing has enabled computer automation to be embedded in a variety of products. One easy way to create new products is to embed dedicated microprocessors in previously *dumb* products. From irons that shut down when left unattended, to autofocus–autoexposure snapshot cameras, to environmental control systems, the proliferation of tiny, low-cost embedded computing devices provides endless avenues for innovation and product differentiation.

Embedding memory and computational power into credit cardlike devices is another approach that downsizing has enabled. Cards with on-board chips enable users to handle financial transactions with improved efficiency and security.

Beyond the advantages just discussed, growing computer power combined with shrinking size and cost enables nearly all the other technologies that can be exploited by strategic information systems. It is the engine that drives changes in other technologies.

Table 12.2 highlights potential uses of processing and storage technologies to support corporate strategies aimed at various targets.

Interfaces

Where once not so very long ago punch card machines ruled, now mice, pens, cameras, and microphones prevail. The region where humans—and the environment—meet computers is marked by rapid innovation. While *traditional* keyboards, CRTs, mice, and tablets continue to be improved, the next generation of devices is beginning to hit the street. Pen-based systems, while still lacking application software, are already available. For individuals working while standing up or moving frequently, either in the field or around their offices, pen-based systems may be the tool of choice. The interface is so natural that pen-based tools may help those not adept at typing, thus opening information resources to a new group of users.[25]

Researchers at the Xerox Palo Alto Research Center (PARC) are refining a series of devices to create a *ubiquitous* computing environment with hundreds of computers in a single room. They have created electronic tabs, much like the post-it notes now affixed to nearly every imaginable document and work surface, and pen-based pads, which are the electronic equivalent of the yellow-lined notepads we use for notes, handwritten drafts, or doodles. They are also using *smart* blackboards—large video screens that can accept input from keyboards, mice, and pens—for group work. Finally, they are experimenting with *active badges,* an alternative to both the common photo ID card and the magnetic striped key card, that combine a tiny computer with a switch and light emitting diodes that allow the badge to identify the wearer to automatic doors, display screens, and location-sensing systems. Altogether, these technologies make up an information-intensive environment that draws on many information resources. Such *invisible* technology could leverage the efforts of white-collar workers—a group that has shown little productivity

TABLE 12.2 Processing and storage

Technology	Target	Corporate Strategy	Notes
Microsupercomputing	Enterprise	Cost Innovation Growth Differentiation	Core or enabling technology
	Customer Supplier	Differentiation Cost Alliance	
CAD	Enterprise	Cost Innovation	Faster product design
Ubiquitous computing	Enterprise	Innovation Growth	Improved work group interaction
Portables	Enterprise	Innovation Cost Differentiation	Increases information "mobility"
	Customer Supplier	Differentiation Alliance	
Embedded computers	Customer	Differentiation Innovation	Make "smarter" products

improvement resulting from past automation efforts—reducing costs and stimulating innovation.

Although limited speech recognition technology has existed for over a decade, only in the early 1990s is it becoming practically feasible. Voice input has two primary advantages: it replaces keyboards, monitors, and mice—unnatural means of communicating—with speech—a perfectly natural means; and it leaves human hands free for other functions.[26] A voice-activated, CD-ROM–based reference manual could be used by a mechanic who could call up relevant diagrams without interrupting work. Voice-controlled robots could leverage a single skilled worker to do either highly complex, interactive tasks or those simply too dangerous for a human to do directly.

Another *old* new technology with potent strategic potential is optical character recognition (OCR). Paper documents are not likely to disappear soon, but the data contained on them could be far more valuable if stored in organizational databases, especially if they are stored as text characters rather than bit-mapped images. The ability to transform paper-based text into database elements easily improves the quality of data resources and can reduce costs and improve access. Information thus captured becomes available for rapid distribution, manipulation, transformation, and analysis.[27] Both page and hand OCR scanners are now cost–effective even for the small office. The immediate benefit would be cost savings, but the long-term effects could include growth and innovation strategies.

Bar coding and magnetic striping are also mature technologies, but they still can be exploited in new settings and in new ways to improve production processes, inventory control, and tracking. The advantage of bar coding is that once an item is labeled, it can be tracked easily by computer almost anywhere. Magnetic striping creates opportunities for more interactive usage. Smart gasoline dealers now let patrons pay at the pump using only their charge card. The appearance of cards with chip memories on-board, rather than just a magnetic stripe, should further simplify computer-aided sales transactions and reduce fraud.

In the music industry, both old (traditional keyboards with electronic outputs) and new input devices (breath controllers patterned after traditional wind instruments) are reshaping the ways music is produced. A variety of control devices can be used by musicians seeking new ways to manipulate digitally synthesized or sampled sounds. Such devices could also be used to control images, light, or even robots. Combined with digital interfaces, such devices enable one person to play all the instruments in an orchestra, permitting sharp reductions in the cost of producing recorded music.

A newly designed device allows users to select items using eye movements.[28] Although this technology will initially have military use (for target acquisition and tracking), once it is perfected and its cost drops, it could be used for a variety of nonmilitary applications. In laboratory settings, it is already being used by marketing research organizations to assess the effectiveness of packaging designs. It also could be built into one of several varieties of *computing suits* or *caps.*[29] These outfits, which are computers that can be worn, consist of a video image projected into the eye (it seems to float in front of the user's face), storage and processor that are built into the clothing, and a simple, preferably hands-off input device. These computing suits are well adapted to delivering information to workers who, like mechanics, need hands-free mobility.

The most extreme form of self-contained computing environment is called *virtual reality.* Virtual reality systems consist of helmets with built-in video and audio combined with gloves or body suits that can translate body (or arm or hand or finger) movement into system input. Applications for virtual reality include entertainment and remote control of highly articulated robots, which might be equipped with image sensors, and tools controlled by body movement.[30] Virtual reality could let humans *experience* a simulated three-dimensional model of a newly designed object to evaluate the design as though it had been built.[31]

Image and analog sensor input is also becoming more common. As processors become ubiquitous, they are more likely to be dedicated to a single task. Sensors provide direct input, freeing up expensive data input resources while providing more accurate data, often from environments too hostile for people, or where the data acquisition rate is simply too high for humans. Some robots have been trained to recognize colors to help in object identification when shapes are unreliable identifiers, as with clothing and soft packaged objects.[32] The CSX corporation is testing a scanner system that *recognizes* freight cars as they roll into a railroad yard.[33]

Progress in developing output devices is equally vigorous. Low-cost laser printers allow virtually anyone to produce high-quality documents, newsletters, and books, opening up vast avenues of growth and product differentiation in the publishing business. The next generation of these machines will provide low-cost color. These innovations are reshaping the graphics arts industry. Computer technology has eliminated many production steps in the printing industry, so that publications can move directly from computer layout to finished plates ready to be placed on the press. The net result of these changes is that high-quality printed material can be produced at lower cost and in less time.

It is now possible to generate inexpensive three-dimensional models of either real or computer-designed objects. Lasers scan real objects and create three-dimensional digitized images. The resulting image files can control laser cutting tools that recreate the object in a variety of materials. Original computer-generated drawings also can be used as a source for 3-D objects, reducing product development time and improving prototype evaluation.[34]

Even in two dimensions, the image control by new computer systems can be striking—even a bit scary. With image manipulation software, it is possible to alter photographic, video, and motion picture film images in ways undetectable by even expert viewers.[35] Is a building in the wrong location in a photograph? Just move it. Is a beautiful landscape photo marred by telephone wires? Erase them. The ramifications of this image-altering ability are staggering and are not limited to the entertainment and advertising industries.

The most readily visible new imaging technology probably will be high-definition television (HDTV). The merging of video that has theatrical film quality with computers should provide stunning advances in interactive product sales, entertainment, and information presentation. High-image resolution and new display technologies promise not only visually striking entertainments but also far denser visual presentations of information for business and technical purposes.[36] The visual richness of the medium could become a significant advantage where large volumes of information must be integrated and presented coherently.

Current trends point to multimedia, which places video, still photos, computer graphics, text, and audio under computer control, thus becoming the desktop system of the future.[37] Multimedia can be used as information reference or for training, entertainment, marketing, system design, product creation, and assorted combinations of these functions.[38] When combined with CD-ROM, a desktop PC with multimedia software can access vast libraries of image, sound, and text. Education can be self-paced while enriched by vivid graphics and high-quality audio. CD-ROMs either could be new products (databases, dictionaries, encyclopedias, fiction and nonfiction trade books, and various forms of entertainment), adjuncts to existing products (such as training or support materials, system documentation, software upgrades), or items for interactive sales and marketing efforts.

Robots can be viewed as a computer interface that directly senses and manipulates its world. While robots are a well established technology, two trends deserve special attention. First, U.S. corporations have been slow to adopt robotics, so innovation is still possible with *traditional* robots. Second, researchers are exploring new approaches to robotics that could provide significant technical advances. One improvement involves the creation of miniature, insect-like, uni-task robots that can function without connection to a large computer. Early results show that these robots are remarkably adaptive, although

TABLE 12.3 Interfaces

Technology	Target	Corporate Strategy	Notes
Pen	Enterprise	Differentiation Innovation Cost	For movers but not "shakers"
	Customer	Differentiation Innovation Alliance	Can reduce training costs, particularly for unskilled
	Supplier	Alliance	
Ubiquitous Computing	Enterprise	Cost Innovation	
Speech recognition	Enterprise	Innovation Cost	Enables hands-off use
OCR	Enterprise	Cost	Publishing, documentation
Bar coding	Enterprise Supplier	Cost Alliance Cost	Tracks wherever an "object" moves
Mag-stripe	Enterprise Customer	Cost Differentiation	Smart cards for customer convenience
Breath control	Customer	Differentiation Innovation Cost	Music industry–specific
Eye tracking	Enterprise	Cost Innovation	High-speed response in "busy" environments
	Customer	Innovation	
Virtual reality	Enterprise	Innovation Differentiation	Allows large-scale visualization of product designs
	Customer	Differentiation	
Analog sensors	Enterprise	Cost Innovation	Replace human inspectors
	Customer	Innovation Differentiation	
Laser printers (plus color)	Enterprise Customer	Innovation Cost	Improves the chance that your manual will be read
3-D model building	Enterprise	Innovation Cost Differentiation	For both reverse engineering and new designs
Image manipulation	Customer	Differentiation	The ultimate in photo "retouching"

TABLE 12.3 (continued)

Technology	Target	Corporate Strategy	Notes
HDTV	Enterprise	Innovation	Wherever high-resolution images are needed
	Supplier	Alliance	
	Customer	Innovation Differentiation	
Multimedia	Enterprise	Innovation Differentiation Cost	Capstone—combines multiple technologies
	Supplier	Alliance	
	Customer	Differentiation Innovation	
Robots	Enterprise	Cost Innovation Differentiation	Can improve quality/cost when combined with CAD

they are endowed only with weak machine intelligence.[39] The second breakthrough is the creation of microscopic machines that can work in highly constrained areas.[40]

Table 12.3 portrays potential uses of interface technologies to support corporate strategies aimed at various targets.

Information Access Technologies

Information access technologies organize data storage and retrieval. They include database management systems, artificial intelligence, associative indexes (hypertext), and knowledge-based and expert systems. Access technologies are the software and sometimes hardware components that define the architecture of information retrieval.

Despite the divergent types of technologies used (e.g., relational database versus expert systems versus neural networks), the goal is roughly the same: to make available the relevant data stored in the organization's computers at the minimum cost, in the least time, with the least extraneous or confusing information, to conduct business transactions, leverage employee skills, improve decisions, control processes, and reduce errors.

Emerging database technologies will address several pressing challenges. The first is the support of very large databases. Scientists already struggle with massive databases from interplanetary probes, long-term environmental studies, and other primary research. Retail stores that record every sales transaction add hundreds of thousands of records daily to their databases. A combination of larger, denser storage media and improved access techniques will be the key to unlocking these data resources for competitive advantage.

The second challenge is to extend database systems to include multimedia information. Groups as diverse as insurance companies, hospitals, and scientists need to store images, graphics, and sound along with text or numeric data. Object-oriented database technology provides one solution to this problem by managing *objects* rather than data, where an object can be an image, a cluster of records, or a block of text. The object-oriented approach improves the application of database technology to office automation, medicine, and science.[41]

Knowledge management is the third database challenge. As databases grow in size and complexity, more intricate rules must guide data storage, maintenance of data integrity, and retrieval.[42] One advanced database technology focuses on retrieving data from dispersed or distributed data sources. Rather than switching between data resources, a worker can use a single interface to access a variety of databases distributed across many servers. Ford developed the VIEW database retrieval system for this purpose: to access directly databases that are organized differently.[43] This approach saves replicating multiple databases, or consolidating many large, costly databases into a single behemoth, while still providing easy access to all the corporate data resources. Researchers at Johns Hopkins University have put together an unusual linked pair of databases of human genetic information.[44] In this early example of a *collaborative* database, the distinction between data creators and data users is blurred, because those using the database also can add to it. In many industries, competitive advantage could depend on intercompany database access. A company could make new designs available to suppliers to encourage early feedback on component prices. In the defense industry, alliances between a prime contractor and its subcontractors could depend on intercompany databases.[45]

A novel alternative to current database searching methods are knowledge robots, or *knowbots*. These software entities will cruise networks or clone themselves in other host computers in search of the information their owners request.[46] With knowbots the user need not know what databases to search nor their internal structure but need only specify the subject of the inquiry. Knowbots could break down the technical barriers between information resources, allowing access to databases not even present on the user's home network.

In yet another approach, Bellcore researchers have developed a new database architecture called *datacycle* that sends the database to the application, rather than the application to the database.[47] Datacycle continuously pumps out the entire database several times a second over a high-speed channel. Application processors on the channel use special filters and search rules to pluck the records needed from the flow in response to specific user queries. The database is updated through a separate channel once each cycle. Because the entire database is read every cycle, no indexes are required. The database is application-independent, and frequent updates on large data sets are simple to do. Bellcore hopes to use this architecture to support a database of "personal" telephone numbers.

After years of inflated claims and disappointing performance, artificial intelligence (AI) systems are finally entering mainstream business computing. Although AI has not lived up to its advanced press, its development has reached the point where practical, successful systems have been built.[48] Even AI's persistent limitations are being addressed, particularly the problem that expert systems are expert only in a very limited domain. Although it will be years before the results are known, progress is being made toward making AI less *brittle* by possessing common sense.[49]

AI can consist of expert (or knowledge-based) systems, natural language understanding, and neural networks. It is best applied to problems not subject to strict rules and rigid structures. Selecting, implementing, and evaluating these systems can be difficult, but some organizations are reporting success.[50] From a strategic standpoint, knowledge-based systems have two desirable attributes. First, while a competitor could copy the *technology* of an expert system—the nuts and bolts of how the knowledge base is organized or the specific technique used—it would be impossible (short of industrial espionage) to gain the advantage provided by the contents of the system: the rules, the fuzzy logic, the algorithms, the knowledge base itself. These valuable assets come from the interaction of the organization with its environment and can be replicated only at great expense, thus becoming a formidable entry barrier.

The second attribute is the ability of these systems to capture, at least to a limited extent, the knowledge and experience of highly valued experts. Encapsulating the expertise of key employees makes a firm less vulnerable to disruption resulting from the untimely loss of those key resources. By leveraging the expertise of professional staff, expert systems can provide cost reductions, opportunities for growth unconstrained by the limited availability of *expert* personnel, and enhancement of product differentiation and innovation. *Smart* systems can improve the quality of decisions and analysis by helping sort through vast quantities of information to identify quickly the best possible solutions or the most well-informed response.[51]

The various AI techniques provide powerful ways to leverage the corporate *knowledge* for competitive advantage in daily practice. Investment, marketing, pricing, and design decision quality can be improved. Customer support can be enhanced. Products and services can be differentiated by speed and *intelligence.* They can uncap growth by freeing up limited professional expertise. AI also can improve product enhancement. Advances in natural language understanding could be used to reduce the resources needed to capture and store text into databases.[52] For controlling complex activities in unstructured domains, AI can direct robots and automated systems in real time, using direct input from sensors.[53] Some components of AI can be added to many traditional systems for strategic advantage.

In the information systems domain, *computer-aided software engineering* (CASE) is a specialized application of access technology designed to simplify system development through systematic knowledge organization. In its simplest form, CASE consists of a database about a computer system. In its most advanced form, CASE combines this database, or repository, with a variety of design tools. The tools are often graphical and use expert system technology to improve programmer productivity. The goals of CASE are cost reduction (by reducing the time needed to develop and implement systems), quality improvement, and growth and differentiation (by creating new opportunities for development).

Object-oriented programming (OOP) is an access technology that promises to revolutionize the computer software industry. OOP eliminates the traditional separation of data and function in computer programs. Data and function are combined to form objects, which may be assembled easily into complex programs. These objects also may be reused, often with extensions and enhancements. OOP can improve system modularity, simplify system design, and speed up development. Among PC software firms, Borland has proven especially adept at applying object-oriented technology to allow it to reduce development time, while maintaining a low-cost strategy. Computer maker Hewlett Packard has also embraced OOP, hoping to create more flexible and extensible products. Some pundits feel that those companies that exploit OOP the best will dominate the computer industry.[54]

New technologies also are reshaping personal information delivery. Using existing technologies, people could have *personalized* newspapers assembled for them based on a user-maintained list of topic preferences. Alternatives to this model might include the daily distribution of topic or article lists, from which the subscriber could select the articles of interest. Or a *hard copy* newspaper could provide the new summaries in the style of *USA Today* but provide, with the wave of a scanning wand over the paper, a far more detailed report on demand. The same approach could be used for interactive television news, where the subscriber would have the option to select "details, please."[55] In each case, interactive delivery systems replace passive systems. Products are differentiated by how much they enable users to customize the product.

Most approaches to information management in the 1990s will be focused on organizing data to support more selective targeting in the marketing and distribution of products and services. Large databases filled with detailed consumer information will increasingly provide companies with the ability to tailor their products to specific groups. Many individuals fear the "big brother" aspect of large databases—the potential for invasion of privacy. But the *scary* invasiveness of *private* information storage is balanced by the cost efficiency and responsiveness resulting from the ethical use of this information. One can use the example of a meaningful wink between two friends to illustrate the power of shared experience to increase the *bandwidth* of human communication.[56] The more focused intelligence resident at each end of a network connection, the less data must be transmitted to accomplish the same purpose. Whatever the specific technologies chosen, mastering this type of information exchange will provide the technologically advanced company with powerful levers to improve service, cut costs, and provide innovative products and services.

Table 12.4 illustrates potential uses of information access technologies to support corporate strategies aimed at various targets.

Telecommunications: Network Bandwidth and Delivery Channels

*Independence in space and time is the single
most valuable service and product we can
provide humankind.*

Nicolas P. Negroponte[57]

Following the introduction of the IBM personal computer in 1981, there has been a virtual explosion in the number of computing devices operating, so that in 1991, there were over 50 million personal computers in use.[58] Many organizations are approaching the point where there is one PC for every worker. With computers (and advanced elec-

TABLE 12.4 Access technologies

Technology	Target	Corporate Strategy	Notes
Distributed database	Enterprise	Cost Innovation	Enables more informed decisions
	Supplier	Alliance	
	Customer	Differentiation Innovation Cost	
Knowbots	Enterprise	Cost Innovation	Personal agents across the network
Datacycle database	Enterprise	Growth Innovation Cost	Bring the database to the application
	Customer	Differentiation	
Artificial intelligence	Enterprise	Cost Differentiation Innovation Growth	To capture and leverage the expertise of your firm
	Customer	Differentiation Innovation	
CASE	Enterprise	Cost Innovation	Specialized for IS development
Object-oriented programming	Enterprise	Cost Innovation	Especially in computer industry or any large software-using field
	Customer	Differentiation Innovation	
Interactive delivery systems	Customer	Innovation Differentiation	Electronic newspapers

tronic games) becoming as commonplace as appliances like the telephone and television, they have reached a critical mass, enabling an era of exploding interconnection. The *infrastructure* is now in place to capitalize on distributed computing in a way that could not have been imagined in 1981.

To meet the growing demand for interconnection, rapid technical advances are improving network bandwidths and increasing the number of alternative channels available for data transmission. For at least two decades, both computing and communications cost performance ratios have been improving significantly every year. Across the country, copper wire has been replaced with glass fiber, which has thousands of times more signal-carrying capacity. No other area of information technology offers so much strategic potential for the savvy organization as the interconnection of computers in local, campus, metropolitan, and wide-area networks.

The speeds of both local and wide-area networks have been increasing. In at least one location, a local telephone company is providing networking services on glass fiber at 100 megabits per second using the fiber distributed data interface network standard.[59] The high-performance parallel interface (HIPPI) was proposed as a network standard for scientific systems in 1987. It currently operates at the Los Alamos National Laboratory on copper wire at 800 megabits per second.[60] Experimental networks have been established to test the synchronous optical network (SONET) at speeds greater than 1 gigabit per second. Combined with the asynchronous transfer mode (ATM) fast-packet technology, SONET could provide nationwide 1-gigabit network services by the end of the 1990s.[61] On such a network, one hour of full-motion video—about the amount of data stored on a compact disc—could be transmitted in five seconds.[62]

To avoid transmission bottlenecks, such networks would depend on extending fiber-optic cabling into the local telephone loop, a task already underway in selected experimental locations. By combining new fiber cables with the coaxial links now used by cable television, most American homes could be wired for high-speed data transmission. There should be little shortage of resources for developing the network infrastructure: venture capitalists have shown interest in telecommunications firms.[63] Counting only wired systems, there should be adequate bandwidth for high-volume data communications available to homes nationwide within a few years.

Other than wired systems, two other wide-area delivery channels will be available in the future. One is location-independent delivery by satellite transmission, while the other uses cellular radio technology. The cellular telephone market has already exploded, and analysts forecast that cellular data transmission will be the next growth area, as the sales of cellular modems expand rapidly over the next several years.[64] Satellite transmission remains a costly alternative but one well suited to certain types of communication (e.g., transoceanic).

In local area networks, both radio and infrared technologies now enable wireless connection within buildings. Often, the cost savings can be substantial. Wireless systems also provide increased flexibility: whole offices can be reorganized in days without concern for the wiring infrastructure. One by-product of wireless networks is the smart *ID* card, by which the network can track staff throughout the physical plant.[65]

Some experts worry about the current and future *bandwidth famine,* where no matter how much the transmission capacity grows, the demand will always exceed it, because computing capacity is growing just as quickly as communications bandwidth.[66] Three factors militate against such a capacity shortfall, each of which could offer a profitable niche for the right companies. The first is the presence of new channel suppliers who will profit by providing capacity when existing providers fail to keep up. The second is the intelligent reorganization of channel usage to maximize efficiency. For example, most broadcast transmission could be moved to cable, leaving the airwaves free for cellular transmission and other narrow-cast signals. Finally, bandwidth demand can be reduced by mundane means: the compact disk (CD-ROM) or a variant can provide an excellent physical channel where information is voluminous and seldom changes. Although it may seem downright antitechnological, sending three CDs by Federal Express from Boston to Los Angeles results in higher throughput than a 64 kilobit per second connection.[67]

As delivery channels increase in number and capacity, the prospect of integrating interactive voice, image, data, and video through a single channel becomes practical, opening the door to many new information services. Although integrated services digital network (ISDN) is designed to do this task, it has not yet caught on in the United States.[68] Improvements in network and delivery system capacity probably will have the most noticeable effect on future information systems. Communications also may provide the best opportunities for strategic advantage. Network links forge alliances, bond suppliers, and entice customers. When high-speed networks are coupled with end-to-end intelligence, market coordination costs drop. Contracting production becomes less expensive than doing it in-house.

Communication technology may be viewed on a spectrum of complexity where simple point-to-point movement of data between two essentially *dumb* machines for later use in *batch* processes is at one end and the full exchange of data and process intelligence between multiple nodes in real time is at the other end. Strategic advantage can be exploited all along the spectrum, but the most advanced technology, and potentially the greatest strategic advantage, occurs at the more complex end of the range.

Electronic data interchange (EDI) is one of the simpler communication technologies. Although EDI is a mature technology in some industries, it remains a ripe opportunity in others. Often, the barriers to implementation can be less technical than political, where resistance to the structural changes that EDI creates can be strong, as in the broadcasting industry.[69] In these situations, the creation of alliances can provide significant competitive advantage. EDI provides lower costs, faster service, and reduced opportunities for errors and forges business alliances that can extend into other arenas. It can reshape markets—it can even create opportunities for new electronic markets. In Japan, a computer runs a nationwide automobile auction almost like an electronic game.[70] EDI can reduce receivables. It can be applied almost anywhere an organization is passing paper documents. The *paperless office* may be a mirage, but the paperless business transaction should not be. The long-term vitality of many organizations may depend on EDI.

On both an intra- and interorganizational level, electronic mail provides a simple and rapid means of moving information among workers, often in remote locations. Electronic mail also opens up the *global village* by allowing the free exchange of ideas between individuals on different continents. By breaking down barriers of time, physical and social distance, and conflicting schedules, electronic messaging allows more rapid and effective communication, thus promoting innovation and growth while reducing costs. Research has shown that electronic communication facilitates open communication far better than face-to-face interviews.[71] So electronic surveys conducted by product or market researchers may be more accurate than personal interviews in assessing trends and values.

Currently, a plethora of incompatible mail and network systems hinder interconnection. So does the desire to move information in a variety of media. The powerful need for integration, however, will drive technology toward the *single electronic mailbox.*[72] In 1993, international bodies were at work developing standards to guide this integration.

The interconnection of networks and integration of media provide enormous opportunities for those firms able to provide effective security systems. The power of the medium may be its Achilles heel if adequate, usable security is not obtained.[73]

When electronic messages involve more than two users, the potential for leveraging knowledge grows. When structure is added to the mix, *computer-supported cooperative work* (CSCW) amplifies what each worker produces with feedback and added information. Tasks that are beyond the scope of a single individual, yet in the past were bogged down in committee, can be liberated by the effective application of CSCW software, or *groupware*. Where participants are geographically dispersed, teleconferencing can reduce both travel time and expense.

Telecommuting is a form of work often seen as benefiting the worker and perhaps the environment. Although both are laudable goals, telecommuting can enable entire new team structures composed of contract workers to be quickly assembled to meet business challenges. By not having to establish an office for such a task force, an organization can move quickly and inexpensively. Independent contractors and staff alike can interact as intensively as needed, using both telecommuting and teleconferencing. Resources from other continents can be called into play, advancing the prospects for global business activity.

In a fixed location, PARC's *ubiquitous* computing environment functions only if supported by radio or infrared local area networks that tie together all the boards, pads, tabs, and badges that exist within a room or a building or a campus.[74] Once PCs are no longer *personal* but part of a networked information resource, their power increases by orders of magnitude: the network becomes the computer, and the power of the network is at the fingertips of the worker. Although this approach to distributed computing has been discussed and even marketed in one form or another for over a decade, only now does a critical mass of computers and networks exist to make such an approach practical.

Many strategic advantages of portable computers are available only when they are part of a metropolitan or wide-area network. Scheduling systems pay off when they instantly receive orders from the main office. Route-finding and locator systems work only when they get their location from a global positioning system. Sales presentations pay off faster when orders can be placed from the field, inventories checked, customer details entered and confirmed, and revenue booked.

The payoffs of network communication are often serendipitous. Phillippe Kahn, CEO of Borland, played a public relations and communications role after the 1990 Loma Prieta earthquake by using his laptop computer to connect with his office via MCI mail when phone lines were down. He then could reassure customers and suppliers worldwide that Borland was undamaged and in business.[75] Although such a situation is certainly unique and hardly a measure of the ultimate value of networked computing, it does suggest the unexpected power inherent in the international web of communication networks.

Ultimately, the network can actually *be* a computer. Networked PCs can be linked to form a single supercomputing resource. Proponents of this approach argue that, with the availability of extremely high-speed networks, there is little difference between a supercomputer with loosely coupled processors and a network of high-powered PCs. Using the underutilized processing capacity in PCs could offer significant cost advantages to organizations with large numbers of PCs and mainframe-size processing needs. Although many speak glibly of the end of the mainframe, this architecture opens the door to the kind of enterprisewide computing power that large organizations need, all based on microcomputing technology. Each dispersed machine is a full participant in enterprise-wide computing, both for processing and storage. At current prices, such an approach offers enticing economics.[76]

Outside the organization, vast international networks open the doors for a variety of information products and services. Personalized information products could include personal newspapers, investment reports, and entertainment. Interactive marketing could provide a host of products for remote shoppers. Could we someday see grocery markets keeping track of our home refrigerator "inventory" to help us shop? Most of the technologies that could enable such an activity are already available. Imagine not having to remember whether you were out of sugar. Your *intelligent cupboard* could let your market know and order a restock! Your only excuse for visiting your neighbor will be to borrow a floppy disk.

Virtually every kind of product can be customized with telecommunications. Your automobile could be made to order based on a computer-generated image. The plans for the car could be sent directly from dealer to factory, where they would control the robots installing interior options, and applying paint and finish trim. You could plan a vacation based on actual images of the accommodations and sights to be seen, combined with up-to-the minute information about prices and availabilities. The clever combination of real-time networking with CD-ROM image and audio storage provides potent marketing tools. The application of networked computers to advertising could make *smart* yellow pages possible. Product availability could be determined from home before purchase, alternative sources and prices reviewed, and feedback given to advertisers.

Although such ideas may seem fanciful and may never occur as described here, they do suggest the kind of power that widespread interconnection can provide.

Table 12.5 suggests potential uses of delivery channels technologies to support corporate strategies aimed at various targets.

SUMMARY: INTELLIGENCE AND INTERCONNECTION

Two approaches to new technology offer the best strategic opportunities. The first is the widespread application of machine intelligence and information storage focused on daily activities. The second is the aggressive use of both local and wide-area networks to connect computers.

The key word is *connection*. Personalization means connecting traits, needs, habits, and values to a particular person. Group work entails connecting local and remote teams to do a single task, or a group of related tasks. Distributed computing uses interconnected machines for high-capacity computing. The strategic advantage in nearly every instance derives from having data in accessible form to attack a particular business problem and the means to move the data instantly to the location where it can benefit people and organizations. Just as now there is (in effect) a single worldwide telephone system, smart companies will start to think in terms of a single worldwide database system, with all the advantages that such interconnection can bring.[77]

TABLE 12.5 Delivery channels

Technology	Target	Corporate Strategy	Notes
High-speed LAN	Enterprise	Cost Growth	
High-speed WAN	Enterprise	Growth Cost	Enables rapid global expansion
	Supplier	Alliance Cost	
	Customer	Differentiation Innovation	
Cellular radio	Enterprise	Cost Innovation Differentiation Growth	Wherever mobility is required to sell, distribute, or even design products
	Supplier	Alliance	
	Customer	Innovation Differrentiation	
Satellite	Enterprise	Cost Growth	Lowers intercontinental costs
	Supplier	Alliance	
	Customer	Differentiation	
Wireless office	Enterprise	Cost Growth	For the office that changes monthly
CD-ROM	Enterprise	Cost Differentiation Alliance	An inexpensive channel for high-volume data
	Supplier	Alliance	
	Customer	Cost Differentiation	
EDI	Supplier	Cost Alliance	Improves speed and accuracy
	Customer	Differentiation	
Electronic mail	Enterprise	Cost Innovation	
	Supplier	Alliance	
	Customer	Differentiation	
CSCW	Enterprise	Cost Innovation	Changes how groups work together
	Supplier	Alliance Innovation	
Telecommuting	Enterprise	Cost Growth	Possible increase in contract workers
Network-as-computer	Enterprise	Cost	Low-cost main replacement
Combination WAN and CD-ROM	Enterprise	Cost	Combine image and sound with currency
	Customer	Differentiation Innovation	

Some technologies are only ideas, while others are already in use in some industries (in 1993). If a technology is not *absolutely* new but relatively new to a specific industry, it can provide as much advantage as the most technically advanced systems, often with less development work and risk. Different industries have advanced at different rates and in different technological directions, so that the hottest new gadget in one field may be obsolete in another. The trick is to find the best fit between the firm and the industry.

Organizations that can control, or control access to, major networks, major data resources, or information distribution paths (such as compact disks) will have a direct competitive advantage in their industry. Those that master new technology first have best chance of getting full value from it. The best way to predict the future is to invent it, so the saying goes.

REFERENCES

1. Weiser, M., "The Computer for the 21st Century," *Scientific American* (Sept. 1991): 94–104.

2. Hopper, M., "Rattling SABRE—New Ways to Compete on Information," *Harvard Business Review* (May-June 1990): 118–25.

3. Warner, T., "Information Technology as a Competitive Burden," *Sloan Management Review* (Fall 1987): 55–61.

4. Sullivan-Trainor, M. L., and Maglitta, J., "Competitive Advantage Fleeting," *Computerworld* (Oct. 8, 1990): 1, 4.

5. LaPlante, A., "The Needing Edge," *Computerworld* (Oct. 8, 1990): 14.

6. Neo, B. S., "Factors Facilitating the Use of Information Technology for Competitive Advantage: An Exploratory Study," *Information and Management* 15 (1988): 191–201.

7. Copeland, D. G., and McKenney, J. L., "Airline Reservation Systems: Lessons from History," *MIS Quarterly* (Sept. 1988): 353–70.

8. Hopper, M., "Rattling SABRE."

9. Viets, R., "Down-Home High Tech Lessons," *Computerworld* (Aug. 26, 1991): 25.

10. Wilder, C., "Storage Coming in Small Packages," *Computerworld* (Oct. 14, 1991): 22.

11. Anthes, G. H., "Computer Still a Baby, Joy Says," Computerworld (Mar. 25, 1991).

12. Dertouzos, M. L., "Communications, Computers and Networks," *Scientific American* (Sept. 1991): 62–69.

13. Verity, J. W., "Rethinking the Computer," *Business Week,* Nov. 26, 1990, 116–22.

14. Dhebar, A. S., Warbelow, A., and Ostrofsky, K., "Batterymarch Financial Management: Information Systems and Technology," *Harvard Business School Case* 9-188-013, Harvard Business School, 1987.

15. Efron, B., and Tibshirani, R., "Statistical Data Analysis in the Computer Age," *Science* (July 16, 1991): 390–95.

16. Schrage, M., "Drug Industry Vision: Faster and Cheaper," *Los Angeles Times,* Mar. 21, 1991, D8.

17. Alexander, M., "Looking Ahead to the Next Century," *Computerworld* (Mar. 4, 1991): 18.

18. Solomon, C., "How They Did That," *Los Angeles Times,* Sept. 22, 1991, 3, 39–40.

19. Saffo, P., "It's an Era of 'Information Appliances,' " *Los Angeles Times,* Nov. 14, 1990.

20. Weiser, "The Computer for the 21st Century."

21. Johnson, M., "New York Life Sold on Laptops," *Computerworld* (Aug. 6, 1990): 39.

22. Carroll, P. B., " Computers Cut Through the Service Maze," *Wall Street Journal,* May 11, 1990, B1, B5.

23. Ostrofsky, K. E., and Konsynski, B., "Personal Portable Technologies: Doing Business Anyplace," *Harvard Business School Working Paper,* Harvard Business School 1991.

24. Wishart, N. A., and Applegate, L. M., "Frito-Lay, Inc.: A Strategic Transition," *Harvard Business School Case* 9-187-065, Harvard Business School, 1987.

25. Carr, R. M., "The Point of the Pen," *Byte* (Feb. 1991): 211–21.

26. Fitzgerland, M., "Audio: The Wave of the Future," *Computerworld* (May 20, 1991): 18.

27. Negroponte, N. P., "Products and Services for Computer Networks," *Scientific American* (Sept. 1991): 106–13.

28. Alexander, M., "Eye-tracking Systems May Let Eyes Replace the Mouse," *Computerworld* (Sept. 16, 1991): 18.

29. "It's the Information Systems You Can Wear," *Byte* (June, 1991): 28.

30. Alexander, M., "Virtual Reality Still Unrealistic," *Computerworld* (June 24, 1991): 18.

31. Alexander, M., "Looking Ahead to the Next Century," *Computerworld* (Mar. 4, 1991): 18.

32. "Robot Color," *Discover,* (May 1991): 16.

33. Alexander, M., "Is It Real, or Is It Digitized," *Computerworld* (Jan. 14, 1991): 22.

34. Wilder, C., "Digitizing Enters Third Dimension," *Computerworld,* (Sept. 2, 1991): 20.

35. Alexander, January 14, 1991, "Is It Real."

36. Negroponte, "Products and Services."

37. Alexander, January 14, 1991, "Is It Real."

38. Phillips, R. L., "MediaView: A General Multimedia Digital Publication System," *Communications of the ACM* (July 1991).

39. Daily, J., "Creepy, Crawly Heroes of the AI Age," *Computerworld* (Apr. 29, 1991): 20.

40. Stix, G., "Golden Screws," *Scientific American* (Sept. 1991): 166–69.

41. Silberschatz, A., Stonebraker, M., and Ullman, J., "Database Systems: Achievements and Opportunities," *Communications of the ACM* (Oct. 1991): 110–20.

42. Cattell, R. G. G., "What Are Next Generation Database Systems?," *Communications of the ACM* (Oct. 1991): 31–33.

43. Ambrosio, J., "Ford Gives Users a Database with a VIEW," *Computerworld* (Sept. 16, 1991): 33.

44. Anthes, G. H., "A Step Beyond Database," *Computerworld* (Mar. 4, 1991): 28.

45. Silberschatz et al., *Communications of the ACM.*

46. Cerf, V. G., "Networks," *Scientific American* (Sept. 1991): 72–81.

47. Anthes, G. H., "Bellcore Database Could Make Phone Numbers Last a Lifetime," *Computerworld* (Mar. 18, 1991): 28.

48. Ryan, B., "AI's Identity Crisis," *Byte* (Jan. 1991): 239–46.

49. Lenat, D., Guha, R. V., Pittman, K., Pratt, D., and Shepherd, M., "Cyc: Toward Programs with Common Sense," *Communications of the ACM* (Aug. 1990): 30–49.

50. Francett, B., "AI (Quietly) Goes Mainstream," *Computerworld* (July 29, 1991): 59–61.

51. See Thow-Yick, L., and Huu-Phuoung, T., "Management Expert Systems for Competitive Advantage in Business," *Information and Management* (1990): 195–201.

52. Barnett, J., Knight, K., Mani, I., and Rich, E., "Knowledge and Natural Language Processing," *Communications of the ACM* (Aug. 1990): 50–71.

53. Payton, D. W., and Bihari, T. E., "Intelligent Real-Time Control of Robotic Vehicles," *Communications of the ACM* (Aug. 1991): 48–63.

54. Verity, J. W., "Software Made Simple," *Business Week,* Sept. 30, 1991, 92–100.

55. Shaw, D., "Electronic Newspaper Emerging After Slow Start," *Los Angeles Times,* June 3, 1991, A1.

56. Negroponte, "Products and Services."

57. Ibid.

58. Detouzos, "Communications, Computers and Networks."

59. Johnson, M., "An Offer They Couldn't Refuse," *Computerworld* (Apr. 15, 1991b): 56.

60. Hildebrand, C., " 'Hippi' Means Speed for Lab Users," *Computerworld* (Apr. 8, 1991): 45–48.

61. Cerf, "Networks."

62. Negroponte, "Products and Services."

63. Gooding, D., "New Age Venture Capital," *CIO* (Apr. 1991): 80–82.

64. Booker, E., "Cellular Modems Put the Office on the Road," *Computerworld* (Mar. 11, 1991): 43–44.

65. Weiser, "The Computer for the 21st Century."

66. Wilkes, M. V., "The Bandwidth Famine," *Communications of the ACM* (Aug. 1990): 19–21.

67. Negroponte, "Products and Services."

68. Keller, J. J., "New Service May Boost 'Telecommuting,' " *Wall Street Journal,* Nov. 27, 1990.

69. Nash, J., "Turning the Tide with Technology," *Computerworld* (Dec. 24, 1990): 47.

70. Konsynski, B., Warbelow, A., and Koluryo, J., "AUCNET," *Harvard Business School Case* 9-190-001, Harvard Business School, 1990.

71. Sproull, L., and Kiesler, S., "Computers, Networks and Work," *Scientific American* (Sept. 1991): 116–23.

72. Craig, F., "Electronic Messaging: Media Integration and Interconnection," *SIM Network* (Jan./Feb. 1991): 2–4.

73. Cerf. "Networks."

74. Weiser, "The Computer for the 21st Century."

75. Barnet, C., "Profiles in Mobility: Phillippe Kahn," *Mobile Office* (Apr. 1990): 26–30.

76. Ryan, A. J., "The Whole World in Your Hand?," *Computerworld* (May 20, 1991): 110.

77. Silberschatz et al., *Communications of the ACM.*

Index